Jossey-Bass Teacher

Jossey-Bass Teacher provides educators with practical knowledge and tools to create a positive and lifelong impact on student learning. We offer classroom-tested and research-based teaching resources for a variety of grade levels and subject areas. Whether you are an aspiring, new, or veteran teacher, we want to help you make every teaching day your best.

From ready-to-use classroom activities to the latest teaching framework, our value-packed books provide insightful, practical, and comprehensive materials on the topics that matter most to K–12 teachers. We hope to become your trusted source for the best ideas from the most experienced and respected experts in the field.

Counseling Toward Solutions

A Practical Solution-Focused Program for
Working with Students, Teachers, and Parents

SECOND EDITION

Linda Metcalf

Foreword by Bill O'Hanlon

JOSSEY-BASS
A Wiley Imprint
www.josseybass.com

Published by Jossey-Bass
A Wiley Imprint
989 Market Street, San Francisco, CA 94103-1741—www.josseybass.com

Jossey-Bass books and products are available through most bookstores. To contact Jossey-Bass directly call our Customer Care Department within the U.S. at 800-956-7739, outside the U.S. at 317-572-3986, or fax 317-572-4002.

Jossey-Bass also publishes its books in a variety of electronic formats. Some content that appears in print may not be available in electronic books.

ISBN: 9780787998066

Printed in the United States of America

SECOND EDITION

PB Printing   10 9 8 7 6 5 4 3 2 1

About This Book

This book was originally written as a handbook for school counselors who wanted to approach school populations with a more positive, solution-focused approach. The original edition covered the basic themes of a school counselor's job and promoted new solution-focused strategies for working with parents, students, teachers, and staff. As schools have evolved, the book too has evolved. In this revised edition, readers will find the same practical and simple explanations about what it means to become a solution-focused school counselor, but with the addition of material on important new issues. New in this edition are ideas for school counselors that show how to work with families to promote student success and increase student performance and attendance. It addresses as well how to help an adolescent change his reputation so that he gets the respect he deserves. And for elementary students dealing with sexual abuse, anger, attention issues, and other mental health concerns, this book shows how changing labels can change behavior. There is more focus on more topics than in the previous edition, so that the application of the solution-focused model can be seen for what it is: not simply a positive strategy or technique, but a way to think about school clients that can change interactions and guarantee success.

To our children, Roger, Kelli and Ryan,
you are my inspiration.

To my husband, Roger,
you help me to believe that anything can happen
when there is passion and determination.

About the Author

Linda Metcalf, Ph.D., is a former middle school teacher, a certified school counselor, a licensed professional counselor, and a licensed marriage and family therapist in the State of Texas. She is an associate professor and director of school counseling at Texas Wesleyan University, where she has developed a solution-focused school counseling program for graduate students. She is an international presenter who has taught the solution-focused approach to many educators across the United States, Canada, Japan, Singapore, Australia, Norway, Scotland, England, and Germany. She is the author of numerous professional articles and seven books: *Teaching Toward Solutions, Parenting Toward Solutions, Solution-Focused Group Therapy, The Miracle Question: Answer It and Change Your Life, How to Say It to Get into the College of Your Choice,* and *A Practical Approach to Learning Family Therapy* (forthcoming).

Acknowledgments

I am a very lucky person. Since the first edition of *Counseling Toward Solutions* was published twelve years ago, I have had the incredible fortune to visit with school counselors and therapists who work with children, adolescents, and families, all over the world. Listening to them, they revealed to me their concerns, frustrations, fears and their successes. They have asked for help with challenging students, questioned the questions that I asked them to ask, and processed ways to help children and adolescents become successful. They have emailed me their own adaptations of the miracle question, the scaling question, and so much more. Each letter was a gift of reassurance that I was on the right track. Thank you for being out there in the trenches each day, working with children, adolescents, parents, and teachers who need you. Together, you are making the difference in education that we need so desperately. By respecting the needs of your school clients, no matter how impossible they may seem, you open the door to possibilities.

To Margie McAneny, thank you for allowing me to write this revision and contemplate how to make the ideas more practical and applicable to today's school counselor and therapist. Your agreement to also publish the companion manual to this book, *The Field Guide to Counseling Toward Solutions,* helps to further my efforts to transform educational relationships into a more collaborative effort for everyone.

To Mansfield Independent School District, my real laboratory of four years, thank you for allowing me to work in your schools. You gave me the opportunity to try the mentor program and work with families to increase student competency. You taught me the important lesson of seeing that teachers and staff members were my school clients as well. I appreciate your fine district and its dedication to excellence. And to the students, teachers, school counselors, and parents whom I had the chance to work with "in the trenches," and still do, as a volunteer, I thank you now and in advance for your stories and opportunity to work with you. You helped me to refine, modify, and create more ways to listen to what you need. It is your voice that counts the most. It is for you that I write this book.

Thanks to Trigg Even, a school interventionist in Mansfield ISD, who always goes the extra mile to reconcile teacher and student needs in a creative manner. You are destined to be one of the best. Thank you also to Linda Fielding, an interventionist in Fort Worth ISD. I wish I could capture and bottle your excitement as you described the story of Julio. To Elliott Connie, a therapist with a solution-focused way of thinking that radiates with his smile and quick wit, thank you for writing about Douglas. Nicole Lucas, you are out in the school community and make a huge difference every day. Thank you for your excitement about Rena, who showed you, too, how the approach could work wonders with parents who are not as involved as you wish. To Ng-Chia Moi Lee of Singapore, your ruler rules with me! Thank you for persevering to reach Singaporean children each day. And Jenny Jacobs, I can still recall the day you told me about the student who envisioned hamburgers falling from the sky in her miracle day. I appreciate your ability to step into her world when others only wanted to protect her. To Nishani Grigsby, you make it seem so simple to be a solution-focused school counselor in a large high school. Thank you for always wanting to learn about the narrative applications that seem to work so well for you. And finally, thanks to the rest of my wonderful graduate students who listened and processed countless cases with me. You make my day, every day that I have the honor to teach you.

As a final note, during the past two years, we have sadly lost only in the physical sense, Insoo Berg and Steve de Shazer, our solution-focused heroes whose wisdom and brilliance brought the model to life and fruition. Their memory is honored each day that those of us who believe in the process use the model with clients. To Bill O'Hanlon, who wrote the Foreword in 1995, your words still resonate with me that you are one of the most creative and influential therapists working today. Teresa Steiner, Michael Durrant, Brian Cade, Eve Lipchik, thank you for opening my eyes to the model of solution-focused therapy in 1991. Thanks to Michael White and David Epston for always being willing to share their work in my publications and whose narrative questions, curiosities, and letters enhance what I do in therapy. The beauty of your work inspires me daily with its rich discourse. To Ben Furman, thank you for your adaptation of the solution-focused process with the delightful program, Kids' Skills. It makes finding solutions so much fun that kids end up dancing with delight all over my office with the wizard!

And to my family who keeps listening as I lament over "one more chapter to go," thanks for your belief in what I do. Ryan, you were only nine years old when you drew the pictures for this book, twirling around the room, doing several of them at once. Those memories are priceless and, apparently, timeless. Your future is bright in film. Finally, to Kelli, Roger Jr., and my husband, Roger, thanks for accompanying me on trips and taking the pictures that remind me daily how fortunate I really am.

Contents

Foreword

If you are a teacher, school administrator, or school counselor/psychologist, you probably remember the sense of excitement you had when you first decided to pursue your career. For some of you, it was a teacher who touched something inside you that inspired your choice. For others, it was a sense that you had something you could contribute to children, and this was a way to do it. But as you acquired more education, training, or experience, some of you might have lost touch with that original excitement or sense of possibility. You may even have become cynical and decided that kids were more unmotivated than you initially thought or that parents weren't that interested in their children's education or that school personnel were being asked to fix society's problems.

This book by Linda Metcalf is a powerful way to reconnect with your sense of energy and possibilities even in the face of serious challenges in schools. Reading this book can be like a massive injection of vitamins and minerals, full of hope and solutions for you.

Without minimizing the serious problems teachers, school counselors/psychologists, parents, and students face in today's schools, she gives a practical road map for rapidly solving these problems. This road map doesn't require massive infusions of federal funding or new students or any other pie-in-the-sky solutions. Instead, it relies on strengths and resources that are already available and dormant within students, parents, and the school.

A revolution is going on in the mental health field, which has for so long been a mental illness field. We are finally focusing on health. We have seen dramatic and moving changes in the people we counsel with the techniques and philosophies explored in this book. School is a natural place to use these ideas. Teachers, administrators, and school counselors/psychologists don't have time to do psychoanalysis with troubled students. Brief, pragmatic, and effective interventions are required. This book has more of those than you need. I got so excited when I read this book that I requested a copy for my son's third-grade teacher and the new principal of his school. I'll bet you'll get so excited, you'll end up buying and recommending this book to your friends and colleagues. But here's a warning: this book could be dangerous to your sense of burnout and discouragement. Reading it could cause persistent episodes of hope and enthusiasm in you and your students. Now you've been warned. Proceed at your own risk.

Bill O'Hanlon, M.S.
Author or coauthor of *In Search of Solutions,*
A Brief Guide to Brief Therapy, Love Is a Verb,
Rewriting Love Stories, and others

Counseling Toward Solutions

Chapter One

Learning to Think with a Solution Focus

You cannot solve a problem with the same kind of thinking that created it.

—Albert Einstein

It was Wednesday morning and Scot, age fifteen, was scheduled to return to his home campus after six weeks at the alternative school. He was sent there due to his repeatedly being disrespectful to two of his seven teachers. While at the alternative school, Scot improved his grades and got along well with his peers. It was a structured, disciplined environment.

In response, Scot was getting along better with his family and had begun to feel better personally. Even his younger brother, ten-year-old Tim, had noticed the difference in the stress level at home, so much that even *he* had begun behaving at school.

With these successes in mind, Scot's school counselor, who had adopted the solution-focused approach for her guidance program, was taking an extra precaution and had asked Scot to stop by and chat with her before he went to his first class. The school counselor had done *her* homework early in the week by asking Scot's teachers at the alternative school to fill out the Teacher Observation Sheet (a reproducible copy is supplied here) that described what worked with Scot behaviorally and academically. Once she had received the report, she made copies and then distributed them to his home campus teachers. The report described Scot as follows:

Teaching methods that work:

1. Hard-working student who responds well to prompts/praise
2. Is reluctant to ask questions but responds well when asked individually if he understands the assignment
3. Has difficulty concentrating during group work but can complete assignments when reminded and in a quiet area

Description of behavior: Please list positive traits that you observed about this student while he/she was in your classroom:

1. A respectful student who seems to have low self-esteem but lots of potential
2. A student who is well liked by his peers
3. A pleasure to have in class

Teacher Observation Sheet: Alternative School Success

Dear Teacher,

Your student, _____, will return to his/her home campus very soon. Your observations of what has been helpful to the student while in your class will be very important to the home campus teachers. Below, please write down what you have noticed as helpful teaching strategies as well as classroom management strategies that seemed to work with this student.

Teaching methods that work:

_____

_____

_____

_____

_____

_____

Description of behavior: Please list positive traits that you observed about this student while he/she was in your classroom:

_____

_____

_____

_____

_____

_____   _____
Your Signature   Subject/Classroom

The school counselor smiled and mused that it hardly sounded like Scot, who was often sent to the associate principal's office with discipline referrals describing him as disrespectful, disruptive in class, unmotivated, and rude. She was pleased that the break at the alternative school had given him a chance to show his strengths. She was also pleased that one of her favorite colleagues at school had agreed to mentor Scot while he was in the school.

As his mentor, the teacher wrote to Scot while he was in the alternative school in an attempt to get to know him—a sort of pen pal who could support his progress. Scot had written the first note to her, a requirement of the mentor program, and had introduced himself and described his life to his mentor teacher using some guidelines given to him:

Dear Mentor Teacher,

I really don't know what I am supposed to tell you. My parents work all the time and I rarely see them. My mother works at Target and my father works for the school district warehouse. When I get home from school I am supposed to take care of my little brother, Joe, but he can be a real pain so I ignore him. I hate school. My teachers don't like me and for the most part, I don't like them. I have two dogs and my hobbies include listening to rock music, getting on the internet to play video games and hanging out with my friends.

Scot

The teacher was excited to receive her first letter from Scot and eager to write back to him. She told the school counselor that he reminded her of her own son, who had disliked school as a freshman in high school but had since grown up and gone off to college. "He sounds bright and in need of someone to give him some time," she had told the school counselor. The school counselor

reminded the mentor that as part of the mentor program, she would be able to see Scot often at school once he returned to the home campus and that the two of them would also be invited to various social events throughout the semester.

The school counselor thought about the many changes that had happened with students since she had implemented the solution-focused program. The faculty members often e-mailed her about their mentored students, confiding in her. The mentor and the mentored students enjoyed the social events. It was endearing to see students deemed to be at risk mingling with their teachers in a positive fashion. It seemed to give many of them a positive adult in their lives, something that many of them had lacked prior to the program.

When Scot arrived at the counselor's office, she could tell from his expression that he was nervous to be back at school. The two of them sat for about fifteen minutes, and the school counselor showed him the Teacher Observation Sheet that the alternative school teachers had faxed to her the day before. Scot was surprised at the remarks of his alternative school teachers and at first was speechless:

SCHOOL COUNSELOR: I have given one of these forms to each of your teachers. What do you think they will say when they see it?

SCOT: They will probably say that it must not be me.

SCHOOL COUNSELOR: Well, let's say that you have accomplished a lot over the past few weeks. Why don't we talk about what you can do when you walk into class this morning, especially with Ms. Lindsey? If I recall, she has not seen this side of you before.

SCOT: Nope, she didn't see me like this, and I'm not sure that I am ready to see her.

SCHOOL COUNSELOR: I can imagine. What do you hope she sees in you when you walk in this morning that will show her what impressed the teachers at the alternative school?

SCOT: That I can be good.

SCHOOL COUNSELOR: How will you do that?

SCOT: Well, I guess that I can walk in and sit down to do my work. But if she starts in on me like she used to do, it will really be hard.

SCHOOL COUNSELOR: I know it will. I'll bet you had challenges at the alternative school too, and it looks like you figured that out. Tell me what else you will do here to show her that you are different from what she thought.

SCOT: If I can sit somewhere in the class where my friends aren't close by, I can probably not talk and not talk back to her. That's something that really helped me at the alternative school.

SCHOOL COUNSELOR: Okay. Let's walk down to your class, and I am going to reintroduce you to Ms. Lindsey and mention the idea you have of sitting away from your friends.

SCOT: Okay.

What Scot did not know was that the day before, the school counselor had talked briefly with Ms. Lindsey and personally handed her the form from the alternative school. When Ms. Lindsey seemed surprised at the form, the school counselor assured her that she would meet with Scot the next day when he returned and set some goals with him. She also reassured Ms. Lindsey that she was there to support her as well as Scot. The teacher seemed to appreciate the information and the offer of support. Before she left, the school counselor asked Ms. Lindsey to do just one thing when Scot came to class the next day: watch for signs that he was trying to do things differently. If the teacher wanted to, she could mention to Scot that she saw improvement.

Scot not only got off to a better start when he was reintroduced to Ms. Lindsey by his school counselor on that Wednesday morning, but he did the same in the other class that he had had difficulties with. The school counselor kept in touch with his teachers through e-mail several times each week and sometimes sent Scot a note by way of a classroom teacher that said, "Wow! You have made such a change. I am impressed with you." As for the mentor teacher, she was also the high school physics teacher, so whenever she saw Scot, she was usually working in the lab. Soon Scot became fascinated with physics. When he visited his mentor, he brought his friends with him to see the mentor teacher instead of standing in the back of the school where trouble sometimes started. The mentor stayed in contact with Scot throughout that school year, and the school counselor took note of the classes and the kinds of teachers who seemed to work for Scot. Each semester as the school counselor and Scot met to plan and schedule the next semester, she asked him what was going well first and tailored his schedule from their conversation. Scot graduated three years later and was the first person in his family to attend college.

Learning to Think with a Solution Focus

An Elementary Student Makes Her Mark

Across town on that same Wednesday morning, an elementary school counselor was meeting with a parent who had called her late on Tuesday afternoon and was very upset. The parent had told the school counselor that her daughter's teacher had sent a note home with her daughter describing how she was not working up to her potential. Apparently the daughter had always done well in school, and now the mother was frantic. She admitted that there had been changes with her daughter recently. She was having stomachaches in the morning and complaining about school in the evening. The conversation started as follows:

SCHOOL COUNSELOR: What can we talk about today that would be helpful to you?

MOTHER: Somehow I have to figure out what's going on with Megan. This has never happened to her before. She has always been such a good student.

SCHOOL COUNSELOR: How will that help you?

MOTHER: I guess if I know what's behind this, I can help her.

SCHOOL COUNSELOR: You mentioned that you have never had this problem before. Take me back to a time when this problem was much smaller or didn't happen at all.

MOTHER: Well, she attended a different school last year. We moved to a different neighborhood during the summer, and I had thought things were working out. She did have trouble making friends at first, but now she plays with the other children quite well in the neighborhood.

SCHOOL COUNSELOR: How about at school last year? What was different in any way that made it better?

MOTHER: I didn't work last year. When we moved, I took a part-time job in the evening to help with the new house payment. Now her stepdad helps her with her homework. Come to think of it, she did better when I helped her with her homework. Her teacher was different last year too. Megan needs to be prompted rather often. She is bright and will do the work for you if she gets praise and encouragement. She needs help to stay on task because she has a tendency to daydream. A few times this year, she has told me that her teacher rarely asked her if she needed help. Megan tends to be shy, and if she doesn't understand the work, she will just stop doing it.

SCHOOL COUNSELOR: So when you helped Megan with her homework, how did that make a difference?

MOTHER: We did it early in the evening and when she completed it, we would watch a movie together before bedtime. We had a routine. With my working now, I'm not sure that the routine is in place.

SCHOOL COUNSELOR: And you said that when her teacher prompted her, that made a difference.

MOTHER: Yes.

SCHOOL COUNSELOR: I know Megan's teacher rather well, and I would like to share your suggestions with her. Would that be all right with you?

MOTHER: Absolutely.

SCHOOL COUNSELOR: Would it also be all right if I went to get Megan out of class for just a few minutes so that we could talk with her?

MOTHER: Sure.

The school counselor went to get Megan from her classroom. She told the teacher that she had been talking with Megan's mother and that she needed to speak with Megan briefly. Together, Megan and the school counselor walked back to the meeting room where her mom was waiting.

SCHOOL COUNSELOR: Hi, Megan. It's good to see you. Your mother and I have been talking this morning about how things are going here at school. Your mother told me some ideas that I would like to share with your teacher, and I wanted you to know about them first.

MEGAN: Okay.

SCHOOL COUNSELOR: Your mother said that last year, your teacher helped you differently than your teacher this year is. Can you tell me what she did?

MEGAN: Well, we had these bookmarks that we had made, and if we had a question, we were supposed to put them on our desks and she would see it and then come help us. She was really nice. I liked her.

SCHOOL COUNSELOR: Your mother mentioned that you did your homework with her last year. Is that right?

MEGAN: Yes, but she works now to get money.

SCHOOL COUNSELOR: If you could teach your stepdad to help you like your mother did, what would you teach him?

MEGAN: (smiling) Me teach him? Well, we would have to do homework at the same time each night because sometimes he forgets until it's almost time for bed, and sometimes I forget what my homework is.

SCHOOL COUNSELOR: All right. And what would you be willing to do in return for your teacher if she tries to help you more in class just for this week?

MEGAN: I would be really good. I might not talk as much. Sometimes I talk when she is talking.

SCHOOL COUNSELOR: Would there be a better place for you to sit in class to help you do that?

MEGAN: Last year I sat up in front next to the blackboard. That's where she wrote the homework assignments down, and I would always remember to write them down that way.

SCHOOL COUNSELOR: Okay. You have both given me some great ideas. Megan, it sounds like it might help if you and your mother could work with your stepdad on a time to do homework. When I walk you back to class this morning, I would like to share with your teacher what worked for you last year. Would that be all right with you?

MEGAN: Yes.

MOTHER: That would be great.

Megan and the school counselor walked down to her classroom and spoke with Megan's teacher briefly in the hallway. The teacher was told that the school counselor was working with both Megan and her mother to help get Megan back on track with her schoolwork. The school counselor shared the ideas that both Megan and her mother had told her about the classroom that Megan was in last year. The teacher was receptive but unsure how to use a signal like the bookmark. Megan said that she would try and come up with something. The teacher was also told that Megan was going to try to behave more in class in response to the teacher's helping her more in class. The teacher was surprised that she had not been helping Megan enough. The school counselor thanked both Megan and the teacher and promised to check in with both of them the next day.

On Thursday, the school counselor sent Megan a note:

Dear Megan,

It was nice to visit with you and your mother yesterday. I learned a lot from you both. I learned that when you get the help you need in class, you do extremely well. I appreciated the way that you volunteered to help your teacher come up with a way to get her attention when you need help. I look forward to seeing your idea when I visit with you on Friday.

Warmly,
Ms. Johnson, School Counselor

On Friday, Megan's teacher came to see the school counselor to compliment her on Megan's new enthusiasm in class. She said that Megan had made a bookmark for her language arts book out of some magazines that the teacher had used in an art project. When several of the other students saw Megan's bookmark, they asked to make one too. The teacher asked Megan to show everyone how she made the bookmark, which instantly resulted in her getting along better with her classmates. Megan's mother spoke with her husband about a consistent time for homework and chose to call Megan each evening from work when she started her homework, which served as a reminder for her stepdad too. Megan's grades improved, and so did her behavior. The teacher still uses the bookmark idea each year.

If You Build the Opportunity for Success, They Will Come!

Teachers, school counselors, and administrators who are in the trenches every day know that students today deal with issues that leave even the most experienced educator stumped. There are grandparents rearing their grandchildren while their son or daughter is incarcerated. Financial worries push parents to work overtime, leaving little time for families to concentrate on school requirements and more time for mischief to evolve during that crucial time after school. While the idea of referring students to outside therapists is a good one, many students and their families can't and don't follow through. Yet the same students keep coming to school, and until they begin making changes, they affect everyone around them. They need help, and they need solutions to make it through the day. The words have to be right and the process has to be brief. The solution-focused approach can do both.

The School District That Did!

These first two stories in this chapter are typical ones in a school district that took a solution-focused approach in response to persistent problems of recidivism in their alternative secondary school and poor student motivation in the lower grades. As the developer and participant in this program, I saw firsthand not only remarkable changes in student behavior but morale improvement among staff members. This new approach of paying attention when students succeed rather than when they fail is a mind shift for many educators, who have only been taught to identify deficits as a way of helping. Many of the staff members were doubtful about whether a new approach would work and responded with concerns:

- Would promoting a welcome-back approach send a message that it was all right to misbehave?
- Would the pairing of a mentor mean that at-risk kids were being given privileges they did not deserve?
- Would looking only for success dismiss the real problems?
- Are we sugarcoating issues?

In response, I learned to ask those concerned staff members about what we had tried and whether those approaches had worked. When they resounded no, I went on to talk about what we were really trying to accomplish: student competency, responsibility, and success. Equally as important, I mentioned that I wanted them, the teachers, to have classrooms where they could teach. When our conversation resulted in defining goals such as getting students to behave, to be more successful academically, and to be more respectful, we were able to determine that the solution-focused program was simply a new experiment. After all, the traditional methods of trying to reach and teach challenging students had failed.

The teachers became slightly intrigued (though it took time) when they recognized that perhaps their classrooms might be easier to manage if the challenging students found some solutions. And I was quick to offer my support and involvement to make that happen for teachers and students. I worked for the teachers as well as the students. Slowly the teachers became interested, particularly when I thanked them for considering the program. During each faculty meeting on the participating campus, the school counselor was given time to inquire about what was working better at school. The counselor didn't stop at a few answers either; he kept asking, "What else?" and, "What else do

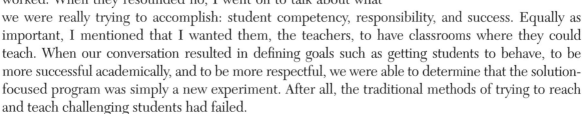

you need from me as we begin to work together on the solution-focused approach?" There was little time given to complaints. As stories of success began to emerge, a paradigm shift took place.

It is that paradigm that makes this approach so timely for schools now. That paradigm shift can create competency among all school clients. This chapter begins to explain the process of thinking that can create a solution focus.

The Power of Doing Things Differently

I recall a day as a young teacher, many years ago, when I sat in the teachers' lounge. I remember finding myself as depressed and frustrated as the other teachers were with some of the negative behaviors our middle school students were exhibiting. I expressed my frustration to several experienced teachers in search of help or advice. I received many empathetic statements such as, "Yes, he's in my class and he's a terror there, too," and, "Her mother has refused to answer my phone calls—one of those families." I am certain these statements were meant to be supportive, but they offered little help.

Fortunately I recalled a professor from one of my college education classes who once stated that the most helpful thing new teachers, or any other teachers, could do for themselves and their students was to stay out of the teachers' lounge—lest they become prejudiced against their students! With this in mind and frustrated that I was not getting anywhere talking to equally frustrated teachers, I retreated to my art classroom on a regular basis with another teacher for lunch and conference periods. We soon found that our more positive conversations at lunchtime were refreshing as we talked about personal issues and productive lesson plans. I noticed how I began to feel differently about my students without the labeling from fellow teachers. Thereafter I also noticed how the students reacted more positively to me when I knew less about their behaviors in other classes. I stayed in that middle school for eight years before returning to graduate school and found my time there quite rewarding.

Consider this question: "What didn't go quite so well last week, yesterday, or today?" How quickly did you recall specific incidences? If you are like most other people, it wasn't too difficult. You might even have a list! That's because when things intrude on our day, they stand out like a sore thumb. It's much harder to think of what did work.

Now consider a different question: "When you think about your week, yesterday, or today, what went slightly better than usual?" It takes more time to answer this question because when life goes smoothly, we mostly breathe a sigh of relief or just enjoy it. We rarely think, "Wow, how did I make this happen? What part did I have in this good result? What was different in any way?" Instead we're just glad we had one fewer problem.

Thinking differently about what we do in our schools means looking for the times when the problems occur less frequently and thinking about what we are doing that contributed to the success. This way of thinking changes the context of the problem from, "Jimmy, you're having a temper tantrum/anger outburst—get some control" to "The temper tantrum/anger outburst is in control again, Jimmy. How can you take over now?" It takes noticing when Charlie sits in his seat, if only for five minutes, while other students are running around the room. It takes noticing that Charlie stayed on task slightly longer today, even though Jonathan was having a tantrum. It may mean noticing that a poem in English class stirred a high school junior to ask a question for the first time this week. What happened during those slightly successful times? It's time that we begin to ask ourselves that question because the answers are our solutions.

It's Time to Close the Book and Open Our Minds

Perhaps in some school settings, closing a book may be more important than opening it, since doing so will force us to see our students differently: as competent people, not people with problems. In addition, it is important for educators to begin identifying their own personal competencies as well. That makes the model part of their life, not just part of their tool kit. For example, answer the following:

- What is your most valuable resource in working with your students?
- What would your students say your most valuable resource is?
- Are you a good listener, a creative teacher, a humorous administrator? If so, how do you do that?
- What would your students say you do that makes such a difference?

The solution-focused ideas in this book contain suggestions for simplifying interactions between educators and students. So begin suspending your thoughts about needing to solve every problem of every student, teacher, parent, and administrator who walks through your door. First, you can't possibly do that, and second, if you did, you would teach them that they needed you to solve their problems again in the future. That's not only overwhelming for you but unfair to them. Think how much better you both will feel when you begin helping them to solve their own problems and they leave your office realizing that they had the tools all along. They will grow, become more successful, and begin believing in themselves for a change. And you might just begin believing too, like the sculptor Michelangelo, that inside every beautiful piece of marble is a statue of beauty, just needing someone to free  it from the stone. You will use different tools to free your students, teachers, and parents from their problems, and they will see themselves as competent, many for the first time. As for the tools? They will show you which ones work for them. You merely have to ask the right questions.

Begin by Helping Students Recall When They Do Well

A very energetic seventh-grade boy once told me that his failure to turn in many other homework assignments caused his grades to stay below the passing level. During one of our sessions, he said that he did well in the classes where he sat in the front row. I suggested, in response to this comment, that he and his parents request a seating change for the remaining classes. But there was more. I asked him, "Tell me more about what else helps you to turn in your homework."

He said that what really mattered was where the classroom was. I was confused, so he explained that he began to notice how he turned in some assignments: he found that he turned in all of his papers when he put his homework in the class textbook and then took the textbook to class.

Unfortunately, he said, he could do so only when his books were in his locker and were near certain classrooms. If the locker was far from his classroom, he did not have time to get his work from his locker and turn it in.

He said that he had never been one for keeping an organized notebook, much to his parents' dismay, because he found it to be too much trouble. But after the conversation and observation about the locker, he turned to me in the session and said, "I just need to put my homework in each of my books and carry all of my books to class in my athletic bag." Although this would not have occurred to me, it worked well for him. His teachers called his parents to report his improvement in turning in his homework. And as for the student, he became quite strong!

Invite the Student to the Conference Table

As you will learn while reading this book, I often visit the schools of my private clients and gather teachers, parents, and students in an informal conference. In a recent conference with an eighth-grade boy who was struggling with paying attention and completing homework assignments, I asked

all of his teachers about the times Tom turned in work, paid attention, and performed other positive behaviors. Four out of eight of his teachers said that he turned in all of his work and that paying attention was only a slight problem. The other four were adamant about his reluctance to turn in work and pay attention. I casually mentioned that I wondered what was going on in four of Tom's classes that encouraged him to participate and complete his work. Needless to say, four of Tom's teachers became very quiet. They began to look in their grade books. Finally, one of the four teachers who had given positive reports said, "Let's ask Tom." Tom was reluctant to respond to his teachers, so I asked him to take his time and to be very specific about what worked. I then asked him how he might use some of the strategies that worked in half of his classes in one or two of his others for just a week. He stated some very specific strategies:

"I sit in the front of the room."
"I complete the homework in class."
"The teacher asks me if I understand the assignment."
"My dad checks my assignments when I ask him."
"When I know Dad will check with my teachers, I get with it."

I respectfully asked the teachers if they would watch Tom for just a week and notice when he attempted to do things differently and to tell him directly when they noticed his new behaviors. I then asked Tom to "do whatever it takes to get your teachers to notice you." The dynamics that occurred were powerful. The teachers who were quick to critique Tom's performance experienced peer pressure. Why was it that Tom succeeded in other classes but not theirs? The student, having stated his strategy in front of all eight teachers and his dad, committed himself to being watched and encouraged his dad's future participation and collegial competition. His school performance improved. An outline of this conference is provided at the end of this chapter on pages 27–28.

First, Believe in Yourself; Next, Recognize Strengths

Looking at students with a new lens is only an external tool if the theory behind it does not make sense to us personally. In fact, one of the tenets of Alcoholics Anonymous that conveys one's honesty in recovery is the idea that a person must "walk the talk." Otherwise, it is merely lip-service. It is quite easy to notice days when school goes poorly. But what about those days when you leave feeling as if you have made a difference, even if for only one student? Those days are treasure chests of solutions.

Moving from a Problem-Oriented to a Solution-Focused View

Educators who use solution-focused ideas have taught me that as they changed their thinking about students and themselves from a problem-oriented view to a solution-focused view, they changed their behavior and became more resourceful with interventions—and so did the student. The case study in the following section describes such a phenomenon.

Getting Through the Day Without Crying

Pat Peters, a fifth-grade teacher specializing in English as a Second Language (ESL), came to therapy as a last resort before she resigned her teaching position. She had taught for twenty years in another city and had recently taken a job at an inner-city school. She told me she was experiencing a depression that affected her so deeply that merely walking into the school building in the morning caused her to burst into tears at the sight of her students.

The students, a majority of whom were dealing with severe problems at home such as neglect, abuse, poverty, and little supervision, would react violently in the classroom toward Ms. Peters when she tried to discipline them with conventional discipline plans set by the district. She had spoken to the principal but received little support except for empathizing.

I began the first session by asking Ms. Peters how she had been able to stay in teaching for twenty years in what I considered to be a challenging teaching position. She responded modestly, saying that she was a good teacher who loved her profession. There had been students over the years who had made it a rewarding career. She said that was the difficult part, for these students were not all difficult. I asked about the students she found less difficult and how she had made it in her current position for the past five months in spite of the difficulties. She responded that there had always been one class in the morning at 10:00 A.M. that she looked forward to. The children in that class could not read when she began teaching them, and now they were progressing. Many of them were adolescents, and since they were nearing an age to drive a car, she had taught them to read a driver's license test booklet since she knew that subject would keep their interest.

She began to smile as she told me of one boy whom other teachers found very violent. She said initially she often placed her hand on his shoulder, and he would wince. Now she could place her hand on his hand, and he smiled at her. I commended her spirit and caring for her students and her practical approach to gaining their interest in reading. While she was glad to be given the

compliments, she still became sad as she mentioned the difficulties at hand. I continued to commend and affirm her professionalism to seek out those who needed her and help them respond to her so warmly. Quietly, she took the affirmation, although reluctantly.

As the session ended, I asked her to do only one task until I met with her again: "During the next week, I would like you to look at your students differently. Instead of seeing them as resisting you and fighting you, I would like you to see them as needing you but not knowing how to relate their needs. I'd like you to pick one student this week and do what you did for the student you told me about. I am asking you to do this for yourself, not just the student, because I can see the joy you receive when you touch a student and make a difference. It seems to work for you. Your smile told me so."

Reluctantly, Ms. Peters said she would try but did not expect to really do it. I told her I realized that this was a tremendous task for someone as sad as she described herself. This realization prompted me to write her a note and mail it the same day as the session:

Dear Pat,

I enjoyed meeting with you very much today. As I mentioned to you, I hold a special feeling for teachers, having been one for ten years. I admired your desire to talk to me about things that were bothering you at school and also your need to have better experiences in your classroom. This week I hope you will look at your students differently. I have a feeling that the magic you worked with [student name] made a tremendous difference in your life as a teacher. My hope for you this week is that you will do this for yourself once again with another student. I look forward to hearing about it!

Sincerely,
Linda Metcalf

Merely focusing on Ms. Peters's problems would have done little to rid her of the frustrations and sadness she was experiencing. Since she conveyed that she wanted relief from her depression and get through the day without crying, it was more helpful to focus on her successes and help her fondly reminisce on times when she did not cry. Many of us enjoy looking through photo albums and recalling happy, joyful, and meaningful occasions. What does reminiscing do for us? It often changes our perception of life events, people, experiences, and even future events. It reminds us that there have been happier times. Most of all, it changes our focus from one of problem saturation to that of a time when problems seemed less dominant. Our successes are like badges of courage, and we revel in our—or family members'—accomplishments. It was important that Ms. Peters recall her teaching successes at a time when she felt that there was little success.

When working with students, teachers, parents, and administrators, searching for more efficient, successful, happier times solicits solutions. Ms. Peters needed a reminder that she was indeed a teacher who made a difference, even in her current situation. She had become "problem saturated," noticing only the times when negative behaviors kept occurring, and her students readily responded to her perceptions. More important, her goal was to "get through the day without crying." If I had appealed to her that her students needed her and that she must give more of herself and put aside her feelings, I would have been giving advice, perpetuating the problem, and losing Ms. Peters's trust by not hearing her goal. Both the teacher and the students would have received a true disservice.

Ms. Peters sought relief from feeling depressed and frustrated. If her goal was "to be less depressed and frustrated," it would have been difficult to project how she would do so, especially since depression and frustration occur intermittently in many people's lives. In addition, being in the context of seeing herself depressed and frustrated left her feeling hopeless. She knew she had a tough population and simply wanted to make it through the day and then possibly make a difference to her students.

Don't Do Something New; Do Something That Worked Before!

The task for Ms. Peters was designed from her previous successes so that she would receive some satisfaction as she had before. It also practically guaranteed that she could do it. I make it a point when using solution-focused ideas never to ask the person in counseling to do something he or she has not done before successfully.  This means I always connect the task to a similar successful action the person has taken previously. For example, Ms. Peters was successful with a student who often experienced violent situations. As I asked her to attempt with only one student what she had been successful at with another student, I asked her only to do what she had been successful at previously. If I had asked her instead to implement a new behavioral program, hug each of her students in spite of their behaviors, and smile when she felt like screaming, I would have been disrespectful to her. I also couldn't have been as confident that she would succeed. In short, I cooperated with her goal. Steve de Shazer, one of the founders of the solution-focused approach, mentioned in his many writings that cooperating lessens resistance and encourages success.

One week later, Ms. Peters returned to therapy, smiling and reporting that her students had been better that week. She thanked me for the note, commented on my taking the time to write her, and mentioned how much that had meant to her. She also said that she was uncertain if she would have followed through with the task if I had not sent the note. She said she realized now that she had just been "thinking too negatively about the kids." I complimented her on this discovery. From that point on, she turned our conversations to other issues of concern in her life. Using the same approach throughout our remaining time together, Ms. Peters's depression and frustration lifted, and therapy ended after six sessions. She was able to complete her school year and then retire.

The Focus Is Now on the Solution, Not the Problem

The solution-focused approach presented in this manual offers a different way of thinking about school problems and assists both educators and counselors in discovering solutions through exceptions that have occurred previously. The ideas of the solution-focused approach encourage the student, parent, or teacher to step outside the problem for a moment and observe the influence of the problem on his or her life. From this observation and from identifying times when the problem is in less control, the student and educator are able to develop their own tasks so that they are in more control. This approach is particularly helpful in work with parents and teachers, for it allows them to notice how they encourage and discourage problems with students. When no centralized blame is placed on a parent, student, or teacher, resistance is lessened and everyone's task is to simply solve the problem.

Guidelines for Using the Solution-Focused Approach in the Classroom

The work presented in this manual is based on a cooperative relationship between the educator, student, parent, and counselor. The following guidelines were developed from the work of William Hudson O'Hanlon and Michele Weiner-Davis, authors of *In Search of Solutions* (1989) and have been applied to the school setting.

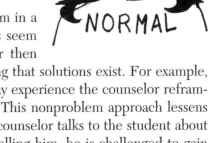

1. Using a Nonpathological Approach Makes Problems Solvable

When the educator or school counselor redescribes the problem in a normalizing manner, hope and possibility emerge as problems seem to become more solvable. The school counselor or educator then looks for exceptions to when the problem occurs, again inferring that solutions exist. For example, a student who is sent to the counselor for being hyperactive may experience the counselor reframing the complaint as "very energetic," a nonpathological term. This nonproblem approach lessens resistance by replacing it with a notion of normalcy. When the counselor talks to the student about the times when he is controlling the energy instead of it controlling him, he is challenged to gain control over the problem, which is interfering.

A high school junior might be referred to the vice principal for an anger problem that often causes disruptions in the classroom. An administrator might notice (as the student sits quietly) in the lunchroom one day that the student could have been tempted to explode in anger but did not. The next time the vice principal sees the student, he might comment on his amazement that the student could have gotten angry but instead refused to explode. He might ask the student, "How did you manage to be in control?" The student might then experience the vice principal differently and become aware of some positive behaviors that he did not know existed.

2. There Is No Need to Attempt to Understand or Promote Insight to Solve Problems

Here's an interesting fact: knowing why we are the way we are doesn't offer solutions. In fact, there has never been any research that deduced, "When you know why something happens, you have a solution for change." Instead, when students, parents, or teachers are given a reason that must be behind their sadness, anger, or anxiety, they often use that information as a symptom and reason for not succeeding. Even in severe cases of past sexual or physical abuse, students who are complimented on their strength to survive rather than given reasons for feeling depressed often blossom into competent, confident human beings who can deal with problems and events efficiently. It is our job to assist them with noticing their competencies.

One of the easiest ways of noticing a student's competencies is to notice if the problem is occurring at the time of intervention or initial interview. For example, a child who is sent to the counselor's office for being very angry may, in that context, appear to be a polite or calm child. That context is important because it produced the desired result. If the counselor asks the student, "How have you managed to control your anger for twenty minutes as you talked to me?" both may realize some more exceptions. Perhaps the child relays that the counselor is kind to him and not punitive. Maybe the time of day is an exception. Either way, the task can be developed according to the student's answers and counselor's observations.

3. It Is Not Necessary to Know a Great Deal About the Complaint

Today many school districts discourage their school counselors from doing therapy. Using solution-focused therapy does not necessitate that the counselor know everything about the problem in order to be helpful or appear to be doing therapy with students. The counselor can refer to the problem as either "it" or "the problem," using the student's language. Referring to the problem in this manner externalizes it, and the student and school counselor align to defeat it together.

A kind and understanding teacher once related a story to me about a seventh-grade student from a neglectful home (under investigation by authorities) who repeatedly came to her for nurturing when she was tearful. The teacher attempted to talk to her about the sadness, and the student refused. The teacher wisely and respectfully recalled times when her own daughters were young and felt a need for attention when they were saddened. She told the student it was fine with her if she needed attention at times, even if she did not want to relay the problem at hand. The student continued to approach the teacher for attention at times and eventually developed more trust with her. The teacher never knew what the exact problem was and did not find that information necessary in order to be helpful with the solution. In many situations, respecting a student's or teacher's need for privacy will lessen the resistance to communication and open up possibilities for solution talk. And it can happen without knowing details.

4. Students, Teachers, Administrators, and Parents Have Complaints, Not Symptoms

Anyone who has ever been labeled knows how it can change self-perception. I recall a young woman who came to counseling and declared that she was manic-depressive, suicidal, and bipolar, and she also was bothered by post-traumatic stress disorder. She even looked the part. She was sad, hopeless about her life, and saw no future with the labels and diagnoses. After hearing this résumé of pathology, I looked at her and said, "Would it be all right, just for this session, to put the labels outside in the hallway and just for an hour talk about what it is that you want to be different?" When the session was over, I asked the question that I typically end with: "What did we do here that might have made a difference?" She said, "It was nice to talk about something besides 'the problems,' because now I don't feel as sick. I don't feel as hopeless as I did before."

5. The School Client Defines the Goal

Consider these unfair statements that well-meaning teachers and school staff all over the world hear:

> "All students who come from single-parent homes are not functional. How can they be? They need an involved parent."
>
> "He already has a police record at fourteen. What kind of future could he possibly have? He needs to stop hanging around the other misfits here at school, or he will surely fail."
>
> "She's being reared by her grandmother, who has three other grandchildren to rear. How can she possibly get the attention she needs at home for her homework? She has to become responsible on her own."
>
> "His brother was a troublemaker, so he must be one as well. He needs to shape up if he comes to my classroom."

For years we have decided what students needed to do because of our unfair observations. There have been tasks designed by counselors, educators, and other experts who saw commonalities in behaviors and subsequently assigned solutions. Many times the suggestions worked after much labor to convince the school client by the "experts." However, the students came to depend on the expertise of the educators, placing more burden on the educators, who eventually felt anxious and resentful for having to do it all. Even worse, the student got little credit except for a pat on the back for following the directions given by the educator. That technique builds dependency, not competency.

Some outstanding strategies for solving the problems of students, teachers, and parents have come from these very populations and are mentioned extensively throughout this manual and the accompanying Field Guide. The solutions develop from exceptions defined by the persons involved. When I wrote down the exceptions that I heard directly from students, teachers, and parents, tasks developed that were achievable. The key to assisting students, teachers, and parents in solving their own problems lies in listening to their definition of what needs to be different and asking when it has been different.

6. There Is a Ripple Effect When One Person Changes

Virginia Satir, an experiential therapist who believed in the ripple effect that happens in systems, often wrapped a rope around a family as a playful exercise. She wanted to make this point: it takes only one person to move and change positions in order to cause other members of the family to move and change positions as well.

When school counselors reach a challenging student in their office and, with the student, come up with a plan, unless the school counselor and student inform the rest of the system what the plan is, the chances are that the plan will fail. The system unknowingly will attempt to bring the student back to the unwanted behavior by roles that stay the same. Those roles are comfortable and easier. It takes just a minute to sit with a student and construct a short e-mail message to the student's teachers or parents. In addition, the task becomes a contractual process, and the student becomes invested. Her task is to show the system the changes she has made. The system becomes intrigued that the student has motivation, and the chance for change doubles.

7. Complex Problems Do Not Require Complex Solutions

When I was a new elementary school counselor, I recall being asked to talk to a fourth-grade boy who had a problem with encopresis. He soiled his pants each morning, supposedly, around 11:00 A.M., and had done so for the past two years. Everyone in the school had a pet explanation of the problem:

- The teacher thought the boy was avoiding social interaction.
- The principal thought he was being defiant.
- The school psychologist thought he had sad feelings about his parents' divorce.
- The school nurse thought he was just too needy.

So, doubtful about what to do, they sent him to me. I was intrigued. He was slightly overweight, polite and kind, and loved to play video games. I asked him some behavioral-oriented questions about what happened when he soiled his pants. He said he would go to the office and call his mother, and she would come to pick him up and take him home to change clothes. There, he washed his own clothes and his mom, if she had time, would make him a hot lunch.

At first, it nearly slipped by me, so I asked more about the lunch. He said his mom always sent sandwiches in his lunch, and he disliked them. He preferred hot lunches, but his mom did not always have money to purchase the school lunch.

I asked the principal if we could get Johnny on free lunch as an experiment for two weeks. I asked Johnny to bring up a few sets of clean clothes in case he didn't get to the bathroom on time. I then told him that the school had discovered that he could get a sort of "grant" from the school that enabled him to eat hot lunches for the next two weeks.

There was only one incident during the next two weeks. We kept him on free lunch for the rest of the year, and the incidents completely stopped.

8. Fitting into the School Client's Worldview Lessens Resistance

Many counselors have encountered students who felt persecuted by a teacher or parent. The adolescent often exaggerates the dilemma and appears to dramatize the seriousness of the situation. Suggesting to an adolescent that she must change is sometimes a guarantee that she will not; it is the nature of adolescence. However, aligning with a student, stepping into her worldview to get the teacher, parent, or administrator off her back, is the quickest way to resolution. Resolved that the teacher, parent, or administrator will not change, the student has no recourse but to come up with ways to resolve the situation. The results are the same: the student behaves differently, and others respond in kind. For example, a high school student who feels the coach just won't get off his back and is full of complaints to the vice principal can be asked:

VICE PRINCIPAL: How will you know when things are just slightly better for you in regard to the coach?

STUDENT: He won't hound me as much. He'll get off my back.

VICE PRINCIPAL: I agree, getting him off your back is a good idea. When, this year, has he been off your back?

It is often helpful to use this approach with students who complain about other teachers, coaches, nurses, and others in school. The goal is the same: to assist the student in creating better relationships. Another approach to this same situation would be to invite the coach and the student for a joint conference. The conference might begin with the vice principal addressing the coach: "Coach, Todd's concerned about the way you and he have been dealing with each other lately. I want you to know that I called you both here because I want you both to get what you want in this situation. Can you tell me a time this year when you didn't find it necessary to keep after Todd?" During the conversation, Todd may hear the coach say that when Todd showed up for practice on time in the fall and worked hard, he had no reason to give him a hard time. This usually comes as a surprise, and Todd may start moving in a better direction. Everyone wins.

9. Motivation Is a Key Ingredient for Change

Many times motivation is not present because people do not know what they want to occur differently and have no specific goal in mind. The way to find out about motivation is to ask  directly: "Are you willing to do whatever it takes to make things better for you?" If the answer is yes, you have a customer. If not, let the student know you are there and that he needs to come back soon when he is ready to tell you specifically what it is that he wants changed. The counselor might say, "Sandy, it's obvious to me that you have some true concerns about Mr. Smith, your algebra teacher. One thing I've learned is that unless you know how you want things to be, it's hard to accomplish anything different. Let's take a break. For the next few days, I'd like you to think about what you want changed with Mr. Smith. You might try paying attention to times in his class that are slightly better for you, as well as in other classes. In a few days, please stop by and tell me what you liked about those times and what you hope will happen more often."

If a student, teacher, or parent desires a change but is not quite sure what it is that she wants to be different or is wanting to change someone else, caution that she cannot change anyone but herself. Then ask the following question to assist in identifying a goal: "Notice this week the times when you feel slightly better. Notice where you are, who is there, and what you are doing. Come back next week, and tell me what part of the week you would like to experience again."

10. There Is No Such Thing as Resistance When We Cooperate

Steve de Shazer (1985) said that when we find ways to cooperate with people, there is no such thing as resistance. This means that we align, sympathize, empathize, and use language designed to connect with the student, even if his or her goal or desire seems impossible. It is important to cooperate in this manner and then renegotiate with the student how things would be different if the impossible goal occurred. This serves to honor the student's wish and help him or her to see other ways to reach that wish. Children and adolescents seek acceptance and validation, so by working in this way, the student is accepted by the school counselor and the goal is heard as a valid one. For example, a student who fights constantly may be perceived as wanting some control in his life and should be acknowledged for needing control; a parent who overprotects can be perceived as protecting slightly more than necessary. These collaborative statements and messages align with whatever the students seek, but the reframing opens up possibilities instead of perpetuating the problem.

For example, students who fight and like being in control can be discouraged from fighting. A principal might say, "Now that you are in the principal's office, it looks like the problem is controlling you! I realize that fighting gives you some control, but now I've got control over you. I'd like to give it back to you. I wonder what you might do to stay out of my office and under your own control?" And a teacher might ask a parent who is overprotective, "You obviously love your child very much. I wonder, though, if it is working for him that you are at school constantly now that he is interested in becoming much more independent. You seem like the kind of parent who would want him to begin finding his own way. I'll keep an eye on him and stay in touch if you like." Both situations cooperate with the school client's view and lessen resistance.

11. If It Works, Don't Fix It; If It Doesn't, Do Something Different

One of the most helpful questions to ask school clients who keep trying the same ineffective strategy over and over is, "Is this working for you?" At times it sounds absurd as they describe their previous strategies of smarting off, stomping out, or fighting in the bathroom. Often both educator and student (or parent) end up smiling, realizing that everyone's strategy can be improved. The session can become more productive by asking the same student, "What has worked for you?" This allows him to recall successful interventions that have worked. The tasks for the days and weeks ahead develop from past successes, no matter how small and insignificant they may appear during the process.

12. Focus on the Possible and the Changeable

Many children would like to be Spiderman, and many adolescents would like to stay out all night. Realistic thinking is the key in solution-focused work, and it must focus on the visible and specific. For example, a child who wants Tommy to stop teasing him can't change Tommy but can change where he encounters Tommy on the playground. An adolescent who complains about his mom's yelling can't stop her from yelling (although she would probably disagree) but can change his responses to those that work at other times with other people (or even his mom).

In addition, the time allotted to work on solutions is important and should be customized to the age of the school client. In elementary schools, a task should not be attempted for longer than an afternoon for a kindergartner to two days for a sixth grader. In secondary school, two days to one week should be the maximum time a task is to be carried out. Performing a task within this short time period is more achievable than attempting to change for an entire term. Besides, children and adolescents conceptualize the future in short time frames. Cooperating with that thinking gets compliance.

13. Go Slowly, Building on Skills and Success

Caution students to not go too fast. Really! You may find that your students want to score a 10 on the scale and be in charge of their life after one visit with you. While you may find it thrilling that they are so motivated, it is more helpful to be supportive and ask them to improve just slightly. Then when they achieve more than you encouraged, they are the experts extraordinaire.

Also, cautioning students to go slowly prevents slow success from being perceived as failing or not happening fast enough. In actuality, when defeating a problem is the focus, not going backward into the grip of the problem should be viewed as success. Make sure you commend students, for example, for not going backward. Another reason for encouraging students and teachers to go slowly is that lasting change takes time. A flutist may find that improvement fluctuates with different musical scores. Change occurs in the same way.

14. Rapid Change Is Possible

Teachers who use the solution-focused approach in classrooms directly are often surprised at how quickly students change behaviors. An elementary teacher told the story of Scott, a kindergartner, who had temper tantrums at least three times a week, usually before 10:00 A.M. Tired from the frequent referral, one morning she went to him and asked:

TEACHER: Would you like to fight off the temper tantrums [his description] just for today?

Scott looked puzzled at first but then said that he wasn't sure if he could.

TEACHER: It's 9:45, and I've just realized that you have not had a tantrum yet this morning. How have you done that?

SCOTT: I just did it!

The teacher continued to remind Scott when he continued to fight off the tantrums during the morning and ask him, "How are you doing this?" Scott did not have a tantrum that day and decreased his tantrums to once every two or three weeks. His teacher rewarded him with being line leader more often, and his counselor presented him with a certificate stating that he had defeated the temper tantrum monster. His mother called and asked the teacher what she was doing because her son was coming home from school so much happier than before.

15. Change Is Constant and Inevitable; Watch for It

When you read a new book, experience a new workshop, or develop a new habit, change occurs. The systems we live in change constantly, which leads to our changing constantly. The process is not always easy, but it is inevitable. When students and parents express the sad notion that "he/she will never change," it is more helpful for the counselor to acknowledge this perception: "I'll bet it must feel that way. When have you noticed [name] making very small changes in other situations?" "Did you have a part in that? How did you do that? How did you see her do that?"

Remember to encourage the school client to "try one thing different" as an experiment and tell you later what the result was. This encouragement places the responsibility back on the school client and increases competency.

16. Every Complaint Pattern Contains Some Sort of Exception

How often have you heard the following statements?

"I'm angry all the time."
"He's hyperactive constantly."
"She never stays in her seat."
"I'm totally stressed out all of the time with all of my classes."

These global statements of complaints are typical from people who feel hopeless and out of control. Yet no one stays angry 100 percent of the time, for they would surely be exhausted. When students talk about school being "awful," ask, "When is it not as awful?" Opening up the possibility that to each problem there is an exception gives opportunities for people to see that they are in control more than they think. Many times, counting the minutes, hours, or days when a problem is not interfering with schoolwork or home makes it seem more solvable and less intrusive in life. For example, of a seven-day week, three days might seem to be slightly depressing and only for three hours of each day. Thinking that 9 hours out of 168 hours are downtime minimizes the effects of the problem, lessens the burden, and helps the student or educator feel more in control.

17. Changing the Time and Place Will Change the Context for a Solution

Students often complain about the teacher who never calls on them or doesn't pay attention to them. However, on examination, a student may realize that it's not the teacher but the timing that's crucial. Sending a student back to class to notice when the timing is better to approach the teacher may give the student a new perspective on how to achieve the goal of getting called on or getting necessary attention. If possible, encourage a teacher to visit with you and the student and ask the same questions. Together, changing the time and place according to what works best will benefit both.

18. Look at Problems Differently and Redescribe Them

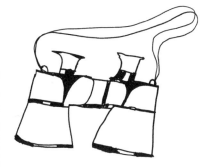

I once remarked to an adolescent in a group who had been placed in a psychiatric hospital–based school how well he did on a weekend visit with his parents. In the past, he had talked to me about his violent outbursts and angry words that truly were interfering in his reconciliation with his parents. He described himself as doing "okay," but said one of the staff members said he was "stuffing" feelings, which made the client feel negative about his actions. I remarked that I saw it a little differently: I saw him as successfully disciplining himself around his parents. He stopped for a moment and then agreed that he had disciplined himself and kept control. From that point on, when another peer talked of "stuffing" feelings, he retorted that the peer was good at self-disciplining. It's contagious.

Summary

Considering and questioning how we think about school, students, teachers, parents, and administrators is vital to this approach because our reactions will differ if we think about issues using a problem focus rather than a solution focus. Our beliefs and theories about people and their competencies are evident from the moment we shake hands with someone in distress until we help them reach resolution. Consider the following questions for yourself:

- How do you think about people and their abilities to change when they are given the opportunity? How have you created that opportunity before?
- Do you believe that your students have competencies—or that they need you to solve all their problems?
- Do your teachers and staff members feel that you work for them as much as you do your students? If so, terrific! If not, what will you begin doing differently to send that message?

Learning to think differently about school clients often leads us to noticing many avenues in which others have discovered the same secret. In an episode of *Northern Exposure,* a popular television show in the 1990s, a scene involving the carving of a flute sends a metaphorical message that can be adapted to our school clients. In the episode, a Native American woodcarver carves a flute as a younger Native American man watches him. The woodcarver is focused and quite careful. The younger man is curious: "How to you know where to carve?" The woodcarver politely and respectfully replies in reference to the wood that he holds in his hands: "Inside every alder branch, there is a flute—your job is to find it."

Now, go find the flutes.

Solution-Focused Training Exercise: Chapter One

The following questions have been designed as a personal exercise to assist in understanding solution-focused ideas. The exercise can be duplicated for faculty meetings. For maximum benefit, discuss your findings in groups of two or three people.

THE PROBLEM-FOCUSED APPROACH

What has been the most frustrating problem for you this year at school? This is the problem.

_____

_____

_____

What did you do to solve your problem? These are your strategies.

_____

_____

_____

Which ones worked? Circle those strategies. Which ones did not work? Draw a line through those.

If your answer was full of success, congratulations! If, however, you were not satisfied with your strategies, please read on. The problem with "problems" is that we notice them only when they're bothering us—when they are present. Clues to solutions lie in the times when problems are not present. These are called exceptions.

THE SOLUTION-FOCUSED APPROACH

What will be different when the problem that has been bothering you at school disappears? This will become your goal.

_____

_____

_____

Solution-Focused Training Exercise: Chapter One (cont.)

When was the last time you were just slightly successful in achieving that goal? (Searching for exceptions)

_____

_____

How did you do that? (Exceptions = strategies)

_____

_____

Where else in your life, profession, job, or personal life are you successful at accomplishing something similar to the above goal?

_____

_____

What strategies do you use to accomplish such a personal task?

_____

_____

If you tried just one or two of these strategies in school for a week, what would you do? What would someone see you doing differently?

_____

_____

_____

Tasks

- Today, notice what goes well. Make notes of what works instead of focusing on what doesn't work in your job, with your kids, or with others in your family. Notice how you feel when these exceptions to life's stresses occur. Consider prescribing this for yourself the next time you need a solution.

- Before the week is over, try a strategy that you identified as helpful in your personal life at school with one student, one teacher, or one parent. Observe what happens.

Teacher-Student-Counselor Conference

Begin the conference by meeting with the teachers as a representative of the student in case the teachers are upset with the student and need to voice their concerns. After the concerns have been voiced, let the teachers know that this conference will focus on what needs to happen rather than why there is a problem with the student. Then invite the student into the meeting.

Say to the teachers: "I am currently working with [student's name], and together we are interested in your concerns. Let's begin by talking about how you would like things to be in the future." This becomes the goal of the meeting. [If the teachers begin to talk about what needs to stop, thank them and respectfully ask for what they want to see instead.]

Make a list of their wishes for the future:

1. _____

2. _____

3. _____

4. _____

5. _____

6. _____

Say to the teachers: "Please each of you look in your grade books or notes and begin to identify times when a little of that happened for [student's name] in the classroom. Make a list:

1. _____

2. _____

3. _____

4. _____

5. _____

6. _____

Teacher-Student-Counselor Conference (cont.)

Say to the student: "We are all interested in your thoughts about the times when [the student's goal] happened slightly in a classroom. Tell us what a teacher did that made the difference for you." Make a list:

1. _____

2. _____

3. _____

4. _____

5. _____

6. _____

Say to the student: "What did you do during those times that also helped these successes to happen?"

_____

_____

_____

Say to the teachers: "What did you say that [student's name] did to help these successes to happen?"

_____

_____

_____

Say to the teachers and the student: "If over the next week, we were all to try again what has worked before, what would you each suggest we try based on our discoveries here today?"

_____

_____

_____

Chapter Two

Creating Possibilities Through Language

If in our world language plays a very central part in those activities that define and construct persons, the redescription of persons is called for.

—David Epston and Michael White (1990)

We describe our world with language. Problems to one person are not always problems to others because of the meanings attached to them. Because language plays such a central role in how we perceive ourselves and our behavior, redescribing situations can often lead to different perceptions and differing behaviors. It makes sense, then, that assisting students, teachers, and parents to see themselves as competent may require redescribing their concerns with a more solvable description. Ours is a problem-focused world, and most of us go through our days noticing primarily the obstacles placed in our way. For example, consider for a moment the worst situation you dealt with yesterday. Remember the details?

Now consider another situation—the best situation you encountered yesterday or the day before—one that you would like to repeat today or tomorrow. Slightly more difficult? Be assured that you are not alone in having difficulties remembering the times life worked. Now consider living your life in a new way, learning what worked and doing more of it.

Life's Little Experiences

Epston and White (1990) mention that people give meanings to their lives through the stories of their experiences. The description an individual gives in her storytelling is her unique reality, and that reality directs the way she lives life. Most of us seem to notice the tragedies in our stories

and ignore the rich unique outcomes or alternative stories in our lives that might make the story less dreary if we added them. White (1989) encourages us to notice the unique outcomes, similar to the "exceptions" in solution-focused therapy, and insert them into our life stories in place of the problems, thereby creating new possibilities in which to live and perceive our experiences. The following explanation of this process by Epston and White (1990) is very interesting: "As unique outcomes are identified, persons can be encouraged to engage in performances of new meaning in relation to these. Success with this requires that the unique outcome be plotted into an alternative story about the person's life" (p. 41).

Label No More

How much power does a label have? Enough to keep a high school graduate from applying to college after being told she's not college material because her PSAT score was too low. Enough to stop a student from trying to complete his math homework because he's been told he doesn't concentrate well enough and has attention deficit disorder. Enough to convince a parent that her elementary school child may not be able to perform like the other children because the child did not attend preschool. When labels start looming over students and parents, self-esteem drops and conventional ways of teaching the student are tried; when those ways don't work, the label gets the credit for the problem. Staff begin to feel as if their hands are tied. Students feel defeated and quit.

Labels are for soup cans, not for students.

While diagnoses are important for classifying many students into categories that can lead to different kinds of instruction, special services, interventions, and even medication that is often very helpful, the solution-focused school counselor must try to add a new description to the situation when labels interfere with the solution. Otherwise teachers and administrators feel limited in how to teach students and talk to parents. Everyone feels stuck when their approaches fail. Some even stop trying. The biggest loser is the student.

The Honor Student Who Wouldn't

The following case taught me more about working with a solution-focused approach and involving the system than any other case. While my approach in working with adolescents stayed the same, my approach with collaborating with the school staff changed dramatically as a result. The case shows the importance of involving everyone who is part of a student's day in the intervention. It also shows the power of changing descriptions of a school client during parent conferences and teacher conferences so that everyone grasps the new description.

Marty was thirteen, and according to his mom, he had made A's in elementary school, and when he got to middle school, he was placed in advanced classes such as algebra 1 and Spanish 1 because his test scores indicated that he was college material. However, during the past few months prior to our meeting, Marty had stopped doing his homework and often fell asleep in class. Then Marty's mom found marijuana in his sock drawer, confirming her suspicion that Marty's behavior changes were drug related. Shortly after, he was expelled because he had brought the marijuana to school. That was the final straw that caused her to make an appointment for counseling.

Marty's parents were divorced, and his mom was a teacher. When Marty's behavior continued to get worse and he wouldn't listen to her, Marty's mom had his grandparents take Marty to his dad's house, where Marty slept in a refurbished barn in the back yard that had only the bare essentials: heat, electricity, and water. Marty had tried to get things back on track, but his dad continued to put him down emotionally, saying that he was a disappointment to him and his family. Marty responded with more rebellion, smoked pot in the barn, and spent his time going back and forth from one parent's house to another.

When I met Marty, he was convinced that his parents thought of him as "a bad kid with no future." We talked that first day about what the substance abuse problem had done to his relationship with his family:

LM: I know that you say you like smoking marijuana. I understand that it relaxes you and that you do it with your friends. But it also looks like it is interfering with some things in your life. Tell me how marijuana has interfered with your family life, school work, and friends.

MARTY: Well, I only smoke it with my friends, except when I am at dad's house. I am mad that my mom went through my stuff. She's never done that before. But I guess it interferes with school because I just don't want to go anymore. I'd rather sleep.

LM: What about your relationship with your parents?

MARTY: My mom yells, but then she has always yelled. My grandparents, they come on way too strong. They come over when my mom calls them and take me out of my own house to my dad's house. That is not cool. Then my dad gripes at me the entire time I am there. The whole thing makes me mad.

LM: It seems like your parents aren't seeing you anymore; they just see the problem with the marijuana.

MARTY: Yeah. Actually, I don't think they have ever really seen me anyway. And now they just think that I am a bad kid.

LM: How do you wish that they would begin seeing you?

With that question, Marty began to sob openly, saying that there was no point in any counseling because his parents would never believe in him again.

LM: I know, but I am still wondering what you wish they would see in you and believe in again.

MARTY: That I am a good kid. I am really. I did get good grades. I did take care of my sister when my mother used to ask me to. I did get along with my stepbrother at my dad's. No one ever thinks of those things. They only see me one way.

LM: Right. What do you think that you could begin doing that would help your mom and dad begin to see you differently, like the good kid you just mentioned?

Creating Possibilities Through Language

MARTY: Probably not make any more holes in the wall at my mom's house. That really ticked her off. And probably stop smoking dope. I don't have to do it. I just like it.

LM: What else?

MARTY: Probably listen and do what Mom says when I am at home.

LM: What about Dad?

MARTY: He's close to impossible, but if I lay off the dope, he might stop griping about that.

At that point, I went out to get Marty's parents, both of whom I had invited to the session. I had begun inviting both parents to sessions when I started using a solution-focused approach because I found that they often contributed ideas of what had worked with their child in their respective homes or in other places. In addition, when working with a child who visited both parental homes, I felt it was important for both parents to agree with the interventions that we developed together.

I stopped Marty's parents in the hallway and spoke to them:

LM: I know that your son is doing some things that you disagree with. I also know that you both are trying very hard to get him back on track. Dad, you have tried staying on him, and Mom, you have tried talking loudly to him and getting your parents to help. Would you say that these strategies have worked to accomplish what you want?

PARENTS: Obviously not.

LM: Then when we go back into the session, I am going to use a new approach, mostly because I am concerned that the old approach that you have been trying may cause you to lose your son, and I get the impression that you don't want to do that. Together, we are going to help him become responsible for gaining your respect back.

When parents become as obsessed as Marty's parents were, punishing their son in the hope of making a point, they make things worse. For some adolescents who rarely get into trouble, consequences such as those tried by Marty's parents work. But for adolescents who feel lost and are involved with drugs, such as Marty, consequences don't work. For that adolescent, there is no way out. This had become the cycle where Marty made a mistake, was punished, and was never acknowledged for anything that he tried to do better. At thirteen, he had given up on himself. That led to more time with his drug-using friends and more negative actions toward his family.

We went back into the room, and Marty was waiting with anticipation. The tears had dried, but his eyes were still red. His parents were surprised at his emotions.

LM: Marty, I would like for you to share with your parents how you want your parents to begin seeing you.

MARTY: (quietly) That I am a good kid.

LM: Tell us what you think you would need to begin doing so that they see you as a good kid.

MARTY: Probably stop smoking and stop making holes in my walls.

LM: What do you think your parents could do to begin helping you to accomplish that?

MARTY: I want to live with my mother all of the time. No offense, Dad, I like coming to see you but not living with you. The barn is cold, and you never spend time with me anyway.

LM: Mom, what will Marty need to do to stay with you?

MOM: He can do what he just said.

MARTY: And I don't want my grandparents spying on me. I can do this.

MOM: They were just helping me.

MARTY: I don't need their help. You and I just need to get along better.

MOM: Like how?

MARTY: Like we used to do before you started working. Now you come home late and just give orders to me to take care of this and that. We used to get along better when you didn't yell as much either.

MOM: All right, if you can stop making holes and even begin patching the ones that you have already made, then I will watch the yelling and keep my parents away.

MARTY: Okay.

MOM: And I intend to give you a drug test every few weeks to make sure you are not using. It isn't allowed in either house.

MARTY: I know.

DAD: What about school?

MARTY: I can get it together in school. I always have.

At this point, the session ended, and Marty moved home with his mother. I continued to see them for a month until his mother said that things were going so well that they could stop coming until school started. Over the summer, they both took time to get to know each other better, and the mother thanked her parents for their help but assured them that she could handle things from there. Marty went to summer school and passed with A's the classes that he had been failing that spring. Soon he was ready to go back to his middle school the next fall. He and Mom were getting along well, and his dad had backed off from negative comments. He was showing them "the good kid."

When Marty returned to school on the first day of the fall semester, he was optimistic. Then an administrator stopped him when he walked in the door of the school and said, "Why did you even bother to come back? Don't you know you are not welcome here?"

Marty turned around and walked out the door. Three miles later, he was at home. The school called his mother to report his truancy. His mother and I called the school and did what we could to tell the administrator that he had been in counseling, had made changes, was no longer using drugs, and was motivated to begin school again. Although the principal scolded the administrator for his action and called Marty herself, it did little to raise Marty's spirits. His mother eventually placed him in a private school that fall, and although he did well there, the rebellion he had tucked away surfaced at times.

As for my lesson, I learned to stay in touch with the new school staff since Marty and I talked occasionally, giving him a chance to be seen differently and more successfully. When that finally occurred, Marty retrieved his confidence and continued as an honor student, and his relationship with both parents got better.

Seek Always the Worldview

As school clients describe their stories, they tell us about the experiences that directed their past behaviors and contributed to their current problems. It is important to listen to what de Shazer (1985) calls "the worldview of the client" because it helps the solution-focused educator know how to assist in coauthoring the story. Listening and suggesting different descriptions of the story is a way of assisting students, teachers, and parents in new ways of seeing their problems. This reauthorship may then encourage new behaviors and relieve the person of feeling hopeless, motivating him or her to engage in new behaviors that do not support "the problem."

A way to change the focus from doom to dream is by redescribing the presented problem into solution talk. The lists below were composed by school counselors and educators who received training in the solution-focused approach. They listed the common complaints they experienced in their schools as problem talk and then developed a more solvable solution talk list:

Problem Talk	Solution Talk
Hyperactivity	Very energetic at times
Attention deficit disorder	Short attention span sometimes
Anger problem	Gets upset sometimes
Depressed	Sad
Oppositional	Argues a point often
Rebellious	Developing his or her own way
Codependent	People are important to him or her
Disruptive	Often forgets the rules in class
Family problems	Worries about his or her home life
Shy	Takes a little time to know people
Negative peer pressure	People try to influence him or her
Feelings of rejection	People forget to notice him or her
Isolating	Likes being by himself or herself

The lists do not in any way minimize the severity of the problems identified as problem talk. However, school clients often feel heard when their problem is redescribed to them and relax at the suggestion that things are not as bad as they thought. This doesn't minimize the problem; it maximizes the chance of a solution. Describing a problem as terrible and difficult rarely motivates people to change. How could they? For example, if you have the choice to be described as having a major depressive disorder versus being sad, which would you rather be labeled as having?

Which one seems temporary and which incapacitating? New descriptions assist students, teachers, and parents by helping them feel more normal. The descriptions do not change the problem; they change the meaning ascribed to the problem. The school client is more likely to change the meaning personally of who he or she is and can become.

Getting Specific

An integral part of becoming solution focused is learning to develop realistic and specific goals with school clients. The two lists of problem talk and solution talk show the difference between a vague goal and a specific goal. The solution-focused educator can assist in the process of writing and developing new stories with students, teachers, and parents by helping them define the desired future behavior specifically. It is better to work toward a specific goal, such as "talking to a new friend," rather than "being happier at school," a vague goal. One way to help a school client go from vague to specific is to ask, "What will I see you do when you are [happier, less angry, less sad]?"

The clarity of the goal promotes the solution-focused process because it allows the solution-focused educator to press on toward exceptions. Adolescents have different perceptions of things such as cleaning their room, being home on time, completing assignments to the best of their ability, and using effective study habits. The language must be specific and competency based if it is to create an atmosphere conducive to responsibility and cooperation. When new, specific descriptions are given, new behaviors can then emerge and possibilities for solution exist.

The following two lists show how goals can be redescribed so that they are specific, observable, and realistic:

Vague	Observable
I want my father to listen to me more often.	I will talk to my father in a quiet, calm voice so he will listen.
I want to stop being sent to the office every day.	I will follow directions in class and do my assignments on time.
I will stay out of fights.	I will walk away from trouble in the cafeteria and go to the gym.
I want to get out of this alternative program.	I need to stay in my seat and let the teacher see me raise my hand so she knows I won't need the alternative program.
I want Ms. Jones to get off my back.	I'll do what Ms. Jones thinks I should do in class to stay out of trouble: do my homework and sit far away from my friends.
I just want to be happier.	When I make new friends and do fun things with them I will feel happier.

Learn to Assume That Change Can Happen

The attitude and perspective of the solution-focused educator when working with school clients are as vital to the process of assisting people as are the questions asked. The following suggestions are ideas that educators can use for presenting an assumption that change is imminent:

• *Talk about the experiences of the school client as if they were in the past, available for reference, but also workable enough for redesigning in the future.* For example: "Sue, I certainly understand how moving four times in the past two years has made it difficult for you to feel as if you are part of the social life at high school. Since I have learned from you today how important it is to feel part of your school, I wonder how you might like things to be different now that you know you will be at this school for the next full year at least."

• *Encourage and invite very young children to imagine describing their story to a child in need of a solution.* Help change their negative experience into a successful triumph over their problem (Keeney, 1994). For example: "Alex, I often work with children such as you who are very angry at their parents for one reason or another. You and I have talked about how you want things to be today and described to me what you are going to do the next time anger gets in your way. I'd like you to tell me in your own words what I might tell the next child I see who is dealing with anger, based on what you now know."

• *Redescribe behaviors that sound pathological into behaviors that seem solvable and common:* "So you get upset sometimes when people tell you what to do. Gee, it sounds like you've got your own ideas and people aren't listening to you right now. That seems to happen to many students. How would you like your teachers to see you: As an angry student who closes her mind, or as a creative student who has questions and suggestions about assignments?"

• *Normalize behaviors for the student, teacher, or parent.* Help them feel as if their situation occurs commonly and that they do not have a severe problem. "Ann, I am really impressed that you have stayed in the geometry class this year. Many students wouldn't have forced themselves to get tutoring or persevere like you have. Even though your grade is low, you keep on going. How do you manage such drive to finish this class?"

• *Pretend that the student's life is considered to be act 1 in the Play of Life.* Now construct "act 2" with the student. Change the characters, interactions, and behaviors into a new scene in which the student does things differently. Ask the student how his peers, teachers, or parents would like to see him in act 2: "John, until now, things have been tough as your parents divorced. Now that you have moved here and you say your mom is happier, let's consider all this act 1 in your life of sixteen years. Now let's talk about how you want act 2 to go. If we used your friends, mom, and other close relatives in your life as the audience, how do you think you and they might write act 2?"

• *Assume change will occur or has already occurred:* "Lauren, someday soon when the sadness about your grandfather's death is not bothering you as often as now, what will you be doing more of?" "Jonathan, when you bring your grades back up to passing in the next few weeks or so, what will be different here at school and at home?" "Mr. Smith, when Priya begins to comply with your rules at home, using the ideas we have discussed here today, what do you see as happening more often at home, or in your relationship with her?"

Notice how encouraging the language is in these suggested dialogues. Using *when* rather than *if* sends a message that the changes will happen. This use of presuppositional language is a suggestive way of not only suggesting success but obtaining answers. If, for example, a student is asked, "If things change for you, what do you think might be different?" the chances are that the student will say, "I don't know." But if the same student is coaxed again by words such as, "Tell me what will change for you when things are different soon," this becomes a sort of command to look into the future and identify what will be better. This use of language is particularly helpful for students who are not as verbal as the educator might wish. It not only helps school clients to solidify what they want to happen, but it helps them to recognize that it can happen. This increases motivation.

A Case Study: A Short Story About School Refusing, by David Epston

The following case, contributed by David Epston, shows how a new focus on an old problem motivated the student to change his behavior. The case illustrates the use of various narrative ideas so that the adolescent concerned begins to see himself differently and gives up negative behaviors for new ones. Because Epston wrote the case study, the "I" mentioned throughout refers to Epston.

Fifteen-year-old Ronald was the very intelligent only son of a frail 70-year-old father and 54-year-old mother. This family had been known to our agency for some time. His father had retired recently and ever since that day, Ronald started refusing school. My colleagues asked me to see this family, as they had grave fears that Mr. Peterson, who had had open heart surgery recently, would not survive Ronald's temper tantrums, which involved breaking windows and smashing furniture. Mrs. Peterson also suffered from angina and there was concern for her health too. Several things impressed me upon reading the file. Ronald, despite his infrequent

attendance at school, was maintaining an A average. Secondly, he had suffered from a neurological disorder as a three-year-old, and, despite reassurances from a neurologist, pediatrician, and child psychiatrist, that this had resolved itself without incident, Mr. Peterson remained unconvinced.

The family entered my room with Ronald at its head followed by his mother and then some time later by his father. I asked Ronald why he wasn't attending school. He said: "Because of the headaches!" Before the word was hardly uttered, Mr. Peterson offered me the medical history of

Ronald's neurological disorder. When he was finished, I said: "Ronald, what did you get in history?" He said: "A." I turned to his father: "Mr. Peterson, do you think some of your son's brain is missing?" "No!" he said with increasing gusto. "Ronald, what did you get in biology?" "A." "Mr. Peterson, do you think your son's brain is moulded?" "No!" I then turned my attention to Ronald: "Ronald, how long did your last headache last?" He told me proudly: "Half an hour." "That's nothing! Why last week I met a boy your age who had a headache for three days. Matter of fact, he sat in the chair you are sitting in now. Guess how long it took for his self-hypnosis to work?" Ronald said, "I don't know." "Twenty minutes. That's all. Do you want to ring him up? I know he'd be glad to tell you all about it. He's a smart kid like you." As usual, he declined my offer, but showed a keen interest in "self-hypnosis." "I suppose you want to learn about hypnosis?" He agreed. I outlined what practice was required of him and ushered the Peterson family out of my room. They were surprised that their consultation had lasted over twenty minutes. I sent them the following letter:

Dear Friends,

Ronald has agreed to return to school in return for hypnotic anesthesia training. I will expect 95% attendance and that sickness be defined as at least 101 degrees Fahrenheit. Ronald will practice having headaches at home for one hour per day. His parents have agreed to leave him alone for this period of time. Ronald has agreed to keep a daily record of the time he induced his headache, the time he stopped his headache, what was going on, etc. In general, Ronald will take over responsibility for his headaches.

I will contact you on the first day of the next school term to see if you have proven yourself.

Good luck!

Yours sincerely,
David Epston

I contacted the family on the arranged date. Ronald's attendance had been 100% since I saw him and he had gone happily off to school for the first day of this term. There had been no headaches or "temper outbursts." Mrs. Peterson also noticed that he had even shown restraint on a number of occasions.
I wrote Ronald the following letter:

Dear Ron,

I know you have lived up to your side of the bargain and that your headaches have disappeared. If you wish to commence your self-hypnosis training, fine. Ring me. If you feel it is no longer necessary, get in touch with me when you stop attending school the next time.

I know I can depend on you.

Yours sincerely,
David Epston

Sending Notes

David Epston makes it a habit to write notes to his clients. His habit developed when he recognized that he needed to take case notes anyway, so why not send along a copy to his clients? This is another way of reinforcing a school client's new discovery and changing his or her thinking with language. Remember when someone in your life put a note in your lunch box, or when your spouse remembered to write down just the right message on your anniversary card? How about your relative who searched for just the right Christmas present? The teacher who takes the time to write a special note or compliment on the back of a report card is remembered for years. Michael White (1989) says that a note sent to someone in counseling is worth six visits of counseling in terms of influencing the school client to see himself or herself differently.

Notes can be sent after sessions and given to the teacher of the child or adolescent in a sealed envelope during class or at the end of the day. When Terry Walkup, a school counselor in Plano, Texas, learned that an adolescent he had been working with had walked away from a gang fight for the first time that year, he quickly wrote a note to the student, commending her on the courage it took to walk away. At their next meeting, the student acknowledged how nice it was to get the letter and for him to notice. The note took about two minutes to write; the effects lasted the rest of the term. The student might not have acknowledged that it was her courage that helped her back down until the counselor took the time to describe it as such. The student, having thought of herself as stuck in the gang, changed her thinking after reading the note.

Take the time to notice when life works for your students, and write it down. The language of possibilities can convey support and belief in a school client.

Using Solution-Focused Language to Convey Hope

The manner in which questions are constructed with solution-focused language makes the questions themselves interventions. Observe how the following questions convey the probability of a hopeful future:

- What new behaviors will tell you when your daughter is capable of being responsible for her curfew? When have you helped her achieve this behavior in the past?

- When this problem is no longer intruding in your life at home, what do you think you will be able to do that you haven't done in a while with your mom?

- Someday when this problem is not bothering you as much, how will you know? What will you be doing, exactly, that will tell you things are much better?

There are several key words and phrases to notice in these questions:

sometimes

part of the time

not yet

instead

for a while

until then

These phrases and words are helpful in assisting school clients to see their problem as temporary. For example, if a teacher says that she simply wants a student to "stop behaving so badly in my class," asking the teacher, "What will the student be doing instead when he stops behaving badly?" will probably yield more concrete behaviors to focus on with the school client. Students need to know exactly what teachers expect of them, as do teachers need to know what students need.

Those Successful Times—They Are Exceptional

Many educators have been taught to work with students by trying to identify an underlying problem, discover why it is a problem, and determine what occurred to cause it. Unfortunately, understanding is often not enough to produce change. The solution-focused educator has little time for insightful sessions. The guiding ideas of the solution-focused approach suggest that insight is not necessary for change. Knowing what is wrong does not provide suggestions for doing things better. However, gazing into past successful behaviors, or exceptions, gives clues to doing things successfully once again. These become solutions for change. Exceptions are:

- Times when a problem occurs less often
- Times when a person is able to refrain from participating in the problem
- Times when a problem does not interfere with a person's life
- Times when the problem does not seem as intense

How do exceptions help us to move in a future-oriented direction? If a nine-year-old soccer player understands why he does not kick the soccer ball into the net (he's not fast enough for the goalie), that alone will not tell him how to kick the ball into the net. However, if he and his brother practice one evening and he scores, somehow catching his brother off guard, he learns that there may be a way he can do it again. A football quarterback may take the time to watch films of his performance at Friday night's game. As he sees his mistakes, he becomes familiar with plays that did not work. However, watching plays that did work will give him more clues to being successful. If I want to learn how to play the piano, I might not learn well if I hear someone playing the wrong notes. However, hearing the correct notes and practicing until I can play them may help me learn how to play. In the same way, checking with students the times when they have experienced success becomes what de Shazer (1985) referred to as "exceptions" to the problem. The exceptions are the music of the solution-focused approach.

Bill O'Hanlon and Michelle Weiner-Davis (1989) talk of searching for exceptions as ways to direct clients to search in the present and past for times when problems occurred less frequently. It has been my experience that many counseling tasks fail when people are asked to do tasks so foreign to them that they simply do not have the skills to carry them out. By focusing on current or past exceptions to the problems and assigning tasks familiar to those who are in counseling, the chances of success increase. I make it a habit never to ask people to do something they have never done before unless they suggest it. Instead I try to connect familiar behaviors that work for them in other areas of their lives.

Using Exceptions in a New Context

A teacher came to counseling to learn to deal with stress. She was recently divorced and was experiencing difficulties with her two children. She said that the children refused to do chores, listen to her expectations, or come home on time. She was sure that her parenting skills would end up costing her custody of the children. She said her goal was to "learn how to get my children's attention, so they know I am serious about my expectations." After asking about her occupation, I learned that she had taught fifth grade for almost ten years. During that time, she told me she had received excellent reviews and was team leader for her grade level. I asked how she managed to run such an effective classroom. She then told me her solution:

> I have rules to go by; the first day of school I go over them until they are crystal clear. I stick to my guns about the rules. I'm fair but I always follow through. With fifth graders you have to, so they don't run over you. I give assignments that are fair. If the students want to question my assignment, I go over it with them and compromise. I'm really consistent. When I say I'm going to do something, I do it—that goes for rewards and punishments.

After she described the effective way that she managed her classroom, I commended her on her ability to run things so smoothly and then wondered out loud how she might begin to apply the same excellent methods at home. She became very quiet. She then said that home was different, with different types of relationships. I agreed with her yet wondered out loud if the skills might just be as effective with her children (ages ten and twelve) as they were for the  approximately same-aged child in fifth grade. She said she would try. In two weeks she returned, saying that her children were behaving better and she was less stressed. I complimented her on her ability to transfer what worked from school to home. I saw her twice.

Sample Questions for Focusing on Past Exceptions
"Tell me about the times when you were able to speak to your mother in a calm way. How did you do that? What would she say you did?"

"When was the last time you were successful in school? What did you do then that worked? How did you do that?"

"When was the last time you noticed Roberto sitting still in his seat? What was going on in class at the time? Where was he sitting? Who was there?"

"How have you controlled this problem with anger before? How did you do that so you were in control?"

"I see that you passed six out of eight classes. How did you manage to pass them? What would the teachers in those classes say you did that worked for you? What did the teachers do that worked for you?"

"You have been off drugs for almost two months now. I am so proud that you've stayed away from marijuana that long. Today you are telling me how hard it is to be around it at times. How did you make it for two months? What was your strategy?"

"Your concern about alcohol at the next party is admirable. Not many kids can tell me about their fear of alcohol. You seem like the kind of person who really takes care of yourself. How have you avoided similar situations in the past?"

"The idea of sex with your boyfriend is a real worry to you. I'm proud that you took the time to talk to me about this. I've noticed over the past months that you are a very careful young lady. You choose your friends carefully, and you take the right classes for college-bound students. How have you made such effective decisions in the past? I wonder how that might help now?"

"Mr. and Mrs. Zappen, you must be extremely proud of your son chosen by four top colleges for admission. Henry, I am very excited that you have been chosen for admission to Harvard, Stanford, Rice, and Baylor. What a tough decision! How have the three of you made decisions in your family before? What do you know about your son, Mr. and Mrs. Zappen, that could guide your decisions further?"

Sample Questions for Focusing on Current Exceptions

"Tim, I've noticed that you haven't let 'energy' take over this morning and keep you out of your seat in class. How have you done that?"

"Todd, I can't believe your performance on the court today. How did you pull it together out there?"

"Latisha, your teacher sent you to talk to me because she was worried about your being so quiet in class. How have you managed to talk to me so freely for the past twenty minutes?"

"Jacob, your vice principal sent you here and said you were very unruly and angry in the lunch line about twenty minutes ago. I'm wondering how you calmed yourself so quickly. Does this happen often—that you calm yourself so well? How long does it take and how do you do that for yourself?"

"Pushkala, your mom said you forget papers in your eighth-grade math class very often. Today I sent for you early in the morning, and it's 2:30 now. You brought me the pass I sent you at 8:30 this morning. How did you keep from losing it?"

"Ann, your grandmother died so suddenly last week. I am amazed at the peace in your eyes as your talk of your special times with her. How have you managed to deal with her death so peacefully?"

The language used in these lists of questions assumed change would occur or was occurring. The school client was addressed by name, the presenting problem was mentioned clearly, and then an exception-searching question was given. The intervention ended with a curiosity-based question similar to, "How did you do that?" As the exceptions develop, tasks are assigned, based only on the exceptions and presented with an attitude of, "Since you've successfully done this before, let's do more of it. It works!"

The following collaborative task assignment basic principles were contributed by William Hudson O'Hanlon, coauthor of *In Search of Solutions* (1989), from a handout at a national conference:

Collaborative Task Assignments: Basic Principles

- Task assignments are to help bring about changes in doing (action/interaction) and/or changes in viewing (perceptions/attention/frame of reference) in the situation involving the complaint or negotiated problem in therapy. They are directed toward having people make changes outside the therapy session.

- The assignment should emerge from the conversation and be cocreated and negotiated between school clients and the educator. Be sure to include or preempt any objections or barriers to carrying out the task assignment before finalizing it. This is a collaborative intervention, not one that the therapist imposes on the person in counseling.

- Frame the task assignment as an experiment. The clients are to make no conclusions before doing the experiment. Make it time limited and adjust the assignment as needed.

- Use presuppositional language when giving the assignment, e.g., "After you do this, I will want you to tell me exactly what happened, as if you could have seen it on a videotape."

- Direct the assignment to breaking up patterns of doing and viewing. Find the places where the pattern seems especially repetitive and predictable and direct the assignment to making the smallest noticeable difference.

- Include multiple levels of meaning (symbols and metaphors) that may speak to the multiple levels of meaning of the situation, if possible.

- Write down the assignment and keep a copy for your files to increase the likelihood of follow-through and continuity.

- If the assignment isn't done between sessions, don't immediately assume resistance. Discuss the matter with the person and, if necessary, make adjustments in the assignment until one is found that works for all parties. The solution-focused educator looks at a reluctance to follow the task as *his* problem . . . he must find a way to cooperate with the school client.

Forget Praise: Be Curious Instead

It has long been a motto among many educators that you will get more with sugar than with vinegar when it comes to responses in the classroom. When my daughter was in elementary school, she was enrolled in a gifted program. The first day of school many years ago, I went to meet her after school

as the bell rang and found her teacher speaking softly to the children in her class: "Students, in all my years of teaching, I have never experienced such a wonderful first day of school with such wonderful children. We are going to have a great year."

As I approached her and watched inquisitively, she turned to me and said, "Linda, I can't believe it; they are all angels." The children glowed, lined up for their bus trip home, and seemed to float out of their classroom like angels. Across the hall, I could hear another second-grade teacher, who apparently did not have such a favorable day. She wasn't speaking softly; she was screaming: "This is the first day of school, and already you are not following the rules. Move here! Stay in line! No talking! Stop that!"

I again watched inquisitively as the children followed suit to her description and reacted accordingly—disrupting the hallway and giving the teacher a hard time. Her attempts were too direct; her affect conveyed her frustration, and the children responded in kind. While this is also an example of the ripple effect, it proves that reinforcing with curiosity and compliments is much more effective.

The "Columbo" Strategy

Reinforcing preferable behaviors using the solution-focused approach is different from strict behavior modification approaches because of the method of delivery of the reinforcement. There is a different relationship between the problem and solution. One way to approach and reinforce an educator or student is to act honestly perplexed and ask, "How did you know to do that?" The solution-focused educator can compliment a student effectively by acting puzzled—the "Columbo" strategy. By doing this, the educator gives all of her curiosity to the student, who then feels quite powerful that he confused a competent adult with his skills! The glow on his face is priceless:

TEACHER: Bobby, you know, you had such a terrific morning, doing your work and staying on task. I am baffled. How did you manage to be so responsible?

BOBBY: I don't know.

TEACHER: I don't know either, but I can't wait to see what you do this afternoon. You are quite amazing.

Notice how the teacher complimented Bobby. If she had simply praised him, she might have said: "Bobby, you did a fine job finishing your work this morning. I am proud of you. I hope you do the same this afternoon." What's different? Here, the teacher is the expert, giving out her approval to the student. In the previous dialogue where the teacher is more curious, it is the student who is the star and the teacher merely an observer. This builds self-esteem more quickly than praise.

Learn to Ask What Works for Students

While working on my dissertation, I researched the dynamics of change (Metcalf & Thomas, 1994) and found that teachers are one of several provider groups that rarely ask what they do that work. As with many professions involving provider-receiver relationships, theories or philosophies based on previous successes are reasons for delivery of certain strategies to the receiver. However, by using the idea of a competency-based program such as the one described in this book, it makes sense to ask the very population we are serving: "What do I need to know about how you learn best?" Many responses may seem a little unrealistic, but the educator can assist the student in identifying a strategy that fits for both of them. The research concluded that when people feel heard and have the opportunity to give clear reasons for seeking help, their needs for help are satisfied more often. Again, giving responsibility for their own success often diminishes resistance and allows self-esteem to blossom in students, parents, and teachers.

Don't Internalize; Externalize!

Epston and White (1990) describe externalizing the problem as "an approach to therapy that encourages persons to objectify and, at times, to personify the problems that they experience as oppressive. In this process, the problem becomes a separate entity and thus external to the person or relationship that was ascribed as the problem" (p. 38). Children and adolescents like to talk about problems as if they were outside of themselves. An adolescent understands easily how "attitude" gets in the way of a good relationship with his teacher. A child understands how the "talking habit" keeps her from recess. As school clients begin to see themselves as intruded on by problems, they begin to move around the problem to get back on track. The road may have two routes: one route may be scenic, taking in all kinds of issues, looking at the back roads of history, and the other route may be the freeway, getting to the destination faster, without all the intrusions and scenery.

School counselors don't have time to take the scenic route. The solution-focused approach is the express route. Knowing how to get to the desired destination means looking for the unique outcomes, or times when the road is clear. These are similar to the exceptions that de Shazer (1985) conceptualized as being most helpful.

As Michael White (1989) began using a narrative therapy approach with families in 1980, he found that his client families often felt like failures, since everyone had tried various ways of solving the problem. Working with ill children primarily, he began to externalize the problem as an entity in itself that could be maintained or dissolved. As he offered this suggestion for families, the families and children felt empowered and decided to eliminate the power of the problem over their lives by externalizing it and not allowing its influences to intrude as often.

Externalizing problems helps school clients see the problems as separate from themselves and see themselves not as failures but intruded on. White (1989) mentions what externalizing the problem accomplishes:

It decreases unproductive conflict between persons, including disputes over who is responsible for the problem.

It undermines the sense of failure that has developed for many persons in response to the continuing existence of the problem despite attempts to resolve it.

It paves the way for persons to cooperate with each other, to unite in a struggle against the problem, and to escape its influence in their lives and relationships.

It opens up new possibilities for persons to take action to retrieve their lives and relationships from the problem and its influence.

It frees persons to take a lighter, more effective, and less stressed approach to "deadly serious" problems [p. x].

The following steps show how the process might unfold when working with a young child. The school counselor can use stuffed animals or ask the student to draw the problem and, later, the solution in an animal form:

1. Identify or give the problem a name. Ask the school client to help with this. Keep a display of stuffed animals handy, and invite the student to choose a stuffed animal that represents what the problem might look or feel like to him or her.

2. Talk about the problem externally by asking the school client to describe what happens when the problem is too close. For example, when the anger monster takes over, what happens to the school client? Talk about who notices and who reacts.

3. Ask the child to put the problem (or stuffed animal) far away for a minute, and imagine what it would be like if a new creature that was more helpful appeared. Help the child to find a name for the solution, or ask her to choose another stuffed animal to hold tightly, imagining with you how the new solution would change the way her day goes. Talk at length about how things would be different, who would notice, who would be surprised.

4. Come up with a plan to invite the "solution" to stay around more often than the "problem." (Make sure to use the language of the child as you talk about problems and solutions.) Help the child be specific in detailing what she will do to keep the problem at bay. Invite the child to share the information with her teachers and parents by writing a note with you that can be distributed to them.

5. When the school client begins to have success, draw up a certificate of success with the child to award to her, proclaiming her as more powerful over the problem. Print the certificate, and ask the child to take it home or back to the classroom to keep on her desk with the teacher's permission.

Consider the following dialogue with a teacher about depression, and notice how externalizing helps the school client to gain composure and direction:

COUNSELOR: How has this depression interfered with your ability to teach effectively?

TEACHER: It keeps me from enjoying my students, being creative in the holiday activities I used to love, and from looking forward to the next day.

             Counseling Toward Solutions

COUNSELOR: How have you let the depression take over and intrude in your life, keeping you from these things that you just described to me?

TEACHER: Well, I go home and just sit, or I go to school and think about how bad things are since Bob left me, or I think that things will never get better.

COUNSELOR: How many hours a day would you say you let depression interfere like that?

TEACHER: It's worse in the morning for about an hour and then at night for about three hours.

COUNSELOR: Really, so about four hours a day?

TEACHER: Yes.

COUNSELOR: What about the other waking hours of the day? How many would that leave?

TEACHER: About eight, I guess.

COUNSELOR: Does the depression bother you as much during those hours?

TEACHER: No, because I'm here at school or doing things for my kids at home.

COUNSELOR: How do you keep the depression from bothering you so that you are able to do things for your children or at school?

TEACHER: I have to. I have to do certain things to survive.

COUNSELOR: That's great—wow—with all of this going on, you still think ahead, about surviving, and do it because you have to.

TEACHER: Yes, my kids depend on me.

COUNSELOR: You certainly are tuned in to what others need from you. Based on what you've told me this morning about how you keep the depression from interfering as much for eight hours a day, what do you think you might try to keep it away, say, for nine hours?

The dialogue suggests how externalizing the problem of depression as being maintained or not allowed to intrude in one's life can convey a person's strength and create an environment in which he or she feels competent to solve the problems. The reference to the depression as external helps it to become a target to defeat. Since the depression did not paralyze the teacher's life completely by diminishing her ability to go to school and care for her children and herself, the counselor assumed that she was winning the battle with the depression at least part of the time. The solution-focused educator simply pointed out her competency. This normalizing of how she handled the depression encouraged her since it meant she was not paralyzed by its influence. A note from the counselor to the teacher shortly after the meeting might be constructed as follows:

Dear Peggy,

I was glad to meet with you today. I have always been impressed with your dedication to teaching, and after meeting with you today, that impression proved correct. You truly have your priorities straight. You want things better in your life and even though you are dealing with some depression, you gallantly keep going, saying, "I just have to." I was touched by your determination to do something different; I still am amazed that you fight off the depression so well, allowing it to bother you for short periods of time in a very long day.

My hope is that you will continue this, as it places you in control. This next week, I hope you will continue to notice your ability to keep the depression from bothering your enjoyment of school and your children. My feeling is that you may be surprised at how the depression won't stand much of a chance when your strength takes over.

Sincerely,
Counselor

Externalizing problems and assisting school clients to move away from problem maintenance and the influence of the problem frees them to imagine how life will be without the problem. Elementary students will enjoy naming their problem. Then ask the student to tell you how the problem interferes in his or her day. Afterward ask the student to put the problem physically far away, or even throw the problem away in the trash can. Try using stuffed animals, pictures, or even cards that show a variety of emotions, such as Strength Cards, manufactured by Innovative Resources in Australia. Ask the student to pick a card that looks like the solution. Have the student tell you how the stuffed animal that looks like a solution or the Strength Card will help him to have a better day. Ask what the new "solution" will tell him to do when the old problem tries to interfere. This creative approach to most problems will be fun, freeing, and helpful to young students who are not as verbal as their peers. The following case illustrates the possibilities that can develop when problems are externalized.

The Temper Tantrum Is Really a Snake

Kathy, age six, her two siblings, and her mother came to visit the counselor after Kathy was reported to have temper tantrums in school as well as at home. Her mother reported that she had recently divorced the children's father due to his alcoholism and that all the family members had been experiencing difficulty with Kathy's tantrums, which disrupted the household. The mother described her older children as "taunting" to Kathy, which encouraged the tantrums. Kathy had a difficult time sitting still in the meeting, trying to capture the attention of everyone. The family presented a goal of "getting along better." When asked how that would take form, the mother described a possible scenario of Kathy being calm and the older children being more cordial to her.

The counselor presented Kathy with several stuffed animals from which to choose "the temper tantrum animal" and "the calm animal." Kathy quickly chose a bright snake for "temper tantrum" and a soft white elephant for "calmness." The counselor mentioned to Kathy that the "calm animal" was magical (White, 1989), and as long as she clutched the animal close to her, it would keep her calm. The counselor gathered the older siblings around Kathy and told them, with Kathy's agreement, that as long as Kathy held the "calm animal," it was a symbol that they could not taunt her. The older children seemed quite intrigued by the idea and on hearing their role, left the immediate area to play quietly by themselves. The mother liked the idea and promised to remind Kathy of the "calm animal" and its powers, should Kathy forget. Kathy soon felt more powerful in her life, and her siblings realized her power as well.

Get Rid of That Anger!

Often school counselors have students referred to them for acting-out behaviors such as anger, fighting, talking habits, and disrespect. By using the possibility language and externalizing problems, the sessions take on a whole new look and often result in rapid change.

The following sequence of questions is an example of externalizing an issue such as anger:

1. Tell me about the anger that caused you to be here. When do you notice "it" [emphasize the word] being around? What do you think you do that keeps it [or "anger"] around?

2. When does the anger not affect you as much?

3. What needs to happen with the anger so that you can stay in school, pass your class, and so on?

4. How many days out of a week are you angry? How many hours are you free from the influence of anger on your life?

5. What are you doing differently to be free of anger during those times?

6. Who will notice first when the anger is no longer bothering you? Who else?

7. Based on what you've just told me, what do you think you might try to make the anger less of a problem for you this week?

Language such as this helps children to visualize problems as external and controllable. When counselors later see their clients separately or in the hallway, they can briefly ask, "How big is the anger?" and then, "How are you helping it to be so small?" If the anger reoccurred, as with any other normal human emotion, they can ask, "What did you do before to shrink the anger when it was big like this?" This sequence of questions again places children in the expert role. Counselors simply guide clients back on the route to control by asking competency-based questions.

The My Solutions! worksheet shown here provides students with an avenue to describe how they are defeating their problem. Copy the worksheet, and complete it with school clients. It is applicable for all ages.

My Solutions!

Name: _____   Date: _____

Problem:

_____

How things will be when the problem is solved:

_____

_____

Times when the "problem" is less of a problem for me (exceptions):

1. _____

2. _____

3. _____

4. _____

5. _____

Tasks for today (this week, and so on) based on the above exceptions:

1. _____

2. _____

3. _____

4. _____

5. _____

Ask: Did we talk about what we needed to talk about? What did we do that helped?

Additional Ways to Escape the Influence of Hurtful Problems

For children dealing with death or loss, sexual abuse, or physical abuse, externalizing the event can be a gentle way of helping them see the circumstances as something they can move away from at times and become free. Contextually, offering support to a child who survived abusive situations and knew to talk to someone is a therapeutic way of saying, "You know how to take care of yourself." It offers a possibility that someday the problem will not be as big, influential, or intrusive in his or her life—that things will get better.

Tricia Long, a school counselor, related the story of a young student currently living with an abusive mother and her companion. The counselor had reported the verbal abuse to the proper authorities, but the child still was not removed from the home. In individualized counseling, the counselor began to brag to the child how brave she was and asked her how she coped with things at home when it became difficult. The child described reading her book, calling a friend, listening to tapes, and holding her stuffed animals when she was sad that her mom yelled at her abusively. The counselor continued to affirm her methods to calm herself and remove herself from the tough situations. The counselor had encouraged her to tell her father, whom she visited every other weekend, about the abuse. The child had refused in the past for fear that her mother would become worse. After two weeks of following the support of the solution-focused approach, on her next weekend visit with her dad, the child told him of the verbal abuse. He filed for custody and won.

Adolescents or children who have survived physical, sexual, or emotional abuse or chemically dependent parents or have observed violent acts, often find great nurturing from a counselor who describes their survival skills as the best she has ever seen. This is quite different from thinking of the school client as a victim. As a counselor expresses to a school client that he is impressed how she has gone on to live her life even though she has experienced awful events, the school client begins seeing herself as victorious over the event. Placing the abuse in a context of being one small part of the school client's long life to come changes the perception that the school client must stay in that story for life. In addition, by talking to the school client as if the effects of the abuse are separate from her personhood, the school client begins to feel freer to escape, survive, and move away from the effects of the situation.

One method that is useful in assisting school clients dealing with traumatic situations is to draw a time line on a large piece of paper or even a chalkboard, such as this one:

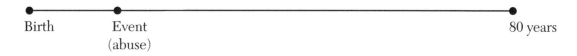

Birth   Event   (abuse)   80 years

A school counselor can help the school client place her birth at the beginning of the time line on the left and then ask the client about the typical life span of her family members. Once this information is added, the client is asked what she would like to call the event that happened to her. The event is named, and the school counselor can begin showing the school client how many years are left in her very long life. Then they begin to brainstorm how it will be for the client to move far away from the event every day. I have routinely used this process with school clients of all ages, genders, and traumas. Typically just visualizing how the client has already moved away from the event brings immediate relief. Then together, the school counselor and school client can glance at the time line weekly and talk about what's gone better as the school client moves forward in her life.

When Casey, age ten, first came to counseling after being sexually abused by an older boy, he rarely got out of a fetal position while sitting on the couch in my office. He refused to talk about the event, so I was quite careful to talk about it differently. When I drew the time line, I asked him to tell me what the event was like for him. With a few small suggestions, he came up with a description that it was like a very deep, black hole. I drew a hole above the time line where the event happened and then asked him to imagine moving forward. He slowly sat up on the couch and became more engaged. I talked too, as I moved my marker along the time line, about how he had nothing to do with what happened to him and that I was sorry that such an event happened at all. Together we colored the black hole a very black color and then began to talk about what he could do for the next week until I saw him whenever the black hole came to bother him. He said:

"Play a video game."

"Go outside and ride my bike."

"Watch television."

"Play with Dad."

"Ride my skateboard."

"Listen to a CD."

Casey continued with his list in a playful manner as I exclaimed each time how brilliant he was to think of such a great strategy to escape from the black hole. He brightened more as the session ended. I made a copy of our paper with the time line and his list of solutions and gave it to him before he left that day. I asked him to use his own ideas to escape the black hole during the next week.

Ideas for the Second Session

When using the solution-focused approach, school counselors may find that most of the work happens in the first session with goal setting and that the second and future sessions become focused on being supportive and success gathering. The second session should center on maintaining the change that has probably occurred since the first session. As the school client returns to the next session, it is helpful to set the atmosphere with the question: "What's been better since I've seen you?"

As the school client begins to recall what has gone better, it is helpful to write down the successes and compliment his abilities. When counseling is completed and the school client is ready to terminate, it is often helpful to review what has worked during the time the school counselor and school client have worked together. A counselor might end such a session with:

"What do you want to keep on doing after our meeting today that is obviously working for you?"

"Like many other problems, the one we have talked about here may resurface someday. What will you do then to control it, as you have before?"

"I am curious. What did we do together during our time that you found helpful?"

The last question is very helpful for both the school counselor and the school client because it punctuates another exception, giving the school counselor an idea of what he did to help the client. This is not only informative; it is rewarding. Another way of reminding a school client of success is to offer a certificate. The certificate might include the problem description, the exceptions that helped solve the problem, and the signature of the educator, like the one shown here. (A reproducible certificate is included at the end of this chapter.) David Epston and Michael White (1990) routinely give certificates to their students and families. The certificate can be a surprise or a promise, whatever is more appropriate.

THIS CERTIFIES

that

Susie Smith

has successfully

defeated the "Worry Monster"

by requesting 10 hugs per day from her mother

and checking the doors only once each evening.

Signed,
School Counselor

This rite of passage can be presented in several ways: in a group setting, teacher-student conference, parent conference, or individual session. Small groups or classes can vote each week and choose who has been the most successful at managing his or her behavior and contributing to the class or group, and so on. The nominations must be accompanied by specific exceptions in order to be considered for election. Hearing about what others think you've done well is usually a morale booster.

Scaling Problems Down to Size with Language

Lipchik and de Shazer (1988) say that scaling questions are therapeutic tools used to measure the effects of a problem on a person's life. The question, a simple line with a 1 on the left end and a 10 on the right end, serves to gauge the health of the solution. This is quite helpful for children or adolescents who tend to be nonverbal. When the scale is used, the problem does not seem as over-powering; often students choose the lower numbers versus a zero. That automatically means that the student has some power over the problem. An example of talking about the scaling question follows: "At 1, the problem is in total control of your life and at 10, you are in complete control of the problem." The school client is asked to tell where he is as the meeting begins. As the meeting progresses, he is then asked to tell where he would like to be by the next time he meets with the educator. The student then describes how he will do that. Here is an example of a session that a school administrator held with a mother and her daughter:

ADMINISTRATOR: Mom, you say that you are having a hard time trusting your daughter, Sarah, since she has failed three classes and skipped school four times this term. Is that correct?

MOM: Yes, it's hard to trust her at all (scowling at Sarah). I would like to trust her again, but it will take a long time.

ADMINISTRATOR: Sarah, where would you say you are right now, on a scale of 1 to 10, where 1 means you are not trusted at all by Mom and 10 means you are totally trusted?

SARAH: About a 2.

MOM: That's even lower than I would have said!

ADMINISTRATOR: Sarah, where would you like to be by the time I meet with you again?

SARAH: At least a 5, but I don't know if that will make a difference to her.

ADMINISTRATOR: Mom, would that make a difference?

MOM: Anything will make a difference.

ADMINISTRATOR: Sarah, you say you are at a 2 now and want to move to a 5 by next week. What would you suggest you do to move up 3 points?

SARAH: Probably come home and do homework so she sees me trying at least. Not skipping would help as well.

ADMINISTRATOR: Mom, would that make a difference?

MOM: Maybe.

SARAH: See, she's so negative!

ADMINISTRATOR: I guess that happens sometimes when the trust level goes down. What I'm interested in, though, are your ideas. They are really good ideas. Have ideas like these worked before to gain trust?

SARAH: Sort of. I think she trusted me last year when I studied at home and didn't skip.

ADMINISTRATOR: Is this true?

MOM: Yes, I remember; last year was a good year.

ADMINISTRATOR: Looking back, where would you have placed Sarah last year on the same scale we've been talking about?

MOM: Probably about an 8.

ADMINISTRATOR: That's great. What did she do then to be that high on your trust level?

MOM: She did study, and her grades were good. She came home when I asked her, her friends came over, and I got to meet them instead of wondering who they were.

ADMINISTRATOR: So, Sarah, you already know how to do this.

SARAH: I guess.

ADMINISTRATOR: Go for it. Sounds like a 5 is very reasonable for this week. I want you to keep thinking too where you want to end up on that scale eventually, okay?

SARAH: Okay.

ADMINISTRATOR: Mom, I'd like you to notice specific things Sarah does this week that make your trust level rise. Okay?

MOM: Okay.

Scaling questions assist school clients in defining their goals specifically, thereby making them easier to achieve. When they become stuck and have difficulty identifying exceptions to their concern or imagining a time when things were better, scaling questions offer small steps to take to slowly move away from the problem's influence.

Summary

Bruce Kuehl (1996), a professor at the University of Wisconsin, Stout, has said that it is not necessarily the model of counseling that makes for success; it is the relationship between counselor and client. His seminal work has encouraged counselors of many theories to confidently work with clients, putting aside the mechanics of therapy and focusing on the relationship between counselor and client. This chapter emphasizes the use of language that is possibility oriented rather than problem focused, providing not only dialogues between school counselor and school clients that offer hope but a means for developing a relationship of trust and respect.

As you begin to use the language suggested in this chapter and the useful idea of externalizing problems, you may find that your counseling load lightens. You may also find that you leave each day more hopeful yourself.

On a Friday afternoon, several years ago, a vice principal approached me as I left for home and asked me this question: "How do you do this? Don't you carry home the burdens of your students on the weekend and worry about them?" When I heard myself tell her, "No, I don't, because I believe each one knows how to take care of themselves," I smiled to myself and realized that the solution-focused approach is not just for school clients; it is for us, the school counselors.

Believe.

Certificate of Success

This certifies that

_____

has successfully

_____

_____

This success was achieved by the following:

_____

_____

_____

Signed, this _____ day of _____, _____

_____

56

Solution-Focused Training Exercise: Chapter Two

Today, consider writing someone you work with a note. Remember a note you might have received once and how it made you feel about yourself or something you had done. Noticing is detective work! Exceptions abound but are often difficult for people to notice. Today, notice what someone does well and see it as exceptional:

- A teacher who always seems to have her students' attention

- The principal who puts in long hours

- The janitor who smiles and jokes with students in the hallway

- The bus driver who waits for that one last student to board

- The parent who has too much to do but still manages to participate in class activities

- The secretary who remains level-headed and focused on the most hectic days

Write a note using one of the forms shown here, describing what you noticed him or her doing that seemed to make a difference. Watch the reactions!

⁃⁃✂

Dear _____:

I am amazed at you! How did you do that?

_____

_____

_____

_____

_____

"Secret Admirer" Signature _____

⁃⁃✂

Solution-Focused Training Exercise: Chapter Two (cont.)

·· ✂······

Dear _____:

No one does it better than you. I am proud to know you.

_____

_____

_____

_____

_____

"Secret Admirer" Signature _____

·· ✂······

Chapter Three

Competency-Based Conversations

We first raise the dust and then claim we cannot see.

—Bishop George Berkeley

One morning at school, a ninth-grade girl wandered into my office "by mistake," she said. Julie seemed quite agitated and said she wasn't sure whose office she was looking for, but she needed to talk to someone because she was getting ready to fight another girl in the cafeteria. Apparently the "enemy" had been harassing her at school, and Julie had enough.

I introduced myself and told her that I was delighted that it was my office that she wandered into, as I liked getting to know the ninth-grade students on the campus. After a few minutes, I asked if talking to me would work, and she said, "I guess." I soon learned that Julie had moved from another city three months ago and had enrolled at our school early in the school year. At first, she seemed reluctant to talk a lot about her old school, but soon told me that she had been in trouble there regularly. Here is how our conversation evolved:

LM: So, tell me, how have things been different for you since you moved here?

JULIE: Well, I haven't been in any trouble. Last year, well, getting in trouble was a weekly thing for me. After a while, I didn't care. But I have been good here, and today is the last day for me to be good. I have had it with that girl putting me down in front of my friends.

LM: I'll bet you have had it. But tell me, how is it that you have been able to maintain such dignity and integrity for the first three months of school here?

JULIE: Heck, I was grounded almost every weekend last year. I wanted to go out and do things at my new school.

LM: And has that been happening for you?

JULIE: Yes, until last weekend when I stayed out an hour later than I was supposed to. But other than that, yeah, things have been going pretty well.

LM: That is really remarkable that you had the courage and fortitude to change your reputation like that. Tell me, who noticed the change in you this year?

JULIE: I guess my mom did. I live with her and my grandmother. They both tell me sometimes that things are better for them this year since I am doing okay.

LM: You know, should you decide not to fight the girl in the cafeteria today, I would really like to know about it. I will be here tomorrow, and if you stop by and tell me that you decided to keep your dignity and integrity along with your new reputation, I will write your mom a note and commend her on having such a respectable daughter.

Silence.

Julie left my office calmer than she entered. She came back to my office the next day and informed me that when she left my office and headed toward the cafeteria, she decided to sit at another table, away from the girl who harassed her. Together, we composed a letter to her mom, describing her daughter as one who valued her own integrity and dignity enough to make wise decisions on how to handle problems. Julie picked up the letter and said to me, "You know, this actually might help me get out of being grounded. Thank you!"

Building Competency Increases the Capacity for Change

If I had been problem focused, I could have talked to Julie about the consequences of fighting at school. I could have also talked with her about not undermining herself after having a successful three months of school. I could have inquired about what she had done at the other school—again, if I were problem focused. But none of that information would have helped me help her deal with the situation in a competent manner.

Instead, Julie looked at herself differently when she left my office that day, as a successful student who had put aside old habits and behaviors and tried to maintain dignity and integrity. While I doubt that she would have used the term "dignity and integrity" in her self-description, she undoubtedly listened to me and began to describe herself as such. The result? New behaviors due to new descriptions. And the note didn't hurt; it reinforced to her family system the changes Julie had made at her new school, helped them to recognize who she was becoming, and resulted in a phone call to me from her mom. In tears, the mom conveyed that she had never received a letter like that from her daughter's school. She told me that she was going to have it framed. I told her that I hoped she would continue to watch for the changes her daughter was making and tell her whenever she noticed her daughter trying to maintain her dignity.

Julie made it through ninth grade without misbehavior of any kind.

The School Counselor Defined

A closer look at schools today reveals school counselors and administrators placed in the position of being asked to fix problems. Students and parents who seek help often feel as if they have failed or that someone else has a problem. Working with the solution-focused approach, students, teachers, and parents come to the counselor or educator with little thought about how they can solve their problem but often leave looking to their own competencies to solve it. This is because solution-focused school counselors rely on the competencies they codiscover with their school clients, not on themselves as problem solvers. School counselors see their job as that of a consultant: a codiscoverer who simply points out and helps students, other teachers, and parents to see the exceptions to the problem. This makes the life of a school counselor less stressful and immensely rewarding.

As school counselors begin to consult with school clients and set the stage for competency-based conversations, it is helpful to use some guidelines in formulating questions that solicit competency. The suggestions presented here will assist school counselors in identifying competent behavior in students and teachers that can then develop into solutions.

Suggestions That Build Relationships with School Clients

Socialize with the School Client

Listen to the school client's language, metaphors, and self-description so that you can align yourself to that description. Ask about success—possible topics such as occupation, school, hobbies, and other areas of interest. Find out who your school client is before you begin the conversation toward solutions. Learn about her hobbies, what she does for fun, what she enjoys about school or work. This genuine approach to learning who your school client is conveys your warmth and sets the stage that says this counseling session is different.

Listen Closely for the School Client's Problem Definition

When school clients visit with school counselors, they typically perceive that it is important to tell the counselor the details about the problem, unless, of course, the school client is a student who has been sent to the counselor. If you find yourself talking about the problem, get each person's view of it, such as the teacher's view or the parent's view. This will give you information on how others perceive the problem. Pay attention to language that the school client uses, and use it throughout the session. Your school client will then feel heard and respected.

When Setting Goals, Let the School Client Lead the Way

If a student is sent to the school counselor by a teacher with a note on what the teacher thinks needs to change, it is important to listen to the student first. This does not mean that the teacher's concern should be disregarded, but it does mean that by asking what the student wants to be different, there is more of a possibility for change to occur. It is helpful to use language that reflects an assumption of positive change. Start small, be concrete, and compliment the school client often on his view of how things need to change. By giving credit to the school client in your office, you will join with the client, who will feel respected and heard. This leads to cooperation and collaboration.

Separate the School Client from the Problem Whenever Possible

Externalizing problems has been my favorite bauble in the solution-focused treasure chest of tools. When the counselor helps the school client begin recognizing the influence of a bad reputation, a dangerous habit, a talking habit, anger, depression, anxiety, and more, the client begins to take ownership in his contribution to the problem and takes on a strategy to defeat the problem. Everyone wins except the problem.

To externalize problems, listen for language that school clients use, such as, "It is always a problem for me," or, "I have a problem with anger," or, "Since this happened, I feel like I am out of my comfort zone and in a hole." Using words such as *it, anger,* or *hole,* the school counselor can begin talking about the influences of such problems on the school client's life and engage the school client in the process of leaving the problem behind. As the client identifies how he participates in maintaining the problem, also consider asking him to tell you how he is thinking and feeling when the problem influences him the most. Then ask what kind of new thoughts need to occur when the problem tries to impose itself on his life again. This will assist the client in future situations when the problem tries to intrude and give him tools to fight off the problem once again.

Learn to Listen Only for Exceptions

Problems do not occur 100 percent of the time. If they did, most people would not make it out of bed, go to work, or take care of their children. The exceptions to problems give clues to solutions. Focusing on the problem gives credence to its existence and can become immobilizing to the school client.

School clients often talk about the problem, but the school counselor who is using a solution-focused approach sees the client's exceptions as the fastest avenue for change. That doesn't mean the school counselor stops the client in her tracks and says, "No problem description needed."

But it does mean that after a short while of learning what brought the school client to counseling, the client is asked, "How would you like for things to be?" This new direction helps the client go down a different path and changes the atmosphere from problem saturation to solution focusing.

Perhaps the client is a parent who, on the first visit, emphasizes that her daughter has never had a problem with behavior until this year. The parent describes her daughter's activities and how she is responsible and caring to others outside school. In these two sentences are two important exceptions: (1) the daughter has not had a behavior problem until now, meaning that she has been successful in maintaining good behavior for several years prior to this one, and (2) the daughter is successful in relationships outside school by knowing how to behave appropriately and be a good friend. These two exceptions are worth noting, particularly if the daughter is currently fighting at school and claiming that she is being bullied. By asking what was different in previous years at school and what occurs outside school that encourages the daughter to have good relationships, the school counselor will have enough exceptions to get started on strategies.

Case Study: Getting to Know You Again

Chris's mother, Linda, brought her seventh-grade, fourteen-year-old daughter to counseling because she was concerned about her daughter's sudden drop in grades (from all A's to some B's) and her isolation from her family. Linda said that Chris preferred talking to friends on the phone to talking to her, and she was concerned that all Chris and she did when together was fight. Linda said that Chris's father agreed that life around the household was frustrating to him as well, especially when he came home from work each night and was asked to referee disputes between his wife and daughter.

Linda mentioned that she had recently been in drug rehabilitation for her use of prescription drugs, and she wondered if that situation had caused Chris to become angry with her. Chris complained instead of her mother's criticizing her friends, her school work, and her appearance. Sitting with her finger over a blemish on her face, Chris explained that she had an allergic reaction to some antibiotics and had forgotten to put cream on the night before. She angrily blamed her mother for her forgetfulness, and Linda looked painfully guilty. Mother and daughter were physically distant as well as emotionally distant in the therapy room, both exchanging angry glances and responding with resentment and defensiveness.

As school counselors know, conflicts between parents and adolescents are part of the normal developmental process; however, they are often the reason for seeking help. Although today's school counselor is not encouraged to be a clinical therapist by certification boards, skills for helping parents and adolescents through communication difficulties are important in order to deal with school issues. There are many influences within the systems in which people live. These influences, if not dealt with in the prioritization brought to the counselor, live on and continue to contribute to the problem. Parents and adolescents, with their conflicting desires for responsibility and protection, on the one hand, and freedom and independence, on the other, easily become caught in interactional patterns of guilt and blame. Telling them what to do differently often doesn't work.

As parents and children begin to disagree during this developmental stage, often labeled as rebellion, many parents bring their children to counseling hoping to mend the conflict that has developed. These conflictual relationships also occur in the school setting between teacher and student, and even between teachers and administrators. The counselor may be presented with a very angry adolescent such as Chris (who blames the parent for the conflict and fears that the counselor may simply be another adult who will take the parent's side) and with a parent who feels abandoned and helplessly frustrated.

The mutual blaming that occurs manifests itself as parents seek some recognition in their being older, wiser, and more responsible, and adolescents seek some confirmation that their parents are being unreasonable. This interaction can be a disaster for counselors who try to assist the parent and child to "work things out" without taking sides. Counselors and other school staff members often get caught between such conflicts in the school setting.

Often school staff deals with parents who expect the school to take over and solve the problem for them. This places schools in a role of (1) being the expert, (2) being responsible for the solution, (3) encouraging dependency by the parent and student, and (4) releasing parental compliance and cooperation. Simple negotiation is unlikely to be effective because both sides are assured that their positions are correct. Attempts to uncover and understand the disputed issues, thereby seeking "the facts," may lead to further arguments, angry accusation, and blame. Even if facts surface and everyone thinks they know why the conflict is occurring, the facts and explanations still do not assist anyone in knowing what will solve the problem. It is at this point that many counselors, teachers, administrators, and parents become stuck. This often results in the school staff offering solutions that may have worked with other students in general. The recipient of the information will either reject the suggestions or give it a try. It has been my experience that the reason most counseling efforts fail is that people are asked to do things so differently from their usual way of acting that they simply do not know how.

School counselors and other educators can avoid the problem focus, lessen dependency, relinquish expertise, and involve the parents more if they move into a solution-focused approach for situations such as these. According to Linda, the problem was the conflictual relationship she and her daughter had. Their goal was to resolve the conflict and develop a communicative and interactive relationship. The mother was also concerned about whether her drug rehabilitation had caused Chris to be distant.

In our meeting, I sought to assist Chris and Linda in identifying those aspects of their previously close relationship on which they might now be able to build:

LM: Chris, what would Mom say she misses the most from your relationship?

CHRIS: I don't know. Ask her; she wanted me to come here.

MOTHER: This is what it's like at home: she won't look at me or talk to me. I don't know what's wrong.

LM: How often is it like this?

MOTHER: Every time we talk.

LM: How often—daily, weekly?

MOTHER: Daily.

CHRIS: When she criticizes my friends and tells me I should do good in school like she did, that's when it happens, and that happens every day.

LM: How long has this gone on?

MOTHER: It started six months ago. I was in rehab two months ago, so for a few months, things were tough when I was having problems.

LM: And how are you now?

MOTHER: I'm much better. I no longer take pain medications. My doctor is giving me muscle relaxers sparingly for my back pain.

LM: How would the two of you like things to be if you both had your say?

MOTHER: I'd like us to talk more and not fight.

CHRIS: I'd like her to get off my back about everything!

LM: Linda, Chris is saying that you criticize her. Can you tell me some of the things about Chris that you appreciate?

MOTHER: No. I can't think of anything that I really like about her now. She's cruel to me, and her friends are not the kind I want her around.

LM: Chris, can you think of some positive things to say about your mom?

CHRIS: Not really. She thinks her hospital thing made me different. It didn't. I'm just tired of being criticized.

These goal statements were constructed initially in what Chris and her mother wanted *less* of: their complaints. When using the solution-focused approach, it is important for the goals to develop into what the parent, teacher, or students *do* want. Often this solution-focused goal develops as exceptions to the presenting complaint are identified. The continuing dialogue attempts to accomplish this:

LM: Chris, take me back to a time when you and your mom got along a little better than now and you didn't feel as criticized.

CHRIS: It's hard to remember. It's been a long time.

MOTHER: (interrupting) Two years ago it was perfect.

CHRIS: (brightening slightly) Yeah, when I was in the fifth grade, things were pretty good between us.

LM: Tell me more, Linda, about what you liked about your daughter two years ago.

MOTHER: She and I did a lot together. We shopped, took walks, you know, she wasn't so worried about boys then, so she and I were really close. There was a lot I liked about her.

LM: Chris, what did you like about how things were two years ago with your mom?

CHRIS: What she said is true: we spent time together, and I didn't mind talking to her. She liked my friends too. That made it easy to bring them home. (glancing) She didn't put me down either. I felt like she was proud of me. She said nice things to me once in a while. (crying)

As Chris and her mom reminisced about times when they got along better, exceptions began to emerge:

CHRIS: I enjoyed my relationship with my mom when I felt she was proud of me, when we spent time together, talked, and she liked my friends.

MOTHER: I enjoyed our time together: shopping, taking walks, feeling close.

The similarities in the goal developments are obvious. Both mother and daughter had been close previously and had accomplished this through mutually enjoying time together, validation, providing acceptance, and offering compliments. With these goals in mind, the dialogue continued, focusing now only on the exceptions that encompassed their goals:

LM: Mom, tell me about some of those nice things you noticed about your daughter two years ago.

MOTHER: She was pretty, as she is now, and she talked to me a lot. She did okay in school, and her friends were pleasant. It seemed like it meant something to her to do things with me. She smiled a lot and helped me around the house.

LM: What about those characteristics today? Are they still there?

MOTHER: You know, I haven't noticed in a while because we fight so much, but I still think she's pretty. It's just that we can't cooperate much today like we did then.

LM: If you could come up with some of the things you and she did then, how would you describe the way you were able to get your daughter to be so close to you?

There were many issues that could have been seen as important in this case. The mother's drug abuse, Chris's isolating behavior, or her father's "triangled" role might have been interesting to explore, but such exploration could have magnified the issues between mother and daughter, increased the feelings of blame, and lessened the hope of reconciliation. The discovery and questioning of past success with current exceptions, however, quickly stopped the resentments from surfacing and allowed mother and daughter to reminisce about good times. In situations such as these, reminiscing about past enjoyable experiences in an hour-long meeting can be like an oasis. The mother's rediscovery of the daughter of two years ago brought back parental memories that obviously were dear to her. The daughter, with her current need for validation and acceptance as an emerging young woman, was able to recall the compliments given to her two years ago and place them in a present state, as if there was an imminent chance her mother would accept her once again.

As the positive events from their relationship began to emerge, each attributed the times when things were better to a difference in each other. However, within the more positive and hopeful focus that emerged, it was easier to ask questions that encouraged the mother to identify her part in fostering the close relationship and Chris to consider how her behavior encouraged her mother not to criticize her. This is very different from asking either of them to tell the other what she wanted changed. By asking each of them to identify past successful behaviors that alleviated the problem, blame was dissolved and competency-based conversations emerged:

MOTHER: Probably in the time I spent with her.

LM: Chris, if you could think of some of the ways you kept Mom from criticizing you two years ago, what would you say you did that helped?

CHRIS: I guess I didn't blame her as much and I talked to her more.

LM: So two years ago when you and your mom talked more and you spent more time with her and she did not criticize you, things were much more pleasant between the two of you. Would that be correct?

MOTHER: Yes.

CHRIS: Yeah.

Through the questioning, mother and daughter came to an agreement that talking together was something that worked in the past. In contrast to the global, all-encompassing picture of their conflict, this was a specific behavior that they were able to agree on. In other words, their previous success became their task.

I suggested a small homework task that used the described behavior, as de Shazer does (1985), by asking them to "do more of what works." Had I simply asked them to spend time together and refrain from criticism in a kind of mediation manner, it would have been unlikely to be successful, since each might still have felt that it was the other who needed to change. In addition, that would have been my task for them, not theirs for themselves. The importance of this task was that it flowed directly from their exploration of previous success and current exceptions. That is, asking them to do more of what they had already agreed worked in the past was much more likely to be successful than if I had simply designed something different for them to try. The following dialogue shows the task development and assignment:

LM: You know, it's reassuring to me that you both have already experienced some really good times together. It's no wonder that you want those good times back. It sounds as if those were good times for both of you. What I'd like to ask you to do this week is what you've told me worked just two years ago. Linda, I'd like you to compliment your daughter once a day based on what you notice that you like about her. It can be anything you notice. Chris, would you be willing to give maybe thirty extra minutes a day to your family time, especially to Mom, if she drops the criticism?

CHRIS: I can try.

LM: Mom, can you agree not to criticize your daughter for just a week, until I see you again?

MOTHER: Okay.

One week later, mother, daughter, younger sister, and father were at the session. Mother mentioned immediately that she and her daughter had experienced a wonderful week. Dad volunteered that he had enjoyed a week of freedom: he had not had to discipline Chris or referee his wife and daughter all week. He said that the atmosphere at home had improved drastically and that he and Chris had also enjoyed more fun times together.

Linda said that at first, Chris came out of her room only for short periods of time each evening, but by the end of the week, she was spending most of her time with the family. Linda also commented that to her surprise, she had noticed many things about her daughter that she liked but had not noticed before. She felt that the compliments had at first seemed artificial to Chris, but as she discovered more of her daughter's positive assets and the compliments continued, Chris accepted them readily.

Jenny, the younger sister, told me that she and her sister had played together during the past week and that she liked the fact that the house was quiet. Although Chris was still concerned about her complexion, she smiled more and began to discuss other issues with me and her parents regarding her friends. The second session continued with much more open communication between her and her parents regarding a friend with whom she was having difficulties. The family dynamics had switched from a focus on conflict between each other to communication with and concern for each other.

As a counselor, my position in this second session was that of cheerleading and asking questions with curiosity, such as, "How did you manage to do that so well?" The developing answers were then credited to the individual family members. This competency-based focus encouraged the family to continue their newly rediscovered abilities to interact positively with each other. The counseling ended after the third session.

This case represented an example of the use of competency-based questions that promoted a rekindling of relationships between parents and their adolescent. Their skills at making their relationship successful, discovered during the counseling sessions and then designed into tasks for mother and daughter, were able to be implemented successfully as they had been two years ago. The ability of mother and daughter to attempt to try these steps was found in their knowledge that they had performed them before. The fondness that existed between mother and daughter at that time in their lives was too attractive in their memories to pass up in the present. The reminiscing changed their strategy from a problem focus to a solution orientation. All they needed to do at that point was to see their successes as a possibility for the future.

Why I Never Ask "Why?"

While doing research for my dissertation, which included a literary review, I did not discover any research that proved how understanding why a problem occurred yielded a solution. None existed. Not one. That experience reinforced the theoretical underpinnings behind the solution-focused approach for me: that it is not necessary to understand why a problem occurs in order to be helpful. In fact, it has been my experience in working with school clients that seeking to know why a problem occurs only gives reasons to focus on why it can't be fixed. Perhaps a child has little supervision at home and can't get his homework done. Maybe an adolescent has too many responsibilities since her single parent works at night. Maybe the angry young middle school student whose parents recently divorced feels abandoned. As school staff, we can't fix these very real personal problems. Focusing on the problems and deciding that we can't do anything until things change at home leaves our school clients stranded with inexperience and us feeling worse.

What does help is watching for times when the school client does turn in work, comes to school, does seem less angry, and does manage to finish an assignment on time or at all. What also helps is thinking of times when the student was on task, did pay attention, did turn in work, and told the truth. What were we doing during that time? What would the students say we did? In these answers, lie solutions.

Building Competency by Becoming Solution Focused in Conversations

The solution-focused process is different from traditional problem solving in that it does not require a lot of information to get started. In fact, you may find that knowing less is more helpful. The solution-focused school counselor begins by focusing on what the school client is trying to achieve and directs efforts toward that goal, no matter what it is, and starts uncovering exceptions. Within this framework, the conversation becomes productive and helpful. The conversation typically consists of the following steps or stages:

1. Identify the concern of the school client.
2. Identify the goal of the school client, and help him or her detail what the goal will look like once achieved.
3. Discover with the client the exceptions to the problem, and connect those exceptions to the goal.
4. Strategize tasks directly from the exceptions, phrasing the tasks as an experiment, and scheduling the tasks for a short period of time based on the age of the school client.
5. Scale the progress of the attempted solution at present and the desired progress to be obtained by the next session.

Let's look at each of these steps.

Identify the Concern of the School Client

School counselors have two types of school clients: those who are referred or sent to them because of poor behavior, and those who voluntarily show up at their door. The first group is the tougher one since that school client does not want to be in the counselor's office. Identifying the concern of referred school clients is crucial and can create motivation for them to talk about what caused them to be referred. Asking questions such as these can help:

"How do you wish your teacher saw you as a student?"

"If you had your way, how would school be working for you?"

"How do you wish things could be for you at school?"

"What do you wish everyone knew that you needed from them?"

"What can we talk about in here that could help you? I'm interested in your viewpoint."

"What do you wish your students knew about you as a teacher?"

"What do you want to happen differently for your son [daughter]?"

What is intriguing about asking these questions is that you will often hear something very different from what you were told in the referral. The importance of listening to the school client first, and moving forward toward goals that he or she has designated, is crucial to satisfying not only the school client but eventually the referring person.

Define the Goal According to the School Client

Goal setting is most effective for school students, teachers, and parents when the goal is stated in specific, behavioral terms. "I want to be happier" is a nice goal but needs to be specific. A school counselor can ask, "What would I see you doing when you become happier?" as a means to identifying a more specific goal.

For example, suppose a student tells you that he wants Mr. Gonzalez to "lay off of him." Suppose a student tells you that she wants her mother to stop yelling. What if a parent tells you that she wants the school to completely redo the discipline policy, which she finds much too punitive? What if a teacher tells you he wants a student out of his class so he can teach? What are you to do with such impossible goals?

Agree with each of them.

What does that answer mean? It means that cooperating with your school client is the fastest road to success. In the solution-focused process, cooperation is the name of the game. For example, let's start with the student who wants the teacher to lay off. First, commend the student for wanting less stress and to be noticed as a good student. Validate his need to get his teacher to lay off. Be curious of how that will help the student when the teacher lays off. Then process with the student how *he* can begin to get Mr. Gonzalez to back off: "What would Mr. Gonzalez say you could do just for tomorrow so that he wouldn't be giving you a hard time?" "What would that look like if I looked in on you while you were doing that? What would I see you doing just for tomorrow, as if you were doing an experiment to get him to lay off?" "Let's write Mr. Gonzalez an e-mail together, notifying him of your plan to be seen differently by him."

These questions are empathetic and supportive yet vigorously encourage the student to be in charge of his own destiny. Most students know what to do when questions such as these are asked.

Sure, it would be easier if Mr. Gonzalez just laid off him, but if Mr. Gonzalez is not in the office and the student is in crisis mode, dealing with what the student wants at the moment is crucial. Plus, helping the student to realize that he can teach people how to treat him is a life lesson.

As for the student whose mother yells too much, validate the student and tell her that her need not to be yelled at is perfectly reasonable. Help her to focus on times when her mother does not yell at her. Explore how the student keeps other adults in her life from yelling at her. While there will always be adults who yell at adolescents, when adolescents realize that their reactions to adults can sometimes modify adults' behavior, they become more aware of their own actions and are more likely to try a new strategy. The following comments might assist a student such as the one described: "While we can't change your mother and since she isn't here to talk with us, one thing that we can do is to explore what you might be doing during the times when she is not yelling or yelling less. Tell me about those times."

What about the parent who expects the school to go above and beyond for her child? School staff members often feel pushed around and threatened by such a parent, and when everyone becomes defensive, nothing is accomplished, and the student suffers. This situation gives the parent more reason to stay defensive. However, when school staff begin to think of such parents differently, such as "passionately concerned," and invite the parent to participate in the solution, the story can turn out very differently, like the one described next.

A parent was asked to come for a conference by the school counselor because her third-grade son was referred to her after being disciplined for throwing rocks at children at recess. The school counselor initially used a problem-focused approach and discussed the situation in an attempt to get the mother to understand what her son was doing. The school counselor told the mother that the son had to stop throwing rocks at recess or he would be sent to the alternative campus the next time it occurred.

The mother refused to believe that her son would throw rocks. She explained that he was a Cub Scout and that she was the troop leader. He was involved in community projects and had achieved many badges. Because of his community involvement and good behavior in Scouts, the mother denied that he could participate in throwing rocks and walked out of the meeting.

The young man continued throwing rocks.

The counselor, frustrated with the situation, consulted me, her colleague, and together we decided to use a solution-focused approach. We began talking about the competencies of the mother so that we could find a way to cooperate with her. We talked about the skills that it took to be a Scout troop leader and were intrigued with the fact that the mother said her son behaved well as a Scout. Apparently the boy knew how to behave in certain situations.

I called the mother and asked her to return for a "different kind of meeting" about her son. This time we began the meeting differently: "We need your help here at school, particularly since you have valuable skills as a Boy Scout troop leader. Surely there are times when some of the boys in the troop need to get back on track. How do you get them to do that?"

The mother responded that she structured the meetings and made sure that she supervised each boy. We then asked her to come and supervise her son for a day or two during the current week to help the school staff learn how to help him behave, much as how she kept her Boy Scout troop on track. The mother said she would be happy to do so, especially so that the school staff would see that her son was not at fault.

The mother never came to school to observe her son. And the boy never threw rocks again.

What happened? We never knew. But I suspect that by being more respectful to the mother and emphasizing that we saw her competencies, she used those competencies with her son in her own way.

Finally, what about the teacher who demands from you or the administration that in order to teach, a student must be removed from his class? Again, agree, cooperate, and collaborate—only do it together with the student:

LM: Mr. Jackson, your concern to teach more effectively in your class is truly admirable. Since I cannot remove Jacob from your class, let's talk about what you need from him. What could Jacob begin doing in your class so that could happen more often?

TEACHER: He could stop making snide remarks. That keeps the class from focusing and disrupts the lessons.

LM: So instead of making snide remarks, what could Jacob do differently?

TEACHER: He could listen in class and wait his turn to speak.

LM: Jacob, what could Mr. Jackson begin doing to help you remember to listen and wait your turn to speak?

JACOB: I don't know. I just never think he likes me, so I guess I don't care to listen.

LM: I see. So what would be signs that he was beginning to like you?

JACOB: I don't know that either. I guess he wouldn't be coming down on me all the time. I have to stand up for myself when he does that.

LM: Got it. Tell me what you think you might begin to do so that he didn't come down on you as often.

JACOB: I guess I wouldn't be talking smart aleck to him.

LM: What else would Mr. Jackson say?

JACOB: I guess that I would listen and do my work.

LM: Sounds like a good idea. What would you say about Jacob's ideas, Mr. Jackson?

TEACHER: Well, if he can do it, but I'm not quite sure he can. Plus, I do like you, Jacob; I just need to be able to teach, and I can't with things the way they are.

LM: Okay. Then let's try an experiment. Jacob, just for the rest of the week, I would like you to do what you just suggested: listen to Mr. Jackson and do your work. Mr. Jackson, when you begin seeing Jacob try to do what you need him to do, let him know.

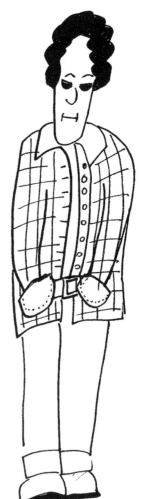

Discover with the School Client the Exceptions to the Problem

A young elementary school student began to cry one afternoon about the recent death of her grandmother, and her teacher sent her to the school counselor. Upon meeting the little girl, the school counselor learned that the grandmother had lived with the girl's family until she passed away. The little girl cried and told the school counselor how sad she was that her grandmother was no longer there with her. The school counselor asked the girl how big her sadness was, and the little girl looked up and said: "It fills this room, goes through the ceiling and all the way up to heaven."

The counselor asked the girl to tell her about her grandmother and the things that she loved to do with her. The girl described playing dolls and going outside to swing and her grandmother would watch. She talked of holidays and how her grandmother liked to read to her. Soon the girl stopped crying and started smiling as she recalled her grandmother, and the school counselor noticed. She then said to the girl: "It seems like you enjoy talking about your grandmother, and I enjoy listening to you. I notice that you aren't crying as much. How big is the sadness right now?" The girl sat up in her chair and put her  hand near her waist and indicated that the sadness had shrunk: "It's about this big now. I really like talking about my grandmother."

The school counselor walked the student back to her classroom and with the student's permission mentioned to her teacher that talking about her grandmother helped her. The teacher told the student that any time that she wanted to talk about her grandmother to her, she could.

In solution-focused school counseling, the exceptions become the basis for strategies. They work because they have worked prior to the current situation. School clients are often more likely to follow through and do them because they are theirs and are guaranteed to work due to their past success. The following statements and questions are helpful when working with parents to identify exceptions:

> "Glance back to the past and recall times when your child was a little more receptive to you or to others. What was different then? How did you or someone else talk so that he listened more often?"

> "This week, ask your son during a quiet time what was different during the times when things were slightly better at home."

> "Watch your own actions this week for times when things seem less challenging with your daughter."

> "How is it that you have reared your fourteen-year-old so successfully for the past thirteen and one-half years? I am quite impressed that it is only for the past few months that things are off track."

These questions focus on times when the problem is slightly better. By emphasizing the words *slightly, less often,* and *a little better,* you encourage the parent to observe things from a different angle. These slight changes become the difference that motivates parents to change.

Strategize Tasks That Come Directly from the Exceptions

I often tell workshop participants never to do anything new with their school clients, which causes many of them to raise their eyebrows. Then I continue to explain the reason for my statement: future success lies in past exceptions. Most people can usually agree to do something that they have done before.

The same idea works with students and teachers. For example, if it is December before a student is referred to you for behavioral issues, inquire from his teacher what worked for the first few months of school. Also explore with the student's other teachers what happens in their classrooms that keeps the student's behavior on track. This information is invaluable to you and to the teacher who has referred the student. Talk with the student, and mention what the other teachers observed about his behavior.

"What is different in your other classes that seem to help you stay on track?"

"What do the other teachers do that helps?"

"What do you do in the other classes that help you to stay on track?"

By talking to the student in this manner, you gather more exceptions that can be helpful to both the referring teacher and the student, since the identification of those exceptions can become possible solutions.

Scale the Progress of the Attempted Solution

When the young girl described losing her grandmother and explained how big the sadness was, she was in effect scaling the effect that the problem had on her life. This approach involves using two methods: externalizing problems and scaling.

Scaling questions (de Shazer, 1985) use a scale and are helpful in focusing on small changes. According to Berg and Steiner (2003), this scaling question helps school clients to gain a perspective of just how much impact a problem has on their lives: "We find that children respond quite well to communicating with numbers, rather than words, because numbers are something they can understand" (p. 21). Using a scale such as this one below can be very helpful when working with school clients:

1	2	3	4	5	6	7	8	9	10
The problem is in control									**The client is in control**

Questions to ask using this scale after goals, exceptions, and tasks have been developed with the school client would be:

"On a scale of 1 to 10, with 1 meaning that the problem is in control of you and a 10 meaning that you are in control of the problem, where would you have rated yourself before we began talking?"

"Where are you now?"

"Where would you like to be before we meet again?"

"What will you begin doing just for the next few days to get there?"

The question can also be used with nonverbal students who feel they have no control over their own destiny. For example, a young elementary student may be bullied on the playground. By talking to him about the bullying as something external to him, the conversation can become more productive: "On a scale of 1 to 10, with a 10 meaning that you are not being bullied and a 1 meaning that you are being bullied twenty-four hours a day, seven days a week, where are you? What's different during those times when you are not at a 1?" Asking the scaling question in this way allows you to learn how often the bullying happens and examine exceptions in the times when it happens less.

Berg and Steiner (2003) also mention that there are other ways to use the scaling question: "Parents and teachers can teach children to adapt the scaling question and apply it to a variety of situations, to monitor their own behaviors. This type of question also makes most children feel competent and successful—it is very grown-up to carry on a sensible conversation with adults" (p. 21). In cases of abuse or trauma, the

question offers a way for students to envision moving forward so that the influences of the abuse affect them less: "On a scale of 1 to 10, with a 1 meaning that the situation that happened to you follows you around and keeps you from doing what you want to do and a 10 means that you are not allowing it to keep you stuck, where are you?" "What are you doing to stay away from a 1?" "What do you think about?"

In addition to using numbers, I have found it helpful to simply ask children, such as the young girl who lost her grandmother, to physically show me how big and how small the problem is at times. For very young children, modeling for them by holding my hands together and saying, "If this means that the anger is never there," and then spreading my arms wide and saying, "This means the anger is there all of the time, where is it right now?" gives children a method of communicating that is easy and understandable.

Making Strides with Nonverbal Students

Truthfully, there will always be school clients who don't talk about, much less know, when things were better. You may hear many renditions of "I don't know" and "I don't care." When this happens, don't change your approach or write the student off as "difficult" or "impossible," and above all, don't think that the solution-focused approach won't work with that student. Instead, see it as a challenge to find a way to cooperate. See the student as stuck in a story that was either written for him or by him and isn't working. Your job is to find a way to present an alternative story. "As this storying of experience is dependent upon language, in accepting this premise we are also proposing that we ascribe meaning to our experience and constitute our lives and relationships through language" (Epston & White, 1990, p. 27).

You can present such an alternative story with students who have trouble identifying what is wrong by drawing a picture together or asking the student to draw what things are like when the

problem is there. Then give the student another sheet of paper and ask her to draw what things will be like someday soon when the problem is no longer there.

If the student is still not as responsive as you would like, let him know that you are fine with meeting again in the near future when he is more aware of what he wants to talk about. Until then, mention that you hope, as he goes through the days, that he will notice when things go better. Tell him you look forward to hearing about those times.

Don't give up, yet don't force the solution talk too quickly. This is more respectful. In the meantime, if you see the student in a non-counseling setting, greet him and talk casually. This builds trust and respect. Many students who had difficulty talking at first can become chatterboxes once they know they can trust you. The solution-focused approach says to cooperate, and if that means waiting, so be it.

Pick One: The Visitor, the Complainant, or the Customer

While this heading sounds rather extreme, it does describe several types of school clients you may engage with who can make your day challenging. Steve de Shazer (1988) identified such clients, and Davis and Osborn (2000) took his ideas and adapted them to the school setting as follows: "Clients and students seeking counseling services are viewed as 'visitors, complainants or customers' and their presenting problem is the result of several unsuccessful attempts to manage difficulties. Symptoms or problems, therefore, do not emanate from sickness, nor are they devised by the student to serve a self-benefiting purpose" (p. 9). Many of these school clients will wander into your office. Before you toss this book because "it won't work on Johnny either," try the following tips that will keep you from giving up.

The Visitor

Realize that this school client is checking out how you can help but is not invested yet. It will be most helpful to both of you that you don't suggest what needs to change. For example, if a student is sent to you by a teacher who is frustrated yet the student does not know why he was sent, help the student to feel that you are on his side by saying, "You know, I realize this is awkward for you. Let's imagine that you don't have to come here anymore. What would be happening that could help that to occur?"

The Complainant

This school client can be a parent who is upset with a teacher or some other school issue. Again, this person's goal is to let you know what the problem is and how bad it is. Listen. This client can be difficult because the venting may be interesting and may get you both off track. Stay safe from this temptation by listening and then saying politely, "I realize this is a real problem for you and your daughter. Tell me what needs to begin happening so that this problem becomes smaller."

Counseling Toward Solutions

By talking in this way, you turn the venting around toward the client, who must then begin to tell you what she wants instead of what she does not want. Typically the client may have difficulty doing this because the complaint is so important to her. Stay patient, and continue asking the same question. If, for example, the client responds, "I want the entire school discipline plan changed," here is how the conversation might play out:

SCHOOL COUNSELOR: That sounds like a good idea. How would having the discipline plan changed help you or your daughter?

CLIENT: She wouldn't be sent to alternative school over silly things like cutting class once in a while, and she would be given more of a chance.

SCHOOL COUNSELOR: And if the school did that, how would that help her?

CLIENT: She would probably have less of an attitude.

SCHOOL COUNSELOR: And what would be going on when she had less of an attitude?

CLIENT: I suppose she would feel treated better and wouldn't mind going to school.

SCHOOL COUNSELOR: Since we can't change the school discipline plan right now, what could we talk about that would tell you and your daughter that she was being treated better?

By talking more with the school client *and* the daughter about what "being treated better" would look like, a school counselor might learn that when a teacher lets her know that she was welcome in class, or when a teacher asked her individually if she understood an assignment, or if a teacher took a little more time to talk to her privately in the hallway when there was an issue, the daughter might feel better treated. A school counselor can arrange for these things to happen by conversing with teachers by e-mail or, more effectively, meeting with the daughter and teachers in a mediation-type setting. As this meeting occurs, it will also be important that the daughter be ready to talk about what she is willing to do to encourage the teachers to try the new strategies. This can be done by asking the daughter with presuppositional language like the following: "Someday soon, when your teachers are treating you better, what do you think they will have seen you do that encouraged them to treat you better?"

Presuppositional language is an intervention in itself: "We intend to influence clients' perceptions in the direction of solution through the questions we choose to ask and our careful use of solution language. Reflection upon these questions helps clients to consider their situations from new perspectives. . . . Presuppositional questions . . . direct clients to responses that are self-enhancing and strength-promoting. In responding to these questions, clients can't help but accept the underlying premise that change is inevitable" (O'Hanlon & Weiner-Davis, 1989, p. 80).

The Customer

The client has arrived. This school client wants your help. He has come either on his own accord or has been sent by someone yet realizes that things need to change. For this client to be successful, you need only create the context for identifying a specific goal and discovering exceptions.

Be aware that often complainants and visitors turn into customers when the solution-focused conversation starts because it is so respectful. As you noticed in the dialogues above, there is no confrontation that "when you are ready to change, come back" because it is the belief of the solution-focused school counselor that people are competent and that it is the job of the solution-focused school counselor to find a way to cooperate with the client. If the client chooses to complain or visit without working on issues, it is her prerogative. However, if she chooses to resolve issues, the solution-focused school counselor is her best ally.

The Solution-Focused Approach to Conversations page is for reference as you conduct solution-focused conversations. To begin, choose one or two school clients to use the approach with so that you become comfortable with it. The guide sheet will take you through the whole process. You may find that you don't complete the entire process during the first session and instead spend the time getting to know the school client and understanding his or her concern. Use the page to help you stay on track and pay less attention to the presenting problem. In time, the process will become more natural. Remember to stay curious. School clients are fascinating!

A Solution-Focused Approach to Conversations: Guiding Questions Cheat Sheet

Concern

"What can we talk about right now that would be helpful to you? I care about what you think and what you need from me."

Goal

"Tell me what it would look like on a small scale when things get better in the near future."

"What would I see you doing in the future if I watched you that would show us both that things were better?"

If the school client tells you how she does not want things to be different, acknowledge by saying, "So instead of that, how would you like things to be?"

Exceptions

"Look back for a minute, and tell me about the times when this has happened on a small scale. What did you do, or what did your parent, family, teacher, or anyone else do, that helped things to be better?"

Task Development

"What do you think you can do for the next day or so based on what we have talked about today? What could your parent, family, or teacher do to assist you in this?"

Scaling Question

"On a scale of 1 to 10, with 1 meaning that things are not working and a 10 meaning that things are perfect, where are you now? Where would you like to be by [insert the date]?"

Finish on a Good Note

"Conversation is, by its very nature, ephemeral. After a particularly meaningful session, a client walks out aglow with some provocative new thought, but a few blocks away, the exact words that had struck home as so profound may already be hard to recall. . . . But the words in a letter don't fade and disappear [the] way conversation does; they endure through time and space, bearing witness to the work of therapy and immortalizing it" (Epston, Freeman, & Lobovits, 1997, p. 112).

Writing your school client a note based on your conversation is an extra gesture that can help ensure that change happens. According to Michael White (1989), a note to a client is worth six sessions in impact. The note should simply be your recap of the session along with encouraging words that empower the school client to do things differently between then and when you see him or her again:

Dear Sue and Family,

I wanted you to know how much I enjoyed talking with you today. I learned about your goals and about the times when those goals happened more frequently. Sue, your goal to be more respectful to your mom this week is admirable. Mom, your goal to give Sue more privacy and allow her to have friends over is generous. I look forward to hearing about your success next week. I am impressed with your efforts to create a more loving family at home.

Sincerely,
Linda Metcalf

How Competent Are You? Check Out What Worked!

If the solutions to problems can be found within our students, so can the most helpful suggestions for helping us develop our skills as school counselors. I have found it personally helpful always to ask school clients about the process of therapy that we just underwent together. The answers increase my knowledge and sensitivity and make sure I am giving the school client what he came to counseling for. When completing my dissertation, I found that most often the reasons for dissatisfaction and failure in counseling were not due to uncooperative people in counseling but to the uncooperative therapists. In other words, the therapist had her own agenda and forgot to inquire what the client really wanted to explore. The following dialogue between a teacher and her student suggests a way of soliciting what works:

COUNSELOR: Thanks, Mrs. Scott and Todd, for coming in today. I enjoyed watching how you both came to some agreements. I wonder, could you tell me what we did here today that might have helped or made a difference?

MRS. SCOTT: I guess I realize that we both have some work to do. It's funny, the way we talked about doing what worked before kind of reminded me that I do need to be more positive.

COUNSELOR: Great idea. I'm glad what we did meant something to you. Gee, Todd, would that be okay with you if Mrs. Scott were more positive?

TODD: Sure.

COUNSELOR: Todd, what do you think helped or made a difference?

TODD: Talking about it helped. I see that I have to do some things too.

COUNSELOR: Looks like you both have things to do, to reach the same goal. Good luck! See you in a few days.

The information gathered from this question, which I ask of my clients, students, and school clients, helps me to know what I did that worked. It also helps my clients know what works for them, giving them yet another strategy for the future.

Summary

The solution-focused conversation is a different way of communicating. School clients come to school counselors to tell them how awful their lives are and need to be listened to. What needs changing, however, is the perspective of the school clients who think that their lives are awful. When a school client leaves your office, she should feel that things aren't as terrible as she had thought. She should leave with specific tools to try, as an experiment, for a short time. This opportunity to try something new and think of themselves differently decreases the fear of taking a risk and increases the possibility of success. You are contributing to life strategies that can help your school clients have better relationships, learn to be more responsible for intrinsic changes, and understand how they learn best. What an opportunity!

Case Notes for School Clients

Name of School Client: _____

Date: _____

Concern: _____

Goal:

_____

_____

Exceptions:

_____

_____

1. _____

2. _____

3. _____

4. _____

5. _____

Task:

1. _____

2. _____

3. _____

Solution-Focused Training Exercise: Chapter Three

Take a personal inventory. The questions here are designed to help you identify your current competencies and help you reauthor the way you want others to see you in the school setting.

What do you do well with students?

_____

_____

_____

With parents?

_____

_____

_____

With other educators?

_____

_____

_____

How do you do that?

1. _____

_____

_____

2. _____

_____

_____

Solution-Focused Training Exercise: Chapter Three (cont.)

3. _____

_____

_____

4. _____

_____

_____

5. _____

_____

_____

What would your colleagues describe as your most valuable qualities?

_____

_____

_____

How would you like to be perceived at school by your students, parents, and teachers?

_____

_____

_____

When have you done this before, in school or in your personal life?

_____

_____

_____

Solution-Focused Training Exercise: Chapter Three (cont.)

How did you do that?

1. _____

_____

_____

2. _____

_____

_____

3. _____

_____

_____

4. _____

_____

_____

5. _____

_____

_____

On a scale of 1–10, where are you now in accomplishing how you want to be at school?

_____

| 1 | 2 | 3 | 4 | 5 | 6 | 7 | 8 | 9 | 10 |

Where would you like to be by the end of the term?

Solution-Focused Training Exercise: Chapter Three (cont.)

Based on how you have accomplished this before, how will you do this?

1. _____

_____

2. _____

_____

3. _____

_____

4. _____

_____

5. _____

_____

Task: Make five copies of the letter that follows. Give three to your closest colleagues and two to students you admire. Tell them you are trying to concentrate on making things work better for you in school. Ask them to fill out the form and return it to you. In return, tell them what you have always appreciated about them.

- ✂ - -

Dear _____,

I am interested in how you see my performance here at school. Your comments are very important to me; I respect and treasure your opinion. Below, please list what you think I do well here at school. It is my hope that your ideas will tell me what I need to keep doing more.

Sincerely,

_____

Comments:

- ✂ - -

Chapter Four

Reviving Piaget

Helping Teachers to Become Solution Focused

*I've come to the frightening conclusion that I am the decisive
element in the classroom. It's my daily mood that makes the weather.
As a teacher, I possess a tremendous power to make a child's life miserable
or joyous. I can be a tool of torture or an instrument of inspiration.
I can humiliate or humor, hurt or heal. In all situations, it is my response
that decides whether a crisis will be escalated or de-escalated and
a child humanized or de-humanized.*

—Dr. Haim Ginott

The solution-focused school counselor wears many hats. Sometimes those hats get snug when the pressure to take care of a student is hindered because her teacher is out of touch with the student's story and therefore the student's needs. The following story is an example of how a student, minding his own business, was sent spinning out of control, only to face consequences that did little to help him. As you read this story, think about how a solution-focused school counselor could have saved this young man much frustration.

Kenny, age fifteen, had lived a few too many lifetimes before reaching his sophomore year in high school. Moving with his family from house to house at least four times that school year, the most recent move due to an eviction, Kenny was bitter. He hated the homeless shelter where his family was living. He disliked not knowing where his family would move next. He worried about his little brother, who got upset when the other people at the shelter stared at him. It was a sad time in his life, but he was determined not to let anyone at school know.

He looked around the classroom most days when he attended school to see other students much better off than he and his family were. They were dressed better than he, and they had their cell phones and MP3 players. So when Kenny's aunt gave him an inexpensive CD player, he was thrilled. It wasn't the latest in technology, but it was his, and having something that belonged to him alone was rare. He treasured it. It almost made him feel like the other kids. He carried his CD player everywhere in his backpack, until one day, late in the afternoon, before the last bell. When his work was done in his last period class, he noticed other students taking out their technologies to listen to music before the dismissal bell. Sitting back in his seat, earphones plugged in like everyone else, CD player in his backpack to hide its obvious technological antiquity, he was surprised that Mr. Locke came up to him, leaned toward him, stared in his face, and demanded that Kenny give him his CD player.

MR. LOCKE: Give that to me. It's not allowed in class.

KENNY: But other students are listening to their players, so I thought it was all right.

MR. LOCKE: I don't care (cursing) what the others are doing. You aren't going to use yours.

KENNY: I don't understand this. I did my work, and I don't think you need to have my player when others have theirs. You don't need to be demanding it from me.

MR. LOCKE: Are you threatening me?

Angrily Kenny leaned forward toward Mr. Locke, who quickly grabbed his CD player and held it behind his back, smiling.

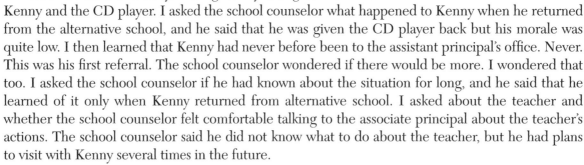

MR. LOCKE: Don't ask for it back. You are going to the office.

With a discipline slip in hand and his CD player in Mr. Locke's possession, Kenny made his way to the office, and once there he met with an assistant principal who apparently was also having a bad day. One look at the referral where the word *threat* was written, and Kenny was on his way to alternative school for six weeks.

When I heard this story, I cringed. My thoughts were with Kenny and the CD player. I asked the school counselor what happened to Kenny when he returned from the alternative school, and he said that he was given the CD player back but his morale was quite low. I then learned that Kenny had never before been to the assistant principal's office. Never. This was his first referral. The school counselor wondered if there would be more. I wondered that too. I asked the school counselor if he had known about the situation for long, and he said that he learned of it only when Kenny returned from alternative school. I asked about the teacher and whether the school counselor felt comfortable talking to the associate principal about the teacher's actions. The school counselor said he did not know what to do about the teacher, but he had plans to visit with Kenny several times in the future.

First, Let Us Do No Harm

Is it possible to make things worse than they already are in today's schools? Yes. Students such as Kenny, in ragged clothes and sometimes unclean due to the limitations of the homeless shelter, could be perceived as threatening to a teacher such as Mr. Locke, who may see students through only one lens. But what *if* Mr. Locke and Kenny's other teachers had received an e-mail note like the one that follows from Kenny's school counselor if he had learned, upon Kenny's enrollment, about his home(less) life.

Dear Teachers,

Kenny Smythe will begin attending your classes tomorrow. Kenny has given me permission to inform you that he and his family are struggling severely and that he would appreciate any emotional support that you can give him. He and his family have moved four times this school year, and in spite of the moves, Kenny has maintained a B average at each high school that he has attended. He said that he doesn't want any special attention, but I would appreciate your understanding that things are tough right now for him and his family.

As his counselor, I will see him occasionally to help support him. Please give Kenny your TLC whenever you can.

School Counselor

I suspect that a note such as this one would have been appreciated by Kenny's teachers. As a school counselor, I always make it my practice to ask permission from students to send such a note to their teachers. No student has ever refused. And teachers often e-mail me back thanking me for taking the time to inform them of something they already suspected was bothering their student. Today's teachers are diamonds in the rough. Full of information on how to help students learn, they are often the least informed on how to help those same students feel comfortable enough to learn. Just a hint of a suggestion by a school counselor can help the misinformed, or uninformed, teacher greet a student, take care to ask if she needs anything that day, or back off if the student seems preoccupied.

When school counselors help teachers alter their perceptions of their students in need, their interactions change and provide opportunities for students that truly make a difference.

No Drama, Please

Such was Maria's need when I met her in a high school several years ago after her father was arrested two days prior for beating up both Maria and her mother. Bruised, with makeup applications to cover as many scratches as possible, she had refused to read a script in drama class, and the teacher, not knowing her situation, had referred her for discipline. The vice principal caught my arm as I walked by his office and told me he was concerned about how to handle the situation discreetly.

Maria, weeping and distressed, told me of the events of that week and how embarrassed she had been for anyone to see her at school. Looking into her eyes, I saw many hidden scars along with the superficial ones that told me the need Maria had for understanding and support. Together we walked down to the drama classroom where her teacher, Ms. Robberts, was directing the play. She walked over to us:

MS. ROBBERTS: Hello, can I help you?

LM: Yes. I just wanted to share something rather private with you about Maria. She has given me her permission to speak to you.

Together the three of us walked into the hallway, where I explained that Maria had given me permission to share that there had been violence at her house a few days ago and she had bruises that she was embarrassed about. That was the reason, I explained, for her reluctance to stand up in front of the class and read.

MS. ROBBERTS: Maria, I am so sorry. If I had known this, I would have never asked you to read. Thank you for letting Dr. Metcalf share that information with me. Why don't we do this: you can sit wherever you feel comfortable in the theater today, and when you are ready to participate again, I will be ready for you.

MARIA: (crying) I would like that a lot. I think I will be fine by Monday.

Later I sent Ms. Robberts an e-mail thanking her for her obvious compassion for Maria. I commended her on her insightful recommendation and told her that I would be available if she needed to speak to me. Maria was able to get back on track on Monday, and she said that she and Ms. Robberts continued to get along very well for the rest of the semester. Toward the end of the year, Ms. Robberts came to my office to thank me for "letting her in." She said that too often, she suspected that students were hurting, but she couldn't always decipher which ones were sincere. She also said that my connection with her gave her permission as a teacher to reach out.

The Go-Between: Ideas for Helping Teachers and Students Resolve Differences

Notice how the dialogue shifted when I spoke with Maria's teacher? Imagine how much more supportive Kenny's teachers could have been with information about his situation. It has become my practice to always involve the system of the student, that is, the teachers and school staff who are involved, when a referral is made. As a family therapist as well as a school counselor, I think systemically. That means I consider how behaviors are maintained and changed through the context of relationships and the interactions of others. For example, think of all the times that you have done good work with a student, and then you return the student to class—where nothing changes. This is because the student went back to the same system that fostered the behaviors to evolve in the first place. That same system will inevitably try to place him back into the same behaviors because the roles of those in the student's system are familiar. Why should they change? They don't have the problem. No, they don't but they still remember how the student had the problem and that is the only way the teacher knows how to relate to the student.

Unless the teacher begins to think differently and do things differently through new perceptions, change will be hard-pressed to last. Although it can be difficult to meet with teachers due to scheduling, it is always helpful to meet for fifteen minutes maximum. A typical e-mail may be sent out regarding such a meeting as follows:

Dear Ms. Joseph,

Thank you for your recent referral of Stephanie Brown. I have met with Stephanie briefly but do not feel that I have enough information to work with her. Since you know her best, please e-mail me back at your earliest convenience and let me know when you are available to spend 10 to 15 minutes with Stephanie and me. This will be a different kind of meeting, one where we look at a better direction for Stephanie. To assist in the meeting, please glance over your grade book for days and assignments where Stephanie did slightly better than usual.

Your help will be invaluable to me as I work with her to improve her behavior and to help you conduct your class in the manner that you wish.

Thank you.

Linda Metcalf

Teachers are typically open to meeting with students if the meeting is brief and they are informed of the process. Meetings using a solution-focused approach are not threatening, leaving teachers more likely to participate willingly. The meeting often encourages a better relationship between teacher and student, and as the issue improves, most school counselors find that their services are rarely needed.

This approach is different from constantly focusing on problems, the primary approach used in schools all over the world. The solution-focused approach stirs excitement within the student as well, and excitement often develops into motivation. When teachers see and hear motivation during solution-focused conversations from their excited students, they often act differently toward the student, and the student behaves and reacts differently in the classroom.

During a recent interview with a future graduate student in school counseling, I verified this idea when I asked him: "What would your students say about you that has made you successful as a teacher?" He replied: "That's easy. It is the relationship that I build with them. All it takes is to go watch them play soccer once, attend a play that they are in or stop them in the cafeteria and tell them what a good job they did on the homecoming decorations, and you have them in your pocket. Then classroom management is a snap."

Relationships do blossom when students see the teacher in a different context, one in which the teacher is not the enemy. As a student hears the teacher describe how he is willing to do something different, the student often becomes motivated as well. Again, the lack of blame encourages motivation on the part of the student. The solution-focused process creates relationships that are based on mutual respect and trust.

The Student-Teacher Conference Worksheet can be used in a student-teacher conference and at all grade levels. Language may be changed or simplified for very young students. The questions use the basic solution-focused ideas in this manual and place them in an easy-to-follow process. Consider copying the worksheet and giving it to both teacher and student after the conference. At a parent conference, the worksheet can serve as a valuable tool not only in informing parents of what works but in demonstrating a sincere effort by the school to resolve the student's concern.

Could it really be this simple? Possibly. Consider the teachers in your school to whom students cling for attention. Those teachers rarely make referrals. Instead, they talk to their students independently. The students respect their efforts. Things get better.

Student-Teacher Conference Worksheet

TO STUDENT

What actions or behaviors would your teacher say he or she would like to start seeing more often?

_____

_____

TO TEACHER AND STUDENT

How would both of you like things to be? (Goal setting)

Teacher: _____

_____

Student: _____

_____

Take me back to a time when that [goal] occurred more often. What was different then? (Discovering when the goal was occurring) Ask for at least three examples.

Teacher: _____

_____

_____

Student: _____

_____

_____

How did you make that happen?

Teacher: _____

_____

Student: _____

_____

Student-Teacher Conference Worksheet (cont.)

TO STUDENT

What did your teacher do that helped [the goal] to happen?

_____

What else worked better for you in class? (Specific, concrete, observable behaviors)

_____

_____

How did that make a difference for you?

_____

_____

TO TEACHER

What did you notice or like about your student when [the goal] was occurring? (Specific, concrete, observable behaviors)

_____

_____

How did that make a difference for you in how you reacted to the student?

_____

_____

SCALE

On a scale of 1 to 10, with a 10 meaning you are both achieving what you want with each other in the classroom and a 1 meaning that neither of you are getting what you need, where are each of you?

Teacher: _____   Student: _____

Where would you like to be when I check in on you next week?

Teacher: _____   Student: _____

Giving Teachers Permission to Connect Emotionally with Their Students

Using a solution-focused approach can often get you pegged as a Pollyanna type who is sugarcoating the problem, particularly when a teacher is fed up with a student or parent. When this happens realize something important: *most teacher education programs rarely teach problem-solving skills, so teachers are often at a loss of how to solve issues with students other than searching for the root of the problem.*

Ms. Peterson came for personal counseling in my private practice because she was tired of "abusive, disruptive students who sabotaged her lessons." She was certain that in all her years of teaching, she had never found such difficult students. As we explored the various times in which she felt good about her day at school, she reported to me that on days when she "worked herself to death to make it interesting," her students complied. She then looked at me and said, "Gee, do you think I need to do this daily?" The answer was obvious. And yes, it may take more work. Consider our competition: video games that make kids feel they are "on site," television shows, movies, music—  interesting things to young, imaginative minds. It is difficult to gain attention from students today.

I asked Ms. Peterson to look over her lesson plans that evening when she returned home and highlight which lectures, activities, assignments, and readings seemed to be more successful than others. She returned the next week to tell me that three of the five days had been good, with students cooperating and minimal disruptions. She said she had realized that the time of day had a lot to do with attention spans and thus cooperation. For example, she said most disruptions occurred in her afternoon classes, so she realized that a movie first, then an activity with an interesting discussion relevant to something they understood, calmed down the students and helped to keep their attention after lunch. I commended her diligence and asked her to do more of what was beginning to work; her students had the answers she was looking for.

Instead of Confronting, Try Respecting

Because of teachers such as Ms. Peterson who lack skills for dealing with challenging students, we must respect teachers for their efforts, even when they are angry, frustrated, and ready to give up. See them as your school clients who are doing the best that they can, and guide them slowly into solution-focused land. While the solution-focused school counselor thinks systemically, he is also concerned with winning compliance from teachers. He knows that when people see a possible benefit to themselves for doing something different, they are more likely to cooperate. When I began using this approach, I encountered teachers who thought my requests of them were odd. Why would I ask them to do something when they expected the *student* to do things differently? I learned that by complimenting and empathizing with the teacher first, assuring them that I was working for them as well as the student, I received more cooperation and collaboration.

Consider this possibility: that the teachers in your school need administrative permission to be compassionate, open, vulnerable, and flexible enough to build relationships with their students.

I once spoke at a faculty meeting about using the solution-focused approach with students, and a teacher asked, "If I begin asking students what they need from me, I open myself up to being vulnerable. Is this what a teacher should do?" Her comments were sensitive and sincere. Her principal stood up, looked out over the audience of teachers, and said: "If we can't be sincere, open, and empathetic with our students, who will be? Many of our students have parents who never take the time to do that. Yes, you all have my permission."

But what do they do next? Most teacher education programs do not offer problem-solving skills to teachers so that they may help students with their personal difficulties. Yet each day millions of students look to what may be the only stable adults in their lives and approach them with the hope that they may connect when things get tough. When they don't connect because their teachers lack the skills to deal with a difficult issue or the confidence to offer themselves as a sounding board, those students often act out, like Kenny, Scott, and Megan did. Then the school staff labels them, and the rest of their time together becomes emotional turmoil for everyone. Taking fifteen minutes during each faculty meeting to train staff to have a solution-focused conversation, as is illustrated in the companion book, *The Field Guide to Counseling Toward Solutions: The Solution-Focused School,* will provide tools that teachers can use every day. When their students respond differently and the parent conferences are more positive, the teachers themselves will begin feeling competent in dealing with a variety of situations. That leads to a safe, secure school environment where more competencies can grow.

Consider asking your principal to say a few words about connecting on an emotional level with students in your school as you begin using the solution-focused approach. Teachers in the 1950s could get away with stern faces and rigid classroom environments; today's students need something different. The world is changing, and as educators, we must evolve with it. No longer can we expect to put students in our box; we must step out of it and find ways to accommodate who they are.

Staying Outside the Box

In his book *Maybe (Maybe Not)* (1993), Robert Fulghum writes about the joy of having a student who created a bit of a challenge for him as an art teacher. The student worked with Tinkertoys whenever he had spare time during class. Instead of pushing him toward another medium, which surely would have made teaching the art class simpler and less cluttered, Fulghum cherished the student because he inspired other students to pursue their own interests as well. The first year I worked as a high school counselor, I learned the hard way that it's important to tread softly in the secondary school classroom. A student dropped by to talk to me about what he felt was an unfair teacher who would not allow him to drop her class, which was advanced. He had been placed

in the class by mistake, he said, and wanted to take another class, which he could pass. It was the fall, and he was on the football team, and in the state of Texas, as in many other states, failing a class meant sitting on the bench for the next nine weeks until he passed each class. This young man was a star athlete, and it was early in the semester, so being optimistic and quite naive, I told him that perhaps if we talked to the teacher together, she might allow me to change his class. I suggested that we walk to her class together.

I greeted and introduced myself to her as new to the high school and asked for her help, which she seemed surprised to hear. I then mentioned that Jimmy was interested in transferring from her course since he felt he could not perform to the level of the other students. She looked at me and said: "Why are you here? I have never met a school counselor who came to my room like this. He needs to wake up, stay awake in class, do the work, and he will pass. Good-bye."

As she loudly spoke to me in the hallway, I noticed that the student, who was initially standing next to me, was now backing off, with a terrified expression on his face. Later in my office, I confided my experience to a colleague, who smiled and guessed who the teacher was. "She takes her course very seriously. He will not be allowed to drop it."

The student did stay in her class, where he performed minimally. The teacher came by my office a week later, angry that I had asked her to watch for what he did better. I recognized that I needed to find a way to cooperate with her language, which was stern and firm. So, firmly, I told her that the student still had difficulties in her class due to her firm approach. He needed some encouragement, I told her, and unless he got it, he would surely not perform in a way that would please her. She backed off considerably and left the office. A week later, she asked me to sit in on a parent conference with his father. I was not only shocked that she asked me; I was shocked that she began to support my efforts. It was a big lesson for me: to remember that my clients at school were not just the students; they were the teachers as well. By letting her know that I feared she would not be able to reach him with her stern manner, she somehow saw me as an ally and began to collaborate. Although we were never close friends, we did begin to respect each other.

A school counselor wears many hats, and in no place is that more evident than in secondary schools. After that experience, I met with my principal, who told me that I had to be careful in asking for help from high school teachers. He said, "They are challenging because they have so many responsibilities, and you must deal with their needs too. You just can't walk in and ask them to do one more thing."

With that information, I learned that I had to find a way to cooperate to stay alive and effective. After that eventful year, I can honestly say that I did learn to cooperate, and I did it by listening to my solution-focused philosophy and applying it to myself. During the next semester, whenever I needed a teacher to observe times when a student did better or a conference with a teacher, I met with the teacher first, got to know him, complimented him on one aspect of his teaching, and told him that not only did I work for students, I worked for him. I wanted his classroom to be the kind of classroom that *he* wanted. I got into the habit of returning e-mails requesting that I see a student with appreciation to the teacher that sent it. I then saw those students as quickly as I could. By the end of the first year as a solution-focused high school counselor, I had rebuilt the reputation from being the school counselor who asked teachers to *watch for what works* (which I still did, only differently) to the school counselor who had a unique way of working with students and teachers, and, most important, *was on their side too.*

Knowledge Becomes Him:
Another Unmotivated Student in Need

There is another kind of student whom school counselors often get referrals on who is sometimes the most baffling of them all. The next story illustrates what many teachers would describe as one of their foremost frustrations: the bright student who "doesn't apply himself."

Sean's dad, a single parent, had brought his fifteen-year-old son to counseling when Sean's report card in January revealed that he was four credits behind due to failing classes. Shy, polite, and slightly timid, Sean said little as I interviewed him about what he wanted to talk about. His dad did most of the talking and stated that he thought perhaps Sean had attention deficit disorder. He said his son loved to read and often read for hours after school in his room, but when it came to homework, he rarely kept focused long enough to complete assignments. He was certain that I simply needed to prescribe medication for his son and the school problems would disappear. When I told the dad that I was "not that kind of doctor" (I am not a medical doctor) but that I did have ideas that might assist his son, he was slightly disappointed yet agreed to continue talking.

After we set a goal of helping Sean pass his classes and begin accumulating credits for graduation, I began asking Sean and his dad some "exception" questions:

LM: Take me back to a time when completing homework was not as difficult.

DAD: That's easy: elementary school. In fact, he was on the honor roll until middle school. He received high scores on the state aptitude tests each year.

LM: What was different then, Sean, that made completing homework easier?

SEAN: I don't know.

DAD: I do. The teachers were great. His current teachers teach only to the state aptitude tests. They don't really care about the kids. I am fed up with the school systems in this state.

LM: So, Sean, what would it take for things to begin getting better for you, if you had your way?

SEAN: I really don't know. Maybe the classes could be more interesting.

The conversation continued to be rather strained, and I began to wonder if Dad's description of the school was influencing Sean's motivation. However, being solution focused, I did not address that concern and instead continued mining Sean and his dad for exceptions. When the session was finished, I was doubtful that attention deficit disorder was the culprit that was keeping Sean from achieving academic success. After all, he had been successful until middle school, and he was able to concentrate not only on reading volumes of history and science books, but also on more challenging projects and papers in some of his classes. But I needed more information on other exceptions that only the school could offer, so I had Sean's dad sign a release for me to contact his son's school, talk to his school counselor, and set a meeting with as many faculty members as I could gather.

Meeting clients at school teaches me about the context in which my clients go to school. After speaking with Sean's school counselor and asking her to arrange for Sean's teachers to meet me, I made sure that the teachers were not inconvenienced and requested only fifteen minutes of their time. I knew the constraints of being a high school teacher and wanted to convey the respect that

their time was valuable. I also requested that Sean attend the meeting, but not when it began. He was to wait in the lobby until I came to get him.

The three teachers who met that morning were curious about an outsider coming to school. I introduced myself as Sean's therapist who was interested in their ideas on when Sean did slightly better in their classes. I mentioned that I wanted to focus on when he was successful rather than when he was not. The teachers immediately looked at their grade books and after a few minutes began to describe Sean in a way that surprised me:

ENGLISH TEACHER: He is one of the brightest students I have ever had in my English class. He reads things that I can't read. He talks about subjects that are way out of the other students' league. He does better when he has a written assignment and can be creative. He can really write. When we discuss novels, he has insight and very intelligent things to say. He just seems to get lost sometimes when the other students act up. Then I see him fold and put his head on his desk.

BIOLOGY TEACHER: Look at his homework grades: he has turned in only two out of ten homework assignments, yet look at his exam grade in biology: it's a 100. I know he is bright. I really enjoy his presence in my class. He is never a problem and always polite. I wish I knew how to get him to turn in his work. I have asked him what I can do and he promises to do the work, but it just never makes it to school.

BUSINESS PROGRAMS TEACHER: I am his computer teacher, and he used to sit in the back of the room until yesterday, when I moved him. He does not have homework in my class, just daily assignments. I found him on the Internet last week and moved him yesterday. He has begun doing the assignments now that he is sitting up front.

The conversation was informative. I was working with a bright, intelligent, yet very bored student. The teachers agreed that if he did his work, he could be in Advanced Placement classes, but without effort, there was no way he would be recommended. I decided to bring Sean into the meeting.

Sean looked terrified as I invited him into the meeting. His school counselor had been talking to him about credit recovery options while he was waiting for me. He looked as if he was going to face a firing squad. Little did he know what was really in store for him.

LM: Sean, I have been talking to your teachers. I am quite impressed with them and have learned that they are very impressed with you. Do you realize how much your teachers think of you?

SEAN: No.

LM: Then I will let them tell you.

Sean's teachers relayed their thoughts about his successes and their beliefs that he had enormous potential. They reiterated our conversation in regard to times when he did things well. They said they were willing to do whatever he needed to help, including providing more challenging assignments. They spoke in such a manner that Sean began smiling and kept smiling during the rest of the short meeting. When the meeting was almost over, I asked his English teacher if she would be interested in recommending him for Advanced Placement English 3 if Sean brought his grade up during the semester, and she said she would. Again, Sean looked at me in disbelief.

Before I left the school that day, I asked Sean what he thought of the meeting, and he said, "I had no idea they thought about me like that. Wow. I don't know what to say." We agreed to meet in a week at my office, and I asked him what he thought he should do at that point. He said, "The least I can do is begin working for them."

A week later, I got a phone call from another teacher who could not make the meeting, and he said Sean was doing all of his assignments. He was much more motivated and attentive. I asked the school counselor to forward the following e-mail to Sean's teachers, with Sean's permission:

Dear Teachers,

Thank you for taking time out of your very busy day to meet with me and Sean Smith last week. I am continuing to work with Sean in regard to his school work. He has told me that he was quite surprised that you thought so much of him. He also said that he plans to show you his appreciation by being more productive in your classes this week. Please watch for times when you see him performing slightly better and mention your observation to him if you have time.

Feel free to e-mail me at any time with your thoughts as you watch this future AP student in action.

Sincerely,
Linda Metcalf

The next week, Sean was much more talkative and animated as he described his reaction to the meeting as "awesome, surprising, amazing." He said he was doing his work more often in several of his classes. After all, he said, he owed it to his teachers. I asked him, on a scale of 1 to 10, with a 10 meaning that he was completely motivated to do his work and a 1 meaning that he was not motivated at all, where he was the first time we met. He said at that time he was at a "3." I asked him where he was today and he said, "I am an 8."

Making Meetings Exceptional

Meetings with teachers such as Sean's should be brief, efficient, and focused on exceptions. The goal is often obvious: change behavior or improve academic performance. Thus, the role of the school counselor becomes one of identifying exceptions. In the meeting with Sean's teachers, we discussed only exceptions, and the possibility of placing Sean in an Advanced Placement class emerged as a reward that seemed rather logical. How different this meeting might have turned out if the focus had been on asking Sean why he was not performing up to his ability. The chances are that he would have left feeling worse than he did when he entered, and the teachers would have less of an idea to help. But by keeping the meeting solution focused, the possibilities blossomed.

Stop Power Struggles Now!

When people are accused of wrongdoings, they often become defensive and sometimes respond by blaming someone. Students, especially adolescents, often feel vulnerable to the expectations of others (parents or teachers) and respond defensively.

The following basic beliefs, suggested by Michael Durrant in *Creative Strategies for School Problems* (1990) are helpful to school counselors when presented with a student or teacher who feels "persecuted":

- Aligning with the student or teacher in his or her complaint and pursuit of justice will lessen resistance. Try saying: "It must be really tough to hear what Mr. Scott says about you so often; no wonder you want things better for you. How will you know when things are better for you in his class? What will I see you doing when that happens?"

- Assuming that the student or teacher has a valid argument and that the argument is a defense mechanism, not an attempt to defeat someone, will "normalize" the student's or teacher's view: "I certainly understand why you're upset and why your mom is worried. Can you tell me times when you don't feel quite as upset? What are you doing during those times that helps you to stay calm and not be as upset by this 'problem'?"

- Wondering out loud what new behaviors might change the "blamed" person's mind about the student will stop the blame and place responsibility on the student: "I wonder what Mr. Scott might see you doing in the near future that would really change his mind about you. I've got this feeling that he really hasn't seen the person I'm meeting with today. You seem so concerned about school. What do you think it would take to get Mr. Scott off your back? Have you gotten him to lay off before? How did you do this?"

- Assuming that the student has accomplished a similar task in other similar situations will encourage his or her chance at success again: "You know, this is the first time I've met with you this year; that tells me you have known how to keep the teachers happy for quite some time. How have you done this? What would your other teachers say you do in their classes that works? Based on what you just described to me, what do you think you might try for just a few days in Mr. Scott's class, to get him to back off?"

What If the Teacher Won't Change?

The previous questions place the responsibility of change on the student and resist the temptation of the student to blame someone else. Peller and Walter (1992) redirect the wish to change someone else by asking directly: What if the other person does not change?

In the following dialogue from *Becoming Solution-Focused in Brief Therapy* (1992), Peller and Walter explore the possibility of the other person not changing and the consequences of that happening. The solution may not contain what the student desires (such as changing the teacher or parent involved), but it opens possibilities to some change by inquiring about what the student can do alone which may cause someone else to change in future interactions:

SCHOOL COUNSELOR: What brings you in, Jack? (Goal frame)

JACK: Mr. Simons kicked me out of algebra class again. That jerk!

COUNSELOR: Really! What happened?

JACK: He does this every time. The whole class can be talking and screwing around while he is out of the room. When he comes back, who does he yell at and kick out? Nobody else but me. He says with my grades I can't afford to be screwing around. He just embarrasses me in front of the whole class. I wish I could embarrass him a few times. I wish I could get out of that class.

COUNSELOR: Hmmm. What are you going to do? (With curiosity)

JACK: I don't know, he's such a jerk. He just decided the first day that he didn't like me and now he is after me every chance he gets. He should retire. He's too old to be teaching.

COUNSELOR: Guess you figure he's too old to change, is that right? (Clarification)

JACK: Are you kidding? He's so crusty. He would crack at the joints if he tried changing. He shouldn't be teaching.

COUNSELOR: Well, you might be right about his not changing. He might be set in his ways. So, if he is not likely to change, what will you do? (Accepting his frame, asking the hypothetical solution, and presupposing that he will do something)

JACK: I am probably going to flunk algebra.

COUNSELOR: Oh, and then would you have to repeat it?

JACK: Yes, and I can't do that. My parents would be all over me.

COUNSELOR: Oh, no! What are you going to do? You don't want that. (Presupposing that he will solve the problem)

JACK: I guess I'll just have to bite the bullet and be mute in Simons's class.

COUNSELOR: Will that do it?

JACK: No, he will still have it in for me.

COUNSELOR: What would he say he wants you to do? (Hypothetical solution, reporting for the other)

JACK: Simons? He would probably say he wants me to "cooperate" in class.

COUNSELOR: What do you think he would say would be signs, in his way of thinking, that you were cooperating? (Hypothetical solution, reporting for the other)

JACK: But I am a cooperative guy.

COUNSELOR: So, what do you have to do to be "cooperative" in Mr. Simons's eyes?

JACK: I guess he would say that I would not be screwing around when his back is turned.

COUNSELOR: So, you would not be doing that. What would you be doing instead? (Eliciting a positive representation for a well-defined goal instead of the negation)

JACK: I guess I would be doing my work or at least keeping my mouth shut.

COUNSELOR: This is what Mr. Simons would say? (Clarification of reporting position)

JACK: Yeah. He would probably say he would like me to volunteer more, too. (Further description of the move)

COUNSELOR: So, you think this might do it and help you pass. Are there times when you do some of this now? (Bringing the hypothetical solution into the present)

In this dialogue, notice that the counselor honors Jack's desire to get Mr. Simons to stop kicking him out of class. If the counselor were to blame Jack for his misbehavior that resulted in his removal from class, the chances are that Jack would have become even more defensive. Instead, by aligning with Jack yet not offering a solution, the counselor guides Jack to a conclusion that he must take responsibility to help Mr. Simons change. The result? A student who discovers how to behave in class to reach a personal goal: staying in class.

What If the Teacher Wants the Student to Change Now?

Consider the following dialogue about a possible referral that never took place:

MRS. JONES: I need you to see Suzanne. She has become so disruptive in my class this week that the rest of the class has a hard time concentrating on anything but her. I need you to see her and find out what's wrong.

COUNSELOR: Okay, I will see her this afternoon. Before you leave, I would like to ask you something. You mentioned that Suzanne has been disruptive this week. How have things been going the last few months of school? Have you found her as disruptive during that time as well?

MRS. JONES: Well, she's been one of those students who talks constantly—you know how eighth-grade girls are. She has all these friends and just can't keep her mouth shut.

COUNSELOR: So does that mean she has been different and not as disruptive earlier in the year?

MRS. JONES: Probably so. I remember one unit we did two months ago, on Shakespeare. She really liked *Romeo and Juliet*. At that time, she talked to me and participated really well in class.

COUNSELOR: Good. When else have you noticed Suzanne not disrupting class and participating just slightly better?

MRS. JONES: She was doing okay until about two weeks ago. This has been building steadily.

COUNSELOR: The disruptiveness?

MRS. JONES: Yes.

COUNSELOR: Okay. Would you do something for Suzanne this afternoon, and for the rest of the week, as a way to identify how she and I can work on improving this disruptiveness?

MRS. JONES: Sure.

COUNSELOR: Here is a teacher referral form. If you would, notice times when Suzanne is not allowing the disruptiveness to bother her. I'd like you to look for times when she is in control of her tendency to be distracted and stays focused. If you will put it in my mailbox tomorrow afternoon, I would really appreciate it so I can assist you with Suzanne.

A Brief Way to Keep Score

Another collaborative way that teachers can make simple interventions and motivate their students is through weekly scaling questions. Ellen Boehmer, a school counselor at Terrace Elementary School in Richardson, Texas, adapted scaling questions into a simple-to-use method for teachers. She duplicated a scale on three- by five-inch note cards (see sample below). When she gave them to teachers of referred students, she explained to the teacher and the students that 1 meant the problem was in control and 10 meant the student was in control. She suggested that the teacher and student collaborate once a week (the day of their choice) about where the student was moving to based on his or her behavior, grades, and participation in school. The simplicity of the card encouraged participation, for all it required was circling a number and noticing the progress. All the teacher had to ask was, "How have you moved from here to here?"

Teacher: _____ Class/Grade: _____

Student: _____ Week of: _____

1   2   3   4   5   6   7   8   9   10

Do You Believe in Resistance?

Most of us become resistant when we are confronted, accused, wrongfully blamed, or rejected. Within school settings, many systemic factors contribute to a teacher's, student's, or parent's resistance. Many times it is lack of information or frustration. Observe the following case study of a psychiatric nurse whom I found resistant to noticing competencies in an adolescent patient I had been working with. She was not unlike many other school staff members who could see only problems, not exceptions.

Sixteen-year-old Steven had been admitted to the psychiatric hospital after he was found drunk repeatedly by his mother, who struggled with alcohol herself. Each week I worked with Steven, and together we noted his achievements in school (which were outstanding) and his participation in the unit group. At treatment team one week, where staff gathered to discuss more diagnosis and progress, I listened as staff discussed what Steven still needed to do according to their diagnosis. After listening to the long litany of complaints and pathological descriptions, I asked the team what he had been doing well. Caught off guard at the suggestion, the head nurse replied that he "never did anything well . . . in fact, he spits, he goes to the gym instead of AA and rarely participates in group."

After repeating my inquiry several times in several different ways, I decided to try a different tack with the nurse. I mentioned to her that she was undoubtedly the most observant member on the team since she saw so much that he did not do well. I then asked her to do something for me that would really help: "Watch for the times next week when Steven does something okay, and tell him about it." She responded quietly that she would try to do that. Before the end of the treatment team, she turned to me and said, "You know, come to think of it, he did pretty well in group this morning; there was a new patient, and he sort of took him under his wing."

Puzzled Looks Galore

Just as teachers need time and patience to understand the solution-focused approach, so do students need time to believe in their own abilities or competencies. It is a different experience (and a very pleasant one) for students to hear what they do well instead of being reprimanded. It will become the norm for puzzled looks to appear on the face of a high school junior who is told repeatedly how interesting his responses are in English class. As her teacher inquires of her humorous approach and helpful comments (even if for only one day in the week), the student fights an internal struggle to believe her and wonder what she's up to. Either way, the walls that had been built when the teacher failed to see her competencies will begin to crumble.

Nevertheless, some school clients are determined to focus only on problems and are quite resistant to noticing anything besides the problem at hand. In keeping with the solution-focused basic philosophy, nothing is 100 percent, and sometimes various approaches need to be taken to approach those who see things particularly negatively. If this occurs, a school counselor can cooperate with the problem focus (by stepping into the problem, negatively, with them), since it is the person's worldview and ask: "This sounds awful for you. When is it the absolute worst?" Then when that time or date is identified, continue: "Then how did it get slightly better the next day?" This attempt to cooperate will be appreciated as the school client feels heard and validated. The solution-focused approach, while initially impressionable as positive, is more than complimenting and talking about wonderful exceptions: it is about connecting with school clients wherever they are emotionally. Once that connection is made, guiding them slowly on a tour of exceptions is enjoyable and productive.

Fifty Miles and Twenty-Five Years

To clarify how this process works, that is, how important it is to "get into the issue with the school client and commiserate a bit," let's look at a conversation that I had with a teacher several years ago. Prior to our conversation, the teacher had tried several strategies with a high school senior who, in her words, "was out to get me." A seasoned and dedicated teacher of twenty-five years, she traveled fifty miles each way to teach at the high school each day and often seemed to be proud of her diligence in doing so. So when she was constantly disrespected by the student, she was not only frustrated and angry; she was hurt. In response to his actions, she told me that she had tried the following strategies, which were not working:

"I tried embarrassing him in front of his classmates by putting him in a corner."

"I tried comparing him to other students during class by being sarcastic."

"I tried ignoring his snide comments in class."

"I tried talking to him after class and telling him I was going to give him a referral."

I was concerned about her strategies, but I also saw her as doing her best to reach the student and set her boundaries. She was a dedicated teacher and did, after all, come to talk to me to make things better. I complimented her on her efforts to try and reach the student and told her that I realized she was frustrated. But adolescents, especially the challenging students, rarely respond favorably to such strategies, so in an effort to help her move forward toward some different strategies, I began our solution-focused conversation.

Step 1: Identify the Concern of the School Client

LM: You've been through a lot with this student. Tell me, what can we talk about right now that would be helpful to you?

TEACHER: I guess, help me to know what to do next. Yesterday another incident happened. I had been standing in the hallway, and the same student had snuck up behind me and waved "bunny ears" behind my head when I was talking to another teacher. That was the last straw.

LM: I'll bet. What was that like for you when he did that?

TEACHER: To be honest, it hurt my feelings. It was humiliating.

LM: I wonder if he knew that.

TEACHER: Probably. But he has no conscience.

Step 2: Identify the Goal of the School Client

LM: You know, you have tried so many things. In fact, I rarely see a teacher as committed to her students as you. And now you are focused on changing a situation. If you had your way, what would you like to see happen between you and this student?

TEACHER: Respect. I want him to respect me.

LM: What will that look like when it happens?

TEACHER: I suppose that he will listen to me and not respond negatively anymore.

Step 3: Discover with the School Client the Exceptions to the Problem

LM: That sounds very important to you. Tell me, in the past, when people hurt your feelings, such as friends, relatives, or other staff members, what did you do to get them to listen to you?

TEACHER: I am actually pretty straightforward. I tell them that they hurt my feelings.

LM: How do you do that?

TEACHER: I get fairly quiet and serious and then just tell them. Sometimes it's embarrassing, so I do it in private.

Step 4: Strategize Tasks Directly from the Exceptions

LM: You know, since you have tried everything else with this student, I want to encourage you to think about sharing with your student how he hurt your feelings in the same way that you would with a friend, relative, or colleague.

TEACHER: You mean, actually tell a student that he hurt my feelings?

LM: Yes, as you have done with others.

TEACHER: I didn't think we were supposed to be so vulnerable with students.

LM: Well, some people think that way, but you seem to be the kind of teacher who could handle that. You did, after all, come to tell me the story, and that tells me you are someone who can handle being vulnerable.

TEACHER: I suppose I could try. I really don't know about this, though.

Step 5: Scale the Progress of the Attempted Solution

LM: Tell me, before we stop, on a scale of 1 to 10, with a 10 meaning that the strategies you had tried before created complete respect from the student and a 1 being the strategies created no respect, where would you say you were when you came in today?

TEACHER: Oh, probably a 1.

LM: What about the strategy that you just came up with? Where do you suppose it might move you as you try it out?

TEACHER: Since I am at a 1, I suppose there is only one direction to go in, and that's up.

We said good-bye, and the next block of classes began. About an hour and a half later, when the block ended, the teacher literally came running to my office, breathing hard:

TEACHER: It worked, it worked!

LM: Okay. What worked?

TEACHER: Before class started, I took the student outside into a hallway where it was quiet and private. Then I told him that when he waved the bunny ears behind my head yesterday, it hurt my feelings. I told him that his disrespect really hurt me too. I told him I drive fifty miles each way each day to teach because I love the students. Do you know what he did?

LM: What?

TEACHER: He dropped his head, stared at his shoes, and, I swear, the boy started to cry. When we went back into the classroom, he said nothing for the entire class period. In fact, he was a model student. But who knows if it will last.

LM: Who knows? But, you know, not only did you do something different, you did something that has worked for you before. That was very wise.

TEACHER: I suppose it was time to do something different.

As time went by during the semester, I had more visits with the teacher, who professed to me each time that her classes were going quite well and that she and the student had not had any more altercations. Each time she warned, "It may not last," and each time I responded, "Who knows, but whatever you are doing, it's working so far, so keep on doing it!"

Summary

What's quite endearing about this last story is that the same teacher had been skeptical and critical of my methods when I was first hired as a school counselor at her high school. She had criticized the way that I visited classrooms to watch for times when students did better work. However, as time went on, she became a good friend and referred many students to me. She also had a good year. And after twenty-five years, she deserved it. She just needed someone to notice her qualities, just like the students did.

The teachers in your school are just as much your clients as are the students and parents whom you work with each day. By letting your teachers know how valuable they are to you through notes, cards, or even an occasional "solution-focused award" at a faculty meeting, you will change more than their attitude. The ripple effect that occurs when one person changes in a system is invaluable. Let teachers know that not only are you working for students, you are working for them so that they can teach as they want. By doing this, you will gain their respect and their cooperation which will help not just you, but the students as well.

Solution-Focused Training Exercise: Chapter Four

The conversations and interactions that you have with the teachers of your students will have a direct impact on your work with the students. This systemic approach is vital to working efficiently and briefly with students.

Write the initials (for privacy reasons) of one teacher in your school who is challenged with problem thinking that might affect the students whom you are working with. Fill in the blanks as indicated.

Initials _____

What are the teacher's traits of concern?

_____

_____

My current strategy with this teacher is:

_____

_____

_____

Is the strategy working? (Circle)

yes   no   sometimes

What do other colleagues do to get the teacher's attention or cooperation?

_____

_____

_____

When you are approached by the teacher or approach the teacher yourself, what is the teacher's language like: critical, frustrated, helpless, linear in thinking, or something else?

_____

_____

Solution-Focused Training Exercise: Chapter Four (cont.)

What would the teacher say she or he needs from you?

_____

_____

When the teacher receives what is needed, how will that help the teacher?

_____

_____

What might you do to begin helping the teacher achieve the goal that he or she indicates would be helpful, using his or her language and the way others approach him or her successfully?

_____

_____

Before the week is over, write a brief note, such as the one below, to the teacher and place it in her or his box so that the teacher gets it first on Monday morning.

Dear Miss Guided,

I wanted to thank you for assisting me in my work with [student]. With the student's permission, I will keep you informed of her progress. I know you are a dedicated teacher with many activities to pursue. The time you spent in the hallway was very appreciated. My aim as the school counselor at this school is to meet your needs in the classroom as well as the student's needs.

I look forward to working with you more often to help you continue to be the teacher that you want to be.

Sincerely,
School Counselor Extraordinaire

Chapter Five

The Miracle Question

Goal Setting for Success

One person can have a profound effect on another. And two
people . . . well, two people can work miracles. They can change a whole
town. They can change the world.

—Diane Frolov and Andrew Schneider, *Northern Exposure*

Travis, age sixteen, had been truant from school for most of the fall semester. He was typically attending one class out of four each day and was making a high grade in that class. At lunch, he sat in his truck and drank alcohol. He had been evaluated by a psychiatrist and had been given several diagnoses, including depression and bipolar disorder. He was taking medications inconsistently and on occasion would take too much and sleep through class.

One morning when Travis did come to school, the associate principal requested that I meet with him and his father. I learned quickly from the father that he and Travis's mother were divorced and that his mother had little to do with her son. This was said in front of Travis, and I noticed how sad he looked as his father continued to describe his mom as a drug abuser and "worthless." Travis chimed in and said that he had been involved with baseball until this school year when his team-mates found out that his mother sold drugs. He said it embarrassed him so much that he dropped out of baseball. Then everything else seemed to go downhill as well.

The associate principal tried to find out what Travis wanted to do in regard to school, and he responded that he wanted to drop out and work: "My friends are older and I relate to them better," he said. He had little motivation to stay in school.

I began talking to Travis, trying to get to know him, and I learned that he lived with his grandparents because he and his dad did not get along. He told me that he had few rules to follow at his grandparents' house; they left him alone for the most part, yet when they did speak, they were critical of him, so he stayed to himself.

I wondered where this young man went for support. It seemed as if he needed a miracle. So I asked him the "miracle" question: "Suppose tonight while you are asleep, a miracle happens, and when you awake tomorrow, you think, 'Hey, I don't mind going to school today!' What would be different as you went through the day that would tell you this miracle had come true?"

For the first time in our meeting, I saw Travis sit up and look interested. Then the conversation took a totally different direction:

TRAVIS: I'll tell you exactly what would be going on. I wouldn't be in classes with freshmen. They are too lame. I am there because I failed some classes last year, but still, they are so immature.

LM: What else?

TRAVIS: I would have more teachers like Ms. Frazier. I always go to her class. It's psychology. I like learning about myself and all the stuff that people say is wrong with me.

LM: What else is it about Ms. Frazier that keeps you going to class?

TRAVIS: I walk in, and she comes up to me and says, "I'm glad you are here, Travis." Then she pats me on my shoulder, and I sit down to work. There should be more teachers like her.

LM: What else?

TRAVIS: I would have friends. I have none, mostly because of the stupid classes that I have with freshmen.

LM: Thanks. You have given me an idea. Since it is December and this semester is almost finished, I think it would be a good idea for us to look at your schedule for next semester and change it to accommodate your needs. Come with me to my office now, and let's figure out what we can do that would help things to get better for you.

Travis agreed to look at his schedule and seemed intrigued that I was so willing to help. I changed the schedule so that he was placed with teachers I knew were more likely to give him the same attention that Ms. Frazier did. I also placed him, with his consent, as an office aide, for which he could earn half a credit doing office clerical work with a secretary in the counseling department. I knew that we had juniors and seniors who were office aides who might befriend Travis. I also knew that the secretary was everyone's "grandmother," and he needed an adult to care.

Travis seemed to like the idea of a schedule, based on what he told me would be in his miracle. Since the next week was the last before the holiday break, I asked him to come to my office before he went to his first class when the spring semester began. I told him carefully, "Do not go to your first class alone. You are important to me, and I want to introduce you to your first block teacher."

He showed up early on the first day of the spring semester, and we walked together to his first class. I introduced him to his first block teacher, and she put her arm on his shoulder and welcomed him into her classroom. I had e-mailed each of his teachers prior to the first day of the semester, alerting them about Travis's need for attention, and each had responded positively.

As the weeks went by, I saw Travis occasionally in the hallway, greeted him, and then followed up by giving one of his teachers a note to give to him that said, "So glad to see you here at school." The secretary I had assigned him to work with quickly became his "grandmother" and began letting him use her desk as his locker. He soon became friends with the other students who worked along with him in the office. The semester progressed. He missed one day of school.

Summer arrived, and Travis put in an application for our district's accelerated high school program and was accepted. He completed two years of high school in nine months, graduated at the top of his class, and won an award for a science-fiction essay. He graduated that June.

In August, he came by to see me and brought with him a scholarship application for college that needed a reference. "Would you be a reference?" he asked. I filled out my part of the application and we had this conversation:

LM: You know, I've told you that I talk about you when I do workshops.

TRAVIS: Yes, you told me. (smiling)

LM: I trust your opinion. Tell me, if you could tell educators everywhere what some people did for you while you were a high school student to turn things around, what would you tell them?

TRAVIS: Tell them to build relationships with their students. Some kids never get anybody to care. Let them know how much they mean to students, even when the students don't show them!

Name That Miracle

Scot Miller, a notable author of several books on solution-focused therapy (Miller, 1996; Miller & Berg, 1992), once told me that "you ask the miracle question when a client really needs one."

Think of your current school clients. How many of them need miracles in their lives? What about the single mother with two jobs who is barely able to get her children to school because she has no help? What about the elementary school student whose father is incarcerated? What about the high school junior whose father has given up all rights to seeing him on visitation? And the parent who has been touted as a troublemaker yet still keeps coming to see you in an effort to get help for her son who just can't seem to behave in class? They all sound as if they need a miracle.

The Brief Family Therapy Center in Milwaukee, chaired by the late Steve de Shazer, began seeing the importance of defining solutions rather than problems: "If the solution was more important than the problem, why not focus more on the solution aspects of the situation? This led to the development of two key elements of their approach, the 'miracle question' and the 'exception question'" (O'Hanlon & Weiner-Davis, 1989, p. 240).

The miracle question is helpful for goal setting in that it temporarily takes the school client away from his troubles and invites him to step into the solution that he desires. School clients provide all kinds of answers, including some that seem impossible:

"My parents would be together again."
"My grandmother would still be alive."

"I would be taller."

"I would have a different teacher for algebra."

"I would be smarter."

"The school would have a better sports program for my son."

"I would not have any behavior problems with my students this year."

Although the first few goals seem impossible, they are still very important and in need of your acknowledgment because the client is sharing with you his heart's desire. Responding with, "Let's be realistic," will alienate and burst the bubble of the school client. Instead, the solution-focused school counselor considers the answers given as clues into what the client desires and sees from his worldview. It is the most important issue of all to the client, and one that he will more likely work toward. By learning this information, the school counselor gets a chance to cooperate with where the school client is, lessening resistance and getting direction. Then the school can continue the process by saying, "That sounds very important to you. Tell me what having a miracle such as that would do for you?"

By acknowledging the miracle and asking further questions about what the miracle would do for the school client, the school counselor is more likely to emerge with a workable goal for the client. For example, if a student talks about her grandmother being alive, asking her how her grandmother being alive would make a difference to her might result in an answer like this: "I would have someone to talk to again." On further curious questioning, the school counselor might assist the student to go on a "friend-hunting spree" and begin noticing people whom she might be able to talk to in some way. This honors the school client's miracle and helps the school client to be realistic about steps to begin taking.

Let us examine how the miracle question can be helpful in a conversation with an elementary student. Take the first goal listed previously: "My parents would be together again."

LM: What would it do for you to have your parents together again?

STUDENT: I would feel like I have a family again. Since my mother left, my father works a lot, and I have to take care of my little brother all the time. There's a sitter, but it just isn't the same.

LM: Tell me about the times when you do feel as if you have a family, just slightly.

STUDENT: On Sundays, when we go to church, we are all together.

LM: When else?

STUDENT: Sometimes when my father gets home, he sits and talks to my brother and me, and he checks on our homework. Usually it's late, but I like waiting up for him.

LM: I wonder if your father knows how important that time is with you.

STUDENT: He doesn't. He's told me that he has a lot of financial problems, so I don't want to bother him with something else.

LM: You are very thoughtful. I wonder, though, is your father the kind of father who would want to know if he needed to do something for you, like sit with you for a few minutes at night?

STUDENT: He is. I don't really need a lot of time, just a few minutes.

LM: How many minutes?

STUDENT: Maybe fifteen.

LM: How do you think it would be best to let him know this? Would you suggest talking to him or writing him a note?

STUDENT: Probably a note. I'm a little embarrassed to ask him.

Together we wrote a note to her father:

Dear Daddy,

I really like it when you spend time with me at night when you come home. I wish we could spend more time together. I only need fifteen minutes a day. I miss you when you aren't here but I understand that you need to work a lot. Fifteen minutes would really help me to feel like we are a family again.

Love,
Ann

The student came in the next week beaming. She told me that her father had spent the entire weekend with her and her brother and promised to give her thirty minutes each night when he came home. Following up with her teacher, I learned that her behavior had changed and her attitude had brightened.

Choose Your Reputation: Complainer or Leader

Adolescents seem to like the miracle question since it gives them a chance to voice their needs. Often they leave their parents baffled as their personalities change along with their bodies and their moods. Their world is a social one, where fitting in and being accepted is their primary concern. When they don't receive that sort of validation from adults, they act out and present themselves in negative ways. Asking the miracle question gives adolescents a way to express what they really need.

Mehmet was a high school student who had been dubbed "the complainer" by some of my colleagues who had worked with him previously. He was an only child who apparently had a voice at home and wanted that same voice at school. When he couldn't seem to comply with his algebra teacher's expectations in class to work silently by himself, he often complained that he just could not stay in that class, so he often walked out. When I met him, it was midsemester and much too late to switch teachers. I asked him the miracle question, and he answered that a miracle would mean that Mr. Jenkins was out of his life. Since I couldn't help him to do that, I asked him what that would do for him and he said, "It would keep him from criticizing my homework and constantly calling my parents." After hearing what the miracle would do for him, we continued our conversation:

> LM: Mehmet, I appreciate your honesty. Unfortunately I can't take you out of his class because it is halfway through the semester and past the transfer date for our school. But let's keep talking. If Mr. Jenkins were in here right now sitting with us, what would he say you could do just for today that would keep him from criticizing you and calling your parents?

> MEHMET: I don't know; maybe not talk when he is explaining a problem at the board. But see, Miss, he just doesn't like me anyway.

> LM: Okay. What else would he say?

> MEHMET: Probably to stop acting up in his class and do my homework and turn it in.

> LM: I haven't heard from any of your other teachers this year, and it's already March. What have you done in their classes to get them to like you?

> MEHMET: If a teacher acts like she likes me, I don't give them a hard time, and I try to work in their class.

> LM: How would you know if Mr. Jenkins liked you?

> MEHMET: If I raised my hand, he would call on me instead of ignoring me. He wouldn't make comments about me either.

> LM: Tell you what, I would like for both you and Mr. Jenkins to meet with me tomorrow morning for about ten minutes before school. Until then, watch for signs that he is not *always* criticizing you. You know, since the class is fifty minutes long, see how many minutes he really spends giving you a hard time. Write them down just for today, okay?

> MEHMET: I'll try.

> LM: I think you are worth our trying something new.

What happened in this conversation? Mehmet was listened to and was respected for his wish to get Mr. Jenkins to stop criticizing him, which was Mehmet's concern. Then I took Mehmet into "responsibility land" by asking him to describe how he had kept his other teachers from criticizing him for almost six months. This approach surprised and empowered him, because he had not thought of himself as successful, and he gave me new information. From there, we decided to discuss the issue with Mehmet's teacher in a different kind of conversation. I invited Mr. Jenkins in for a fifteen-minute meeting.

> LM: Thank you, Mr. Jenkins, and Mehmet, for coming early this morning. I wanted you to be here, Mr. Jenkins, because I know that you are the kind of teacher who wants to do whatever is necessary to help a student.

MR. JENKINS: I would hope so.

LM: As you know, I am working with Mehmet, and we are trying to find times when school goes better for him. He is particularly interested in doing better in your class. I'm interested in times when you notice Mehmet doing better in your class.

MR. JENKINS: Lately, there haven't been many times. Earlier in the year there were a few more times.

LM: Can you tell me what was different earlier in the year?

MR. JENKINS: He would participate in class appropriately.

LM: If I looked in on him during those days, what would I have seen him doing that was appropriate?

MR. JENKINS: He wouldn't be cutting up with his friends or refusing to do his work like he does now. That makes my job pretty hard. I spend too much time disciplining kids and not enough explaining the work to them. I run out of time.

LM: Okay. Wow. I'll bet that is difficult. What would Mehmet be doing differently instead of cutting up?

MR. JENKINS: If he raised his hand before speaking and turned in his work most of the time. He's a bright student, and when he works, he does quite well.

LM: Mehmet, what did Mr. Jenkins do that helped you to raise your hand and do your work?

MEHMET: He explained the work in a way that made it easier to do. I knew the answer so I raised my hand.

LM: How did he explain it so that it was easier?

MEHMET: He would ask if anyone had questions, and I raised my hand, and he went over it with me at my desk.

LM: How long has it been since you raised your hand for help?

MR. JENKINS: (interrupting) A long time.

LM: With this information, what could you each do just for the next few days so that Mehmet gets back on track, like before?

MR. JENKINS: I can come by your desk after I have explained a new problem, and if you need help, you can ask me to help you.

MEHMET: Okay.

MR. JENKINS: I think I have forgotten to do that for a few other students too, since we have been so busy preparing for the achievement tests next month. You will have to remind me, Mehmet. I want to help you. I want to mention one more thing. You know, early in the year, we did group work, and I always thought of you as a natural leader. You have real potential.

LM: Wow, Mehmet, did you think that Mr. Jenkins thought that about you?

MEHMET: Me, a leader?

MR. JENKINS: Yes.

This conversation took about fifteen minutes, and both Mehmet and Mr. Jenkins left my office talking to each other. Mehmet's behavior radically changed, and when I asked him in a follow-up session the next week, "What's gone better?" he told me that his teacher was being nicer to him. My response to him was, "What did you do to help that to happen?" He smiled and said, "I guess I behaved better." Mehmet went on to not only do better in algebra class but began to correct other students in his class when they got off track and stopped listening, according to Mr. Jenkins, who thought Mehmet's new actions were amusing. I suppose he was developing his leadership skills further.

Parenting Miracles: Whatever You Say, Ma'am

The miracle question can also help parents define what they really need when their needs seem insatiable. Perhaps you have visited with a parent whose child is not given enough of the following at school:

- Attention
- Testing
- Time at centers
- Homework extensions
- Freedom to express herself
- Chances at making the team
- Choices of books to read
- Understanding
- Patience

And the list goes on (hopefully not all of these from just one parent!).

Usually when parents make unrealistic requests, school counselors try to convey the impossibilities of the request to the parent, who typically meets them with more resistance and defensiveness. It's time to stop that strategy because it rarely works. But if instead the school counselor honors the impossible request as important and valid and conveys that to the parent, the resistance dissolves. The parent then begins seeing the school counselor as an ally, a situation that leads to a much better conversation. The next story addresses a possible course of action for a parent whose request at first seemed impossible but then turned out workable.

LM: What brings you in, Ms. Sang?

MS. SANG: I am very upset with this school. They are not giving my son what he needs for college. He is a senior and he is not taking enough AP [Advanced Placement] classes so that he can be the top student in his class at graduation. It is September, and I demand that you put him in all honors classes in the spring. In our family, you are supposed to work hard. He works at school and then in our restaurant at night. He studies until midnight, then comes to school. Next semester he tells me that he qualifies for a class period time off since he has taken all of his required classes. He says that he can get out of school at noon. He tells me that there is nothing else to take. This is ridiculous. He needs to study!

LM: This sounds very important to you. I agree that it is a good idea for your son to study hard. But I am a little confused about what we can do. Let me ask you something. If you had your way and our school was doing exactly what you wanted us to do for your son, as if a miracle happened when you woke up tomorrow, what would we be doing?

MS. SANG: You would have my son studying something important that would help him in college next year. He would not have a time off.

LM: Tell me what sorts of classes that you feel have already helped him to prepare for college.

MS. SANG: He is very interested in physics. The more he knows, the better he will do in college. He spends time with Mr. Johnson, his former physics teacher, in the afternoon after school. He is the Physics Club sponsor. It seems that Mr. Johnson is someone he enjoys talking to. He loans him books.

LM: Since we really do not have any other classes that your son could take, let's come up with some sort of way that he could expand his knowledge of, maybe, physics. You said that Mr. Johnson is someone he enjoys talking to.

MS. SANG: Yes, he is.

LM: I wonder what kind of project or study that you could speak with Mr. Johnson about that would be of interest to your son.

MS. SANG: He is very interested in aeronautics.

LM: Great. I would like you to contact Mr. Johnson and let him know your idea. I will e-mail him now before you leave and let him know that you are going to talk to him this week. Would that work?

MS. SANG: Yes. I can do that.

Ms. Sang talked with Mr. Johnson, who then asked her son, Tim, to be his lab assistant during the last period of the day that semester. Not only did Tim enjoy the chance to work with his teacher, he used the experience to write about on his college essay. He is now in college and, I assume, studying very hard.

Tip: Don't Hurry the Miracle

Insoo Berg, one of the founders of the solution-focused approach, always asked the miracle question with such patience and respect that clients felt compelled to answer. I am reminded of that patience that I must take when using the miracle question. For many school clients, envisioning a miracle is far-fetched, and sometimes the school client would rather admire the problem than imagine life any other way. When that school client is a teacher, the tendency is to focus on the problem, so it takes understanding and time to help the teacher brainstorm what the miracle would look like. With students, asking the miracle question gives them hope and the chance to escape, even momentarily, from turmoil that has kept them trapped emotionally.

The following dialogue explains the importance of going slowly and staying patient when asking the miracle question. The school client was a student who was missing her mother's presence at home and was asked the miracle question to help the school counselor understand her needs:

CLIENT: My mother would not be married to Joe. She would not work so much either. I think she just wants money. It gets so bad sometimes that I just stay in my room and cry all night long.

SCHOOL COUNSELOR: What would be happening instead of that in the miracle?

CLIENT: She would spend more time with me. With Joe around, I never see her. He has this truck that he works on, and he's always asking her to go out and sit with him while he works on it. She leaves my brother and me to fend for ourselves. It's not fair.

SCHOOL COUNSELOR: What would you see in the miracle that would begin to tell you that things were becoming a little fairer?

CLIENT: Well, with my father dead, it would finally seem like having my mother do things with me occasionally. That would be a start.

SCHOOL COUNSELOR: And how would that help you?

CLIENT: I guess I would feel like I hadn't lost everything. After my father died, I felt lost too. He and I were very close. We did a lot together. Lately I have been thinking how I really don't have anything.

SCHOOL COUNSELOR: Oh, so doing some things with your mom might mean that you weren't as lost.

CLIENT: Exactly.

Here, the school client is focused on changing someone else in her miracle, which is doomed to fail. By asking about what the miracle would "do for her," she was able to verbalize something more specific. "Feeling like I hadn't lost everything" is a conversation that can deal with identifying times when the school client *did* feel less lost. By helping her to identify those times, her feelings of being insecure begin to shrink.

In addition, writing or calling the client's mother would be helpful. If the mother is not available, writing a letter with the school client in your office and handing it to the school client to take home to her mother would be a helpful way for the school client to learn to verbalize feelings and needs:

Dear Mom,

Ever since Dad died two years ago, I have felt very insecure. I know that you love Joe and that he is important to you, but sometimes I feel like he is more important than me when he stays around so much and takes all of your time when you are not working. I would like it very much if you and I could spend maybe 30 minutes together, two times a week. That would help a lot.

Love,
Sherry

Summary

The two worksheets that follow may be helpful to use when asking the miracle question to school clients. The first worksheet sets out the steps that this chapter has outlined to use the miracle question and stay on track with school clients. The second is an alternative way to talk about the miracle question when school clients have difficulties relating to the question. Life can be hard, and sometimes it can be so challenging that school clients can't think of anything that they would like to be different in their lives. They just know that they want things to be different. This exercise is helpful for school clients who are stuck in problem thinking, particularly secondary students and their parents. For elementary students, it is helpful to ask their teachers to assist the student with this exercise. It will give the teacher knowledge of exceptions and further their ideas about how to construct solutions.

Remember that on any given day, any of us could use a miracle. The miracle question in this chapter is not just for school clients; it can be for us too. When you have a tough day and wish things were different, ask yourself the miracle question and go through the steps described here. It will give you a sense of relief to know what you are really looking for.

The Miracle Question: An Exercise of Hope

1. Ask the miracle question: "Suppose tonight while you sleep, a miracle happens. When you awake tomorrow morning, what will be different that will tell you that a miracle has happened in your life?" Adapt this accordingly for conversations with elementary and secondary students or parent conversations. Help the client to define the miracle in terms of what he or she wants versus what would not be happening. The client has to be able to see the miracle.

_____

_____

_____

_____

2. Define the miracle goal—what the miracle will do for a school client's life—the goal: "Tell me what your miracle [the one listed in question 1] will do for you?"

_____

_____

_____

_____

3. Identify the exceptions—the times when the goal happened slightly: "Tell me about times when a little of this happens now, even in other places or situations."

_____

_____

_____

_____

_____

The Miracle Question: An Exercise of Hope (cont.)

4. Design the action plan—a plan that develops from the exceptions: "From your ideas, let's decide on which ones you would like to try, just for a day [for elementary students] or a week [for secondary students]."

_____

_____

_____

_____

_____

5. Pay attention to the results—observe what changed and how the task worked to accomplish the changes. This step can also be used as a form of follow up-question: "I'm glad to see you again. Tell me what's gone better since I last saw you."

_____

_____

_____

_____

_____

Watch Out for the Miracle! An Exercise for Students, Parents, or Teacher

1. As you go through the next day or week, watch for times when things are slightly better. Write them down.

_____

_____

_____

_____

_____

2. What activities or interactions seemed to work better for you?

_____

_____

_____

_____

_____

3. What did those activities or interactions seem to do for you [or your son/daughter/student]? Write down how you felt and what thoughts occurred during those activities.

_____

_____

_____

_____

_____

Solution-Focused Training Exercise: Chapter Five

Suppose tonight, while you slept, your school became solution focused. What would be happening when you drove up to the building the next morning and went in that would tell you things were very different?

Who would be doing things differently?

_____

_____

How would those changes make your day different?

_____

_____

What else would be happening so that you could be the solution-focused school counselor that you have always wanted to be?

_____

_____

What would that do for you?

_____

_____

Write down what you could begin doing, just for today, to move toward your goal.

_____

_____

Do the same exercise tomorrow.

_____

_____

Chapter Six

Constructing New Stories with Elementary Students

What we remember from childhood we remember forever—
permanent ghosts, stamped, inked, imprinted, eternally seen.

—Cynthia Ozick

Taylor was a bright, precocious five-year-old who glanced through each magazine in the waiting room, reading each page aloud to his mother. Then he tackled the box of blocks with ferocious energy, building a structure that seemed architecturally ahead of his time. Although quite masculine in appearance and behavior, I soon learned that Taylor was teased by the first- and second-grade boys as being gay because he only wanted to play with the girls. This didn't seem to faze Taylor, but it bothered his mother. She was as concerned about his overt feminine side as much as she was over Taylor's tendency to become angry and violent with other boys when they teased him. When that happened, Taylor was punished by his teacher, which again brought him negative attention.

Taylor's teacher often dealt with his misbehaviors by announcing to the class that Taylor was to be "invisible" to everyone, which often meant that he was invisible at lunch, so his classmates sat far away from him. The mother had spoken to the teacher and even the principal about this technique, which she found offensive and cruel. However, both educators dismissed her request for a different approach, saying it was school policy. Taylor increasingly disliked going to school due to the humiliation he experienced from the bullying. When he continued to act out, his mother wondered if he was out of control or a victim of emotional abuse.

With so many strengths in view, I approached Taylor and played blocks on the floor with him for a while, talking to him and asking what his time at school was like. I learned that he played with the girls more often because they were nicer to him. The boys, he said, liked to play rough sports, and he was more into playing school and house with the girls. He loved parts of school, especially library time, when he could read whatever he wanted. He disliked being called "invisible" very

much. As I played with him briefly, I asked him to imagine a new day when school went well for him, almost like a fairy had waved a magic wand and created a new story for that day when he was the star. He told me that on that day, he would not be in trouble because he wouldn't be getting angry and that his teacher would like him. The other boys would also like him. It was getting angry, he said, that got him into too much trouble with everyone.

There were many concerns that I had for Taylor, one being that his teacher addressed him as "invisible." When the teacher refused to change her tactic, I was determined to help Taylor learn that he could control his behavior and avoid the invisible label. His identification of anger, "getting him in trouble," also gave me a reason to try externalizing the anger with Taylor and help him write a new story. Our conversation went like this:

LM: Tell me about getting angry. What is it like for you when that happens?

TAYLOR: I get really mad, and then I hit people. Then the teacher punishes me.

LM: And then what happens?

TAYLOR: I get in trouble, and then my mom gets mad at me too.

LM: So the anger kind of takes over your day at school and makes you do things that you don't want to do, right?

TAYLOR: Yeah.

LM: Tell you what. Here is some paper. Let's draw what that anger looks like when it is at school, following you around, waiting to take over. Tell me what it might look like.

Being a former art teacher, I love drawing pictures with children and often find it a good join-ing technique. Together Taylor and I composed a sort of monster with a huge grin and ugly teeth. He said, "It wears sunglasses because it gets so hot outside sometimes." As we put sunglasses on the monster, it reminded me of Cousin It from the *Addams Family* television show. I told Taylor about Cousin It with his long hair over his face, and Taylor liked the idea, smiling and laughing with me.

LM: So this is what the anger looks like when it follows you. Not too much fun. And, remem-ber, it's not you; it's Cousin It that is the problem. Tell me, what will happen when Cousin It begins to stay away?

TAYLOR: I won't be in trouble, and I won't hit anybody.

LM: Wow. What would be there instead of the anger monster then?

TAYLOR: Something a lot better.

And so we began to draw "something a lot better," which turned out to be a gigantic teddy bear with a smile, soft eyes, and soft fur. Taylor loved the drawing and wrote his name across the top of that page. I then gave both pages to Taylor and his mother and asked his mother to remind him each day to choose between the two pictures as he got out of the car at school. Taylor said that he knew which one that he would choose each day. He wanted to "take" the bear to school. I complimented him on his choice but reminded him that Cousin It might try to trick him into being angry. I then mentioned that there was a good chance that his strength would win over Cousin It. To that remark, he smiled and hugged his mother.

As a safeguard, I mailed a note to Taylor's teacher describing the externalizing process and asking her to notice when he was able to control the anger. Taylor returned with his mother two weeks later, carrying the picture of the bear. He decided to leave the picture of Cousin It at home because he didn't need it anymore. Smiling, he described two weeks of staying out of trouble. His mother, still unhappy with the teacher, said that Taylor had done quite well at home and at school in spite of the atmosphere at school. I applauded Taylor in his ability to keep the bear alive even when it was difficult for him. The mother told me that she had plans to enroll Taylor in a private school the next year.

New Stories, New Characters, New Results

This chapter presents a variety of methods that solution-focused school counselors can use with children in elementary and middle school. The ideas here are not limited specifically to this age group; they are appropriate and helpful in dealing with many issues facing school counselors today, such as anger, depression, grief, fear, phobias, bad habits, poor behavior, violence, divorcing parents, abuse, and low self-esteem. The important component of each of the ideas is the belief that a child who comes up with the strategy is more likely to follow through with it. Therefore, the solution-focused school counselor does not suggest actions or words; instead, he creates the context in which the child identifies what he wants to achieve, feel, or accomplish and then, with the school counselor, discovers how to make it happen.

Externalize, Don't Rationalize

In Taylor's situation, the school and the teacher were not as helpful as I had wished; however, by externalizing his anger, we took the focus off the negative punishment that he received from his teacher and focused on how he was able to get control of the problem. This is quite helpful when working with children who have been given a label by a well-meaning diagnostician or other mental health professional. It also assists the adults in the child's life because they begin looking for different descriptions, thereby freeing the child of negative assumptions—for example:

- "An angry child" becomes "a child dealing with anger at times."
- "A depressed child" becomes "a child who lets sadness take over sometimes."
- "An ADHD child" becomes "an energetic child who forgets to slow down" or "a child bothered by attention deficit disorder or 'energy'."
- "A talkative child" becomes "a child bothered by a talking habit."
- "A child who hits and bites" becomes "a child whose actions control him at times."

Notice the language in the second description. Words and phrases such as "at times," "sometimes," "forgets," "bothered," and "at times" all represent tentative, not permanent, situations. These words and phrases also send a message of hope in that they propose that the situations do not occur constantly. This is far more helpful than trying to rationalize with children about things that they might try to do differently, even if those ideas work for others. The solution-focused model emphasizes the importance of making the client the expert. By externalizing the problem, the student becomes the expert who can gain control over his destiny. There is no more effective self-esteem builder than that of knowing you have worked things out for yourself and succeeded.

And the Winner Is . . .

Sometimes situations can be made into competitions using the scaling question differently. For example, two young boys fighting on the playground can meet with the solution-focused school counselor about the "fighting habit" that seems to have taken over both of them and even restricted them from playing together. Asking the questions on the worksheet for the Competition Scale for Defeating Bad Habits can get things progressing positively. Make a copy of the worksheet and, with student permission, give each of the student's teachers a copy. When the teacher knows the plan, the student gains support and knows that others are watching. This is a subliminal way of sending the message of confidence to the student.

Counseling Toward Solutions

Competition Scale for Defeating Bad Habits

Students:

_____

versus

_____

"Which of you thinks that he/she can be stronger in beating the [name the habit here] habit that keeps getting you in trouble?"

"I am going to draw a scale for both of you. The middle of this scale [show the scale to the students] means that there is no [habit]. The ends of the scale mean there is lots of [habit]. If I were to place each of you on the opposite ends of this scale, where should I put you?"

"[Jill], where are you?"

"[Jana], where are you?"

"What would I see you both doing slightly differently if you each moved up one space for the next week? [Write down the task described by the student under each name.]"

"Who do you think will reach the middle first?"

Student's Name   Student's Name

_____   1 2 3 4 5 4 3 2 1   _____

Solution: _____

Plan   Plan

_____   _____

_____   _____

_____   _____

_____   _____

131

Learn to Brainstorm, Not Blamestorm

Ben Furman is a Finnish psychiatrist and an author of many children's books. In his groundbreaking book, *Kids' Skills* (2004), Furman gives solution-focused school counselors another way to conceptualize how they work with elementary and middle school students.

What if, for example, instead of thinking that Sally needs to stop tattling on Jeanne, her friend, the teacher thinks that Sally needs to learn how to be a good friend and sets up some opportunities during class time to do so? What if a child who needs to stop creeping into his parents' room at night needs to learn how to fall asleep in his room by himself and his parents begin brainstorming with him how that can happen?

Furman (2004) writes that "the kids' skills program is based on the notion that children do not actually have problems, they simply lack skills that they have not yet learned. In other words, most issues confronting children, including fears, bad habits, and disorders involving sleep,

eating, urinating and defecating, can be perceived as undeveloped skills. By learning the relevant skills, children overcome the corresponding problems" (p. 4). This is a refreshing way to redescribe children who others fear have deeply rooted problems.

Furman mentions that thinking about kids' skills prevents "blamestorming," something that happens when parents blame teachers or each other for their child's problems. When using kids' skills, "We do not devote much time to finding out the original cause of the child's difficulty. Instead we focus on what the child needs to learn, thus avoiding those typical faultfinding conversations so characteristic of more traditional approaches to childhood issues" (p. 8).

Furman (2004, pp. 10–11) lists these fifteen steps as important to developing kids' skills:

1. *Converting problems into skills*—Find out what skill the child needs to acquire to overcome the problem.
2. *Agreeing on the skill to learn*—Discuss the issue with the child and agree on what skill he will start learning.
3. *Exploring the benefits of the skill*—Help the child become aware of the advantages of having the skill.
4. *Naming the skill*—Let the child give the skill a name.
5. *Choosing a power creature*—Let the child choose an animal, or some other character, to help her learn the skill.
6. *Gathering supporters*—Let the child invite a number of people to become his supporters.
7. *Building confidence*—Help the child build confidence in her ability to learn the skill.
8. *Planning the celebration*—Plan with the child, ahead of time, how to celebrate when the skill has been acquired.
9. *Defining the skill*—Ask the child to tell you, and to act out for you, how she will behave when she has acquired the skill.
10. *Going public*—Inform people what skill the child is learning.
11. *Practicing the skill*—Agree with the child about how she will practice the skill.

12. *Creating reminders*—Let the child tell you how he wants others to react if he forgets the skill.
13. *Celebrating success*—When the child has acquired the skill, it is time to celebrate and to give her an opportunity to acknowledge all those who helped her learn it.
14. *Passing the skill on to others*—Encourage the child to teach the new skill to another child.
15. *Moving on to the next skill*—Find agreement with the child about the next skill to learn.

In addition to the fifteen steps, Furman designed a fun, interactive DVD, *Bam, the Wizard,* in which a child and an adult sit together and review the skill development. During the DVD, the child is asked a variety of questions, including these:

- How old are you?
- What are some things that you are good at?
- Would you like to change a bad habit?
- Tell how the bad habit hurts you.
- Tell who you would like to have as a support team.
- What would you like to name the new solution?
- How can you get started practicing?
- What would you like your support team to remind you about if you forget to practice?

The child and adult complete the DVD together, and after the child has learned the skill, Bam, the Wizard types out a certificate with the child's name on it that can be printed. The Wizard also writes a letter to the people whom the child chooses as a support team, so that they know their part in the program. The DVD is a great training tool for school counselors to teach themselves the process of choosing new skills for children and to implement as classroom guidance lessons. It is also a great tool for parent training and use at home. (For information on the DVD, go to www.reteaming.com.)

Working with Children Who Have Experienced Abuse

Many schools discourage school counselors from working with children who have been sexually abused since it may take a lot of time using traditional models of counseling. However, if a child is not receiving outside therapy, the school counselor can provide tremendous support. This section provides a unique way for school counselors to approach children who have experienced events such as abandonment, physical abuse, loss, or sexual abuse. It gives children an opportunity to express the feelings that bother them without infringing on their privacy. For the school, this approach is invaluable for supporting students who otherwise may not have any support at all.

The Sun and the Clouds

The following case illustrates a solution-focused approach for working with children who have faced sexual abuse. Although the session took place in my private practice, the strategies used can easily be adapted to the school setting. Annie, age ten, was brought to counseling by her father and stepmother who, only a week before, had found Annie and her brother, age fourteen, engaged in a sexual situation. The parents immediately called Child Protective Services, and the brother was removed from the home. Child Protective Services mandated counseling for Annie and placed her brother in a first offenders program fifty miles away, where he was to live with his uncle.

Annie was quiet and reserved when we first met. Her parents accompanied her, and I invited them into the session so that she would know that I was a safe person to talk to. Soon I learned from Annie that the "situation" had been going on for five years. Prior to her brother, Jim, doing inappropriate things to her, her older stepbrother, Nathan, had also done inappropriate things with her and with Jim. A true survivor, Annie talked about how much better she felt now that "the secret was out." Like many other sexual abuse survivors, she loved her offender and missed him. She did not, however, miss the activities.

The stepmother revealed that since finding out that the abuse had been going on, Annie seemed more relaxed and was even sleeping better. "She doesn't curl up anymore. Instead, she sleeps with her arms and legs spread out." This told me that Annie was feeling safe again. My job was to continue to enhance that safety, and I chose a visual activity during our second session that she enjoyed.

Janet Roth, a talented social worker in Brisbane, Australia, has written of ways in which she uses the scaling question (Metcalf, 1998). She cuts out ten teardrops and asks children to tell her how sad they are by counting out the number of teardrops that measure their sadness. Then together, they discuss what it would take to reduce the number of teardrops, which would indicate that the sadness was lessening. From this example, I asked Annie what it was like when the "secret" (her language) was happening. Using ideas from Epston and White (1990) about externalizing the problem and blaming "it" for robbing her of safety, I asked Annie what her days looked like when the secret was still happening. She said that it was like a cloudy day with no sun. So I cut out ten clouds and a sun and asked her to arrange them on the floor with me so that I could understand what it felt like when the secret dominated her days. She placed them as they appear in Figure 6.1A.

I remarked to Annie how small the sun was and how big the clouds were. Then I told her how brave she had been during those secret days and how glad I was that the secret days were over forever. I reinforced it by saying that she never had to go back to those secret days because now she was safe. I asked her to tell me the supportive people in her life who were making sure that she was safe. She listed her parents, her caseworker, her group counselor, me, and her best friend, Lisa.

I then told her to think about how things will be from now on, since the secret days were over. I asked her if the clouds and sun would look different since things are different at home. She then rearranged the clouds, and when we looked at the sun, it seemed too small. She said it should be bigger. We cut out a bigger sun, and the picture took on a dramatically different look, shown in Figure 6.1B.

Together Annie and I talked about what she would be able to do more of now that the clouds were not covering the sun. She talked about being able to go wherever she wanted in her house without worrying that her brother would make her do things that she did not want to do. She talked about being able to tell her parents the truth more often. Apparently keeping one rather large secret had taken its toll on her truth telling, which her parents brought up later in future sessions. She admitted that she would miss her brother, whom she enjoyed playing video games with, but she would not miss feeling like she was "living a lie."

Annie and I worked together for about six months, and each week we used the sun and clouds as a way to scale her week. If she had a tough week, there were more clouds, and we talked about better weeks where there were fewer clouds. She blossomed into a young preadolescent girl who

Figure 6.1 (A) Problem in Control.   (B) Solution in Control.

took pride in her appearance and made new friends at school. Her teachers noticed a remarkable difference in her personality. Her parents confided in her teachers that they had discovered some sexual abuse issues, and together, the school and parents provided Annie with safety and support. Annie terminated counseling with a positive self-esteem. I encouraged her parents to continue their support by letting her always know that they were there to keep her safe.

Changing the Story to Change the Person

Children and adolescents who experience traumatic, sad events such as sexual abuse often feel shameful about what has happened to them. Without help, they can begin living their story as a sexual abuse victim, and as they grow into adolescents, they may act out sexually toward others. Therefore, in the initial sessions, instead of talking details, which Yvonne Dolan (1991) said once in a workshop, is more abuse, I prefer to draw pictures and use scaling techniques like the sun and clouds, as the children describe how they felt during the time the "secret" was occurring. I have noticed that children feel more at ease with this technique, and together we accomplish helping them to see a future without uncomfortable feelings. They begin seeing the "secret" as something that they can indeed escape from in their mind, with the help of visuals. That escape is emotional freedom, which leads to a new story and a new chance at a happier life.

Tell Me a Story, But Make It a Better One

In the same way that Annie experienced a new vision of her life where the sun was brighter and the clouds smaller, rewriting stories with children like Annie provides an opportunity for a child to take on a new meaning for their personhood, which results in new behaviors.

Berg and Steiner (2003) discuss story construction in a therapy session as one that provides an opportunity for a child to work with a therapist in an effort to tell a story with strong metaphorical content. In this comfortable setting, the child becomes the author of a new story about a character similar to herself who has been in a tough situation but eventually triumphs over past events. Berg and Steiner offer the following steps to take with children in constructing a story (for a summary of this approach, see the My New Story worksheet):

1. Introduce the outline and background for the story. Describe the surroundings, the time of year, the weather, and the activities that are taking place such as celebrating Christmas, or a birthday, or the weather was perfect for a picnic, or hiking in the woods.
2. Introduce the protagonist by describing the character's strengths and what other people appreciate about him or her.
3. Introduce the antagonist in terms of how that person is creating havoc in the life of the hero. Describe the problems in as concrete a manner as possible so that the client can form a clear picture of the problems the hero is facing.
4. Have the protagonist be quite desperate, not knowing what to do.
5. Let the protagonist think of something that was helpful in the past, or let the helper appear, asking the protagonist whether she or he needs help.
6. Have the helper give the protagonist advice. The directions provided with the advice are not easy to fulfill and have to be followed exactly as given. No shortcuts or alterations are allowed.
7. Have the protagonist gain courage. On the way to achieving the goal, the protagonist believes he or she is smarter than the helper, thus altering the advice.
8. The protagonist fails and has to start over again, maybe under even poorer conditions than before, like climbing a mountain.
9. After two or three further failed attempts, the protagonist tries very hard to concentrate on what the helper warned him or her about. The protagonist can find a little trick not to get lost on the way, like counting, singing to overcome fear, keeping his hands in his or her pockets, and so on.
10. Finally the protagonist reaches the desired goal.
11. Have the protagonist realize a difference within him- or herself—feeling a great sense of calmness, having a clear way to think about his or her problems, being able to see or hear better, having more friends, and so on.
12. End the story with a special ritual where the strength and endurance of the protagonist are celebrated [pp. 83–84].

My New Story: A Scribble Sheet for Creating New Stories of Success

Begin by asking the child to help you set the stage: Describe the time of the year, weather, activities.

▬▬▬▬▬

Once upon a time, there was a child named _____. This story

happened during [season] _____.

_____

_____

_____.

[Student] _____ was very strong _____ and was

good at lots of things such as _____

_____.

But there were some people in her/his life that caused _____ to

be unhappy. Those people were _____, _____, and

_____. They had done things that made _____ feel

_____.

She/he did not know what to do most of the time, so instead of believing that she/
he was strong, he/she _____

_____

_____. One day, _____

remembered something that used to help her/him to feel better. It was _____

_____

_____

_____

My New Story: A Scribble Sheet for Creating New Stories of Success (cont.)

_____. Whenever

_____ did those things, _____ felt and

thought _____

_____.

Even though it was still hard to get over what other people had done, _____

_____ saw that when she/he did those good things, everything

was so much better that _____ was able

to _____

_____. People such

as _____, _____, and _____

_____ began to notice when _____ had good

days. They saw _____ do lots of things that told

them all how much [feeling] _____ was.

They were all so happy for _____ that they

celebrated with _____ by telling her/him _____

_____.

The end.

Berg and Steiner (2003) mention the case of twelve-year-old Miguel and his younger brother who were adopted from Chile when Miguel was seven and his brother Pedro was five. His adoptive mother was very concerned and upset that Miguel would never allow her to touch him—because Miguel just did not trust her or had difficulty emotionally bonding with her—even after many years of being cared for and loved by his adoptive parents. . . .

In the first meeting, I [Therese Steiner] learned that in Chile, Miguel had to watch his brother Pedro getting beaten up by his aunt and uncle to the point that he was hospitalized three times.

Miguel's answer to the miracle question was that he would become friendly with his mother, would play nicely with other children, and have friends of his very own [p. 87].

Steiner used the technique of storytelling to work with Miguel and related this story to them:

> There were two sisters. One was two years younger than the other. Both were very pretty, with fair hair and blue eyes. They were brought up in a very hostile family and nobody really cared about them.
>
> One day, the younger of the two girls became very ill. She was so sick that she had to be brought to the hospital several times. There she was looked after very well, she got lots of toys to play with, people smiled at her, and she had enough to eat. Meanwhile, the older sister stayed home all on her own without her younger sister, she was not allowed to go visit her sister at the hospital and nobody would tell her about her sister in the hospital. She had no idea how her younger sister was doing, whether she was safe at the hospital, or was getting enough to eat.
>
> She was very lonely without her younger sister, very miserable and worried about her. In a way, the older sister had a harder time and was more miserable than the sister in the hospital. Nobody took any notice of the older sister because, everyone assumed, she had to be glad that she was not sick and in the hospital; everyone thought she should be happy because at least she was healthy. Nobody even noticed that she did not get enough to eat, was not playing, and was very miserable. After all, a broken heart just didn't count to the grown ups. . . .

Miguel listened painfully to the story and when he returned to the next visit, he shared more of his painful life with the therapist. Eventually, the therapist asked Miguel to finish the story that she had told him. He said it would end like this:

"Somebody, some grown-up person, would spend an afternoon with me and take me fishing and listen to me; the grown-up person would talk and we would have something to eat" [Berg & Steiner, pp. 88–89].

As the therapist began drawing pictures with Miguel going fishing with someone grown-up, that grown-up turned out to be his adoptive mother.

Bragging Rights: Certificates and Letters That Reinforce Better Behavior

After the stories are told and monsters are fought, the use of a certificate brings smiles and a welcome documentation to success. For children who rarely get positive notes sent home from school, constructing such a document not only reinforces the child's changed behavior, it also stimulates the child's system to praise and brag. Epston and White (1990), developers of certificates for problem-defeating behaviors, have written: "We have found children taking fear-busting certificates to school and endeavoring to identify other children who either are in need of assistance or might already be members of the Fear Tamers and Monster Catchers Association" (Epston & White, p. 192).

Documents such as certificates celebrate the new stories that children create in therapy. I have routinely used certificates to reinforce problem resolution and solution development. I have found it the most helpful to design certificates with the children so that they describe to me their own success. As we design the certificate, we reiterate what helped the success to happen, and once these new actions are on paper, they become permanent. The certificate is given to the student to take home and, with the student's permission, the teacher gets a copy. The more certificates are distributed, the more the child's system can support her (see the example of the certificate of success shown here).

Certificate of Success

This certifies that:

Elli

Has done an extraordinary job at defeating shyness.

She has done so by learning new skills such as:

1. Asking her fellow students to play with her, one at a time.
2. Watching for signs that other students like her company.
3. Playing politely alongside other students.

Elli has done a great job.

School Counselor

_____

Elli Smith

_____

Contractual Agreements: A Step to a More Successful Day

In addition to developing certificates after success, I tend to develop solution-focused contracts to reach success. Chris, age ten, was sent to me by his teacher when she grew tired of his tendency not to complete homework. She knew that Chris was bright and that his mother worked two jobs, so she wanted to make sure she gained the mother's attention.

She wrote the mother a note:

Dear Ms. Browne,

Chris is in danger of failing the semester because he is not doing his assignments. Please make sure that he begins completing his homework on a regular basis. Call me if you have questions.

Ms. Jones

This is a typical note that teachers sometimes write. Yet when Chris read the note, he burst into tears and told his teacher that if he took that note home, he would be beaten. Unsure whether Chris was telling the truth, she sent him to me, the school counselor.

When situations like this one happen, I am always curious as to how else a problem can be handled. I began thinking about the purpose of the note: to get Chris to do homework. Since I was also concerned about possible beatings, I spoke with Chris about finding a different way to approach the dilemma, one that he would agree to. I was searching for a way to cooperate with both Ms. Jones and Chris, so I asked him: "I wonder what Ms. Jones would need to see you do this afternoon in order for her to decide not to send this note home today?" Chris immediately sat up and told me the following ideas:

- Complete all homework.
- Pay attention in the morning.
- Pay attention in the afternoon.
- Don't start any fights.
- Help my teacher.
- Listen to instructions.
- Participate in discussions.

I turned to Chris and told him he was brilliant because the tasks he described were exactly what a teacher would want a student to do. When I asked him what we should call the list, he said, "Call it Chris's Successful Day."

Chris and I walked back to the classroom where we showed Ms. Jones the form that we had constructed. (See the sample.) While at first reluctant, she eventually agreed to try the contract. That afternoon, Chris checked off all the tasks that applied on the contract, signed it, asked Ms. Jones to sign it, and walked with him to the front of the school. His mother, obviously tainted by previous "bad notes," frowned as he walked up to the car but quickly smiled as she read the contract. I was glad that we constructed the contract and decided to not send the note home. A day later I learned that Chris's mother had been reported for child abuse several times in the past.

Chris's Successful Day

❏ Complete all homework.

❏ Pay attention in the morning.

❏ Pay attention in the afternoon.

❏ Don't start any fights.

❏ Help my teacher.

❏ Listen to instructions.

❏ Participate in discussions.

_____

Chris Browne

_____

Ms. Jones

Summary

All schools have children who need support for many of the issues discussed in this chapter. Consider forming support groups on topics such as anger, fears, social skills, grief, loss, and even sexual abuse if your school district allows them. Use the scaling question formats as a means of helping children identify how big their problem is and how much they want to shrink its influence in their lives.

As in the movie *Star Wars*, sometimes it will be a challenge to "trust the Force." However, the merits of trying the solution-focused approach will pay you back with success. Think about your own philosophy of people. What is it that helped you to change during various times in your life? Whatever it was, realize that people have a variety of ways to make changes. Trust that your students do too.

Solution-Focused Training Exercise: Chapter Six

Our lives are stories. The characters and events that are part of our lives influence who we are and who we aspire to be.

Perhaps in your life, you have some characters and even events that enhance your life and others that keep you from being the person you want to be . . . for now. But what if you had the chance to write Chapter Two of your own story? Who would you include or exclude, and how would those changes make a difference for you? What else would you include in Chapter Two? Maybe travel, reading more, becoming a dancer, learning karate, gardening more, being with your children or partner more often?

On the lines below, write down some ideas for your Chapter Two. And along with the new adventures that you include in your Chapter Two, list the beliefs about yourself that are necessary to begin carrying out the new chapter.

After all of that, think of times when you had those beliefs. Focus on how you held on to them. Think of how you can reclaim them today.

_____

_____

_____

_____

_____

_____

_____

_____

_____

_____

_____

Chapter Seven

Relationships, Reputations, and Scheduling

Creating Success with Secondary Students

The young always have the same problem—how to rebel and conform at the same time. They have now solved this by defying their parents and copying one another.

—Quentin Crisp

Trigg Even is a licensed professional counselor and interventionist at Summit High School in Mansfield, Texas. Before working at the high school, he was a director at a treatment center for adolescents. As a counselor who always looked for resiliency in adolescents, the solution-focused approach seemed to fit with his ideals and ethics as he began working at a challenging high school that presented issues of cutting, substance abuse, violence, and disrespect. I worked with Trigg for a short time and was always impressed with his casual approach to students, which easily won their trust. In an effort to explain the value of the practical applications that a solution-focused school counselor can take with such students, I asked him to summarize how the solution-focused approach affected his everyday approach to teens and made a difference for everyone, including him. He wrote:

Historically, the practice of counseling has engaged itself in a process of identifying, dissecting, and defeating larger and more looming problems of life and relationships. We, along with our students, too often expect the course of counseling to commence in a like manner. But in doing so, what often happens is that both student and counselor risk feeling defeated all over again without ever truly gaining ground on growth. What a relief, then, to find unexplored promise and possibility—not by necessarily attempting to fix anything—but by learning to "cooperate with the problem."

This concept has drastically changed the way that I practice counseling. By relieving myself of the pressure to fix everyone and their problems and by focusing instead on ways to cooperate, and allowing the student to partici-  pate more fully in the solution-finding, I have discovered a fresh excitement and creative energy that truly results in a more efficient, effective, and enduring counseling intervention. What has happened is that I have changed the way that I think about complaints and how I talk about them with parents, students, and teachers.

For example, when a student, teacher, or parent uses problem language to describe behavior that is problematic for them or others, I acknowledge the inherent potential or advantage of the problem and then ask a simple "what if" question to suggest cooperation. For instance, an adolescent who states that she repeatedly gets in trouble for "telling my teacher off" and "refusing to do my work" might be described as oppositional, obstinate, and unmotivated. However, when asked what her behavior demonstrates about her strengths, she describes herself as assertive, willing to defend her values, and protective of herself. Then, with this description in mind, I might ask her: "What if you were able to be both assertive and protective in a way that helped you get what you want without interrupting your learning? How would you accomplish this?" Then, to include her "system," I might arrange a brief meeting with her teacher and ask: "What if your student was allowed to demonstrate the positive side of herself (assertive, protective, etc.) during your class? What would you be able to do so this could happen in a way that worked for both of you? What would you need from her to assure you that it was worth your effort?"

These questions were utilized with a fifteen-year-old student who developed a pattern of intense emotional reactions to various crises and was referred to counseling. Several times per day, the student would leave class upset and present to the high school counseling center requesting assistance. The problem, according to the teachers, was that this student was failing to complete class work and was simply seeking attention. Furthermore, if the student remained in class, she had a tendency to dominate the class discussion with lengthy and emotional narratives of her various personal and family problems.

When I interviewed the student, she identified the problem as one where she was having serious personal and family concerns to which no one would pay attention to and offer support. She expressed feeling isolated, invalidated, and frustrated. It was clearly important to the student that she be heard; and it was equally important to her teachers that she remain in class able to learn. Cooperation with the problem resulted in the student being offered a "free pass" to the counseling center which was available to use once her work was completed. Upon entering the counseling center, she would be provided a notebook in which she was instructed to write about her crisis. She was asked to hand this to the counselor and return to class. The counselor would read it and, if necessary, follow-up. The following question, which was asked of both student and teachers, served both functions of meeting each party's need and increasing the student's ability to be proactive in handling her crises. "What if you/she were able to express your/her feelings by telling your/her story and maintaining your/her schoolwork?"

By approaching situations in this manner, the responsibility for change was placed in the hands of both student and teacher. By redescribing the student's behavior and alluding to the benefits that the teacher might reap from her own efforts, there was a better chance that both parties would cooperate, and they did.

By thinking differently, the solution-focused school counselor has a better means to discuss the issues of the adolescent and the teacher. By focusing on only the problem, the discussions would simply be a repeat of the complaint and offer no real solutions except that of blaming each other and forcing the adolescent to comply, which rarely works. In the high school setting, thinking instead of how to help adolescents redescribe themselves by rebuilding their reputation is like a breath of fresh air, particularly when the stale air has circulated too long.

Where's Julio?

Linda Fielding is an intervention specialist in Fort Worth, Texas, and as I was writing this book, she relayed to me a story that not only had her excited but had a teacher wondering out loud, "What on earth have you done with Julio, and where has the old Julio gone?" Her story follows.

One of the programs that my school district has put into place is a student service team. This team is designed to counsel with students who are at risk for failing for any number of reasons. One of my assignments was to work with Julio, a middle school student.

Julio had received about twenty-five infractions since the beginning of school and, characteristically, students who have such a history are often a challenge. A school counselor or Intervention Specialist is accustomed to teachers' or principals' saying, "You need to see Julio again; he's still late to my class." Imagine my surprise, then, when one of Julio's teachers stopped me in the hallway one day and asked what I had been telling Julio. The teacher said Julio's behavior had changed dramatically. In fact, he said Julio was now "perfect" in class.

Just before I received Julio as an assignment, I had been reading a book about narrative counseling. Excited about a fresh approach to counseling with students, I decided to make Julio my first attempt. After researching the reasons he was referred to the student service team, I called Julio into my office, where we spent some time getting to know each other. I asked Julio what was causing him problems at school, at home, and with his friends. He said that he had no problems with his friends, but that the problems at home usually happened when he got in trouble at school for things like talking, being late to class, and not doing his work.

I explained to Julio that we all have problems and that what we have to do is learn how to fix the problems. I asked him how he thought these problems affected his reputation with his teachers. He said his teachers saw him as a troublemaker. I asked him if he would like to change the "troublemaker reputation." He said that he would.

I then asked Julio if he felt that he was successful in any of his classes. He said he was successful in English. We discussed specific things that he did in his English class that brought him success. He replied that he sat at the front of the class, which helped him to pay better attention. He said he didn't sit around any of his friends, and that helped him to concentrate and to get his work done. I asked how he could take these successes and apply them to the classes in which he had problems. He said he could ask to be moved to the front of the class or away from his friends. I asked him what he could do to fix the tardies. He replied he would "just get to class on time." I told him these were big changes and a great beginning to fixing his "troublemaker" reputation. I asked him if he thought he could really "fix" these problems. He said that he could.

I was so proud of Julio for beginning to address the problems he was having at school that I asked for his approval to write his parents the following note:

To the parents of Julio:

I am so proud of Julio! He wants to fix the problems that are causing him trouble at school. Julio is a very determined young man and has set several goals for himself. He has decided to get to class on time, pay attention in class, and do his work. Julio wants to be a positive role model in the classroom, and these changes will help him to do just that! I am convinced that Julio is committed to achieving his goals.

Two weeks later, I had another conversation with Julio's teacher about his improvement in his performance. I explained to him that I was using a new technique with Julio and asked if he would reinforce the change in behavior by complimenting Julio on the changes that he had noticed. The teacher seemed delighted to do so. After the conversation with Julio's teacher, I wrote the following note to Julio and his parents:

To Julio and his parents:

Today, I had a conversation with [his teacher]. He was excited about the positive changes Julio has made in class. [His teacher] said Julio was now one of his best students and is a role model for others. He said Julio was turning in his work and paying attention in class.

It's important that you know that I did not seek out the teacher and ask about Julio. The teacher found me in the hallway and began bragging about Julio. It's wonderful to know that Julio has earned [his teacher's] respect. I am so proud of Julio and his smart decisions. I know that you are too.

Linda Fielding, Crisis Intervention Specialist

That day, Julio and I both left school with big smiles on our faces!

Under Construction

Adolescents focus on their self-image more than anything else. That's why they try so hard to look different from yet similar to their peers. Therefore, talking about a student's reputation and the effects of that reputation on the student's life makes a vital connection between school counselor and the adolescent. In this way, the reputation becomes external to the adolescent, allowing both parties to sit back and discuss the reputation and the problem that the reputation causes the student. Then new strategies develop that can catapult the adolescent into new reputation building, pleasing and satisfying all who wander in and out of his social, family, and school system.

Rebuilding Reputations Can Change the World of a Student

When the solution-focused school counselor works with adolescents who are having difficulties with their teachers, administrators, or other authority figures, it is exciting to begin asking them about their reputation. The reputation of any adolescent is particularly important, since the adolescent years are all about identity. Consider the following dialogue:

COUNSELOR: Tell me what your reputation is in Mr. Howard's class.

STUDENT: He would probably say that I am disrespectful to him even though it is he who is much more disrespectful to me. He told me last week that I had a real attitude and that it would probably get the best of me.

This description and defensiveness usually lead an adolescent to show that defensiveness in the classroom, defying the authority more because of the damage done to his self-esteem. Yes, the student was responsible for his attitude in the classroom, but a solution-focused school counselor sees that perhaps another influence encouraged that attitude to be maintained, such as the teacher's remarks. An adolescent's nature is to see himself as invincible, so when an adult tries to destroy his attitude through words, the defense mechanism goes full throttle. By listening to the adolescent and giving him a chance to find solutions to the situation for his own sake, the counselor might continue:

COUNSELOR: That must be terrible for you. How do you wish he would talk to you in class that would be less hurtful?

STUDENT: Something nice for a change. In fact, if he would be nice to me first, I might be nice back. That will never happen though. You don't know him. He just doesn't like me. I can tell.

Here the adolescent reveals what he wishes would happen. While he is still focusing on what the adult is doing, he begins to give the school counselor an idea of what the student might do in response to the teacher's doing something different:

COUNSELOR: You seem as if you are nice already! Too bad Mr. Howard doesn't see that trait of yours yet. I wonder what you think you might do as an experiment, just for tomorrow, that might really shock him and change his belief about you so that he could see this "nice" trait that I see?

This challenge is something that both adolescents and children enjoy. It becomes a game to play that they feel they might win, along with a little coaching from the counselor. And, of course, they love the shock factor that sometimes happens: "Shock my teacher? Yes, I would like to do that."

STUDENT: I would probably have to walk in, sit down, and do my work. He probably wouldn't notice though.

This becomes a crucial point for the solution-focused school counselor to pay attention to. As the adolescent describes what he can do, it is important that the counselor commend him on the idea and then relay the plan, along with the student's help and permission, to Mr. Howard, opening up the possibilities for success. This can be done through an e-mail message or a handwritten letter and should note only what the student is trying to do. Whether or not Mr. Howard is interested in learning that his challenging student is trying new strategies in class is not as important as it is for the student to know that Mr. Howard knows about the plan. This will help the teacher watch the student's behavior. Mr. Howard will have a tough time ignoring the fact that the student makes the changes, and as he notices, he may respond differently to the student. But even if the teacher does not, most students continue with their plan.

COUNSELOR: That is a terrific idea. With your permission, would you help me write an e-mail to Mr. Howard, describing to him that you are working on changing his image of you? I want him to notice the kind of student that I see in my office. You seem bright, interested in being perceived correctly, and you also like to stand up for what you believe. I believe you are all these things and my hope is that Mr. Howard can begin to see it too.

Dear Mr. Howard,

Thank you for referring Ken to me. He and I are working on some issues that you were concerned about, and he has given me permission to write to you. He wanted to let you know that he has some ideas about changing his behavior. Please watch over the next few days for changes that Ken makes in your class. When you notice, I am sure Ken would appreciate your saying so.

Sincerely,
Linda Metcalf and Ken Smith

Even if Mr. Howard never mentions the changes that Ken makes, the fact is that Ken knows his school counselor believes in him. As educators, we know that teachers are stressed and often do not have time to take to reinforce students as we wished they would. That is part of life. The solution-focused counselor may mention to Ken in the future that even though Mr. Howard did not respond immediately, that his reluctance to do so is normal for some people. Then the counselor can talk to Ken about how there may be other people in his life who won't respond to his changes when he wishes they would. By processing this, the counselor can ask Ken what he could think about to keep on making changes in spite of that tendency. This teaches coping skills to students and helps them to begin relying on themselves. In addition, the counselor might mention that although certain people won't respond immediately, others will. By identifying those people, the school client can realize that there may be others who do notice, and his school counselor is one.

Where's the Hammer, Miss?

As a school counselor, I have learned that it is often the toughest students who buy into the idea of rebuilding their reputation. It is as if they know they had apparently dug themselves into such a deep hole with their misbehavior, lack of motivation, and other antics that no one ever thought that they could climb out. Merely suggesting to them that they could climb out and rebuild their reputation and their life must have seemed as if I was lifting them out and up myself. The following questions on the Reputation-Rebuilding Exercise are strategies that conjure up a different type of conversation in relation to reputation rebuilding. The questions can be used with one student, a group of students, teacher and student, or student and family members.

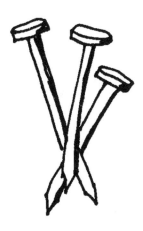

Reputation-Rebuilding Exercise

Step 1: Describe the current reputation.

"Tell me how you and others in your life would describe you now, with this current reputation."

_____

_____

_____

"If you would, tell me about the actions you engaged in to earn your current reputation."

_____

_____

_____

"Tell me what you must have been believing or thinking about yourself to engage in those actions."

_____

_____

_____

"Would you say that thinking or believing like that has worked for you?"

_____

_____

_____

Step 2: Describe how the reputation has interrupted the student's life.

"Tell me how the current reputation has interfered with your life at school, at home, or with friends."

School: _____

_____

Reputation-Rebuilding Exercise (cont.)

Home: _____

_____

Friends: _____

_____

"How unfair is it that your reputation has cast a shadow over who you really are?"

_____

_____

_____

Step 3: Inquire who will notice when the student's reputation changes.

"Tell me who will definitely notice when your reputation changes."

_____

_____

_____

"What will these people be seeing you do that will convince them that your reputation has changed?"

_____

_____

_____

"How will the new reputation help you?"

_____

_____

_____

Reputation-Rebuilding Exercise (cont.)

Step 4: Steps to take to begin changing the reputation.

"Tell me what you can begin doing today to change your reputation gradually so that others will notice."

_____

_____

_____

"What will you need to be thinking of to help this happen?"

_____

_____

_____

"Who in your life can you ask for support as you make these changes?"

_____

_____

_____

"On a scale of 1 to 10, with a 1 standing for your current reputation and a 10 standing for the reputation that will allow others to see you at your best, where are you today?"

_____

"Where would you like to be by the time I see you again?"

_____

Gather Support: Write the Letters

After this conversation, mention to the adolescent how impressed you are with the changes that he or she described. Copy the Reputation-Rebuilding Exercise form that you filled out with the student, and give the student a copy. Then take time to write to his or her parents, with the student's permission, describing how impressed you are that their child is interested in changing things for the better. Let the student read the letter.

Also with student permission, take one more step and e-mail or send notes to each teacher, again describing how the student desires to make some changes in his or her school behavior. Ask the teachers to watch for changes and mention when they notice those changes to the student.

Reputation Rescue

"By noticing something new nobody before had paid attention to, and commenting on it in the form of questions, one is more likely to draw the adolescent's attention to strengths and resources. Discovering the smallest possible successes that are the opposite of violent or aggressive behaviors, and pointing out and highlighting these small successes, is like putting the spotlight on what we want the adolescent to do more of" (Berg & Steiner, 2003, p. 210). When adolescents decide to make big changes like the ones that modify their reputations, they need monitoring to keep them on track. There will be pitfalls: teachers who don't follow through with your request to notice what works and parents who just may not believe their child can change until they see it. Talk about these possibilities, and blame them on the reputation that influenced the student negatively. Normalize the reactions that some people may take. Then focus on what you see the student doing, such as coming back to see you, even if changing the reputation is harder than he or she thought. Then begin  sessions like this: "I am so glad to see you again. Tell me what you have begun doing to change your reputation." Then: "Who do you think is beginning to notice?" If the student says "no one," continue:

> You know it's sometimes hard for people to recognize people like you who are trying to make changes. It's easy to see negative behaviors, but the positive ones take more time. What do you suppose you might try to do more of so that they begin seeing the new behaviors?

When the solution-focused school counselor continues to normalize the pitfalls associated with changing the reputation, the student will feel more in control and continue this journey. It will also help to e-mail the teachers again, particularly if you have not heard from them in a while (which is actually a good sign) to ask them to keep on noticing what the student has been doing better. Everyone needs to be prodded occasionally when there is so much to do, and your reminder may be quite welcome.

Scheduling Classes Using a Solution-Focused Approach

As a middle school or high school counselor, you can't escape from the daily requests and complaints that happen in relation to a student's schedule. Each school has its own scheduling software, and each state has its own credit requirements for graduation. From that description, you might think that scheduling would be a snap. It isn't. During my term as a scheduling high school counselor, I learned about the following road-blocks that often got in my way on a daily basis and kept my nose to the computer screen, fishing for the answers to these dilemmas:

- Parents who wanted their adolescent to be in Advanced Placement classes when he or she didn't qualify.
- Parents who wanted their adolescent to be in another teacher's class because they had heard she taught geometry in a way that students could understand.
- Students who hated their teacher and wanted a schedule change.
- Students who went out for sports and, ten weeks into the semester, needed a schedule change to accommodate the sports class and practice time.
- Seniors who, six weeks into the course, discovered that they had sufficient credits to graduate and wanted their well-deserved senior release time, a reward for high school seniors with enough credits. However, they didn't realize that they couldn't drop the course after three weeks.
- Transfer students or homeschooled students whose courses didn't meet state requirements and whose parents had been told that those courses would count.
- Students who did not pass the state aptitude test and were required to take a review course. That meant a schedule change.
- Students who were accepted at the college of their choice by early decision and therefore thought they didn't have to take the last math course in the spring semester.
- And even the lead counselor, who designed the schedules and wanted the numbers to be balanced, had to be consulted constantly for special permission to change a class. Of course, I always forgot and changed it anyway.

And the list went on. My colleagues told me when I began working at the high school to beware of MSRS: the Mortal Sin of Rescheduling Students. I have to admit that being the parent of three adolescents, I often sinned by changing schedules for students who gave me what I considered to be important reasons for needing the changes. Luckily, those students were more successful after the change, giving me reasons to continue to sin, and I did. I was more interested in matching up students to contexts where they could be successful and working out details with their teachers instead of telling them what the rules were. To this day, I still feel proud of changing the schedules as I did, and despite some threats from my colleagues that I would have more students "lining up outside the door for changes," that didn't happen. I did have a lot of students lined up outside my door, but usually to tell me thank you. That was enough for me.

Each school has its own protocol for scheduling classes. In some schools, students just fill out their course selections, add a few electives, and the school counselor punches the course numbers into the computer. However, what if there was more collaboration, particularly for students who are not as successful as they could be? The solution-focused school counselor listens to students for exceptions that help to guarantee a successful school experience by asking questions like the following:

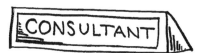

"When you look at the list of required courses for your freshman year, which ones do you suggest taking this first semester? Second semester?"

"When you think about participating in the marching band this fall and the rigorous schedule of practicing after school, what courses do you think you could handle?"

"When you look over the courses that most colleges expect applicants to have, which ones do you think would work best for you during your junior year?"

"What kind of teaching style fits the way that you learn best?"

"What have you found works for you in regard to study habits?"

"What do you need your teacher to know about you?" For a needy student, send an e-mail to the teacher with this information.

"When you think about college, what majors or careers interest you the most?"

"When you think about working during high school, what kinds of jobs interest you?"

These questions give you a chance to get to know your students better and give them a chance to identify their strengths, dreams, and needs. Suddenly the courses that they take are those that they choose because they know what path they want to take. There is less complaining because they chose the classes, and when they are scheduled with the right teacher, you will have more time to counsel on personal issues.

The College Application

When students in high school begin thinking about college applications, they are often at a loss unless an older sibling has already been through the process. I once had a senior student come into my office, sullen, with her SAT scores in hand. She said, "I don't think I can go to college. I heard that your SAT should be 2000 and all I got on mine was a combined score of 1345, so I didn't even complete the common application." In shock, I assured her that she was definitely on her way to college, and together we called her mother who cried on the phone as her daughter told her the news and then got online to apply before the deadline.

Misinformation is rampant in high schools, so it is important that both high school and middle school counselors consider how to get the right information to each student on everything, from taking algebra in middle school, to the usefulness of the PSAT and the importance of AP classes.

While this dispensing of information is very difficult in high schools where the senior class tops out at over a thousand students, giving each student information firsthand is a must. To accomplish this, consider in your high school how other information filters through to your students about various kinds of try-outs, meetings, sports events, musicals, tournaments, and other events. Use whatever means there is to gain access to students so that, together, you can help them choose what they need to be successful.

When it comes to helping students decide on which college to apply to or what type of college to consider, the following solution-focused questions may provoke ideas for students to consider (Metcalf, 2007):

- What has worked for you in the past when you had to plan on a future project?
- How have you organized yourself in other projects so that you could get the job done?
- How have you approached your parents on other decisions?
- How do you make your own decisions? Which ones have you made before that worked out well for you?
- When you think about your personality and traits, which seems to fit: a junior college near home or a four-year college away from home?
- When you think of your personality, what size of the college town or city would suit you best?
- For those who are taking the ACT or SAT: When you think how you have studied for class tests before, what did you do that worked?
- If you woke up tomorrow and it is five years in the future, what would you be doing after college graduation that would make you feel good about your accomplishment?

And for the parents who are trying to plan for their adolescent's college future and just can't seem to get them to apply on time or apply at all, the following questions may save the day:

"Tell me what you have been doing for your daughter to help get her motivated to apply to each college that she is interested in. Which strategies worked?" If the answer is few or none, continue.

"When you think about how you have been able to motivate your daughter about other situations before, what did you do then that worked even slightly? What would your daughter say worked?"

"What would your son say would be the most helpful to him right now as he thinks about which college to apply to? What will you need to tell yourself so that you can begin doing some of that, just as an experiment, to see if it helps him to get started?"

Consider meeting with both parents and student as a mediator to learn what stands in the way of moving forward. Perhaps the parents are pushing for a student to attend their alma mater, and the student wants to go to a different school. Maybe the student isn't ready to launch and would be better off at a local college. Or maybe the student is worried about his single-parent mother, who will be alone if he leaves. Helping to bring out the concerns that keep future plans from happening will give everyone a chance to brainstorm and talk about what could be helpful.

It is a relief for some students to know that their parents will be all right without them. There can be many thoughts and beliefs that keep adolescents stuck when it comes to this big decision. By helping them to identify how they have made decisions before, the path opens up as everyone learns their part in the journey.

Becoming a School Counselor Extraordinaire

If the ideas so far in this book seem too good to be true, you are correct. They take time and patience, particularly with secondary staff members. Secondary school and elementary school staff are like oranges and apples, and rightfully so, because they each have roles that are essential to launching healthy, motivated students.

Begin practicing the approach in your secondary school by trying out the following idea as a way to begin helping the adolescents you see each day with a solution-focused approach.

For the next week, choose two or three students who have come to your office more than enough times. These are the students who sleep in class, rarely turn in their work, and tell you they don't care. Make yourself a promise to find a way to cooperate with these students, and don't give up. Everyone else has, and they need you to believe that there are possibilities for them. You can even say, "I am trying to find a way to cooperate with what you need, and I am stuck. Help me to learn what you need from this school. I am willing to wait. You are that important to me." You will be amazed at their reactions.

Let's say that the student tells you that he really wants to:

1. Quit school.
2. Have different teachers.
3. Get other peers at school off his back.
4. Make the team.

Be respectful, smile, and agree that his ideas sound great and very important to him. Ask him what achieving those ideas would do for him; then sit back and listen some more. It will take time, but the conversation will take you to a different, more possible goal such as the following answers, which I have received (and are matched with the preceding problem-saturated statements):

1. I wouldn't have to do work that I don't know how to do.
2. I would feel like school was an okay place to be.
3. I wouldn't feel like I had to be ready to fight every day.
4. I would feel a part of things.

Then ask: "What would you be doing when a little of this happened?"

1. I guess I would know how to do the work, and I would be passing my classes.
2. I would relax and probably be nicer to people.

3. I would probably stay out of trouble and hang out more.

4. I might join something and feel better about myself.

From here, you can begin talking about how to achieve just a small part of the goal. By going from a global, seemingly impossible goal to an achievable, specific one, you learn what will make the student tick and from there, deduce how you and school staff can help that to happen.

Summary

At the end of the week, think about what's gone better for you as you took a new approach to the problem. Did it give you hope? Did it make a difference for one student? Realize that one student who makes a slight change affects a classroom, maybe six or seven classrooms, and that many teachers as well. As Linda Fielding wrote in her story about Julio, his actions made his teacher excited, which probably carried over to the other students in her class who often did not get as much attention because of Julio's acting out. That's the systems theory at its finest.

Solution-Focused Training Exercise: Chapter Seven

Our reputations become the guiding force for how others treat us. Some of us are cautious and don't take risks. That may lead us to have a reputation that we are inflexible. Some of us are too understanding and sometimes get taken for granted. Still others of us are so busy we are unapproachable.

How do you want your reputation to be with your school staff? Write down your answer.

_____

_____

_____

_____

_____

What will you need to begin doing to create that reputation on a small scale?

_____

_____

_____

_____

_____

Begin the week by noticing how others receive you. Then begin implementing some of your own suggestions on a small scale.

Chapter Eight

Working with Families to Change the Lives of Students

If you cannot get rid of the family skeleton,
you may as well make it dance.

—George Bernard Shaw

If you were to stroll through the hallways of your school today, the chances are that you would see many children or adolescents who have come to school with the weight of family problems in their backpacks. Many of the "symptoms" that students bring with them are often family related. However, when teachers, staff, and even school counselors are unaware of home issues, they often attribute such symptoms as personal ones, meaning that they see students as unmotivated, lazy, compulsive, belligerent, or defiant. What if there was another explanation? What if that explanation revealed that the problems at home were directly influencing the student? And what if there was a way for the school counselor to address those issues?

Research has suggested that students react to changes and stress within their families and often act out or become emotional as a result. In fact, according to systems theory, those acting-out behaviors often serve a purpose: to draw attention to the parental unit because something is wrong with the family. This attention-seeking behavior also serves the purpose of distracting parents from their issues.

When I was working in a residential treatment center, I recall a ten-year-old boy who was placed there for having severe temper tantrums after his parents decided to divorce. He had been diagnosed as being oppositional and defiant. Later, when I was working with him, I asked him how the temper tantrums knew when to come along and bother him. He replied: "When my parents fight, I have a tantrum. Then they stop. It works."

163

Imagine, then, the well-intentioned school counselor who is working diligently to help that student give up the temper tantrums when the family system is working to defeat her efforts at home. By checking in with a family and inviting them to family counseling at school at least once (as suggested to the family), the school counselor may make more of an impact than she realizes:

- A more productive distraction occurs, one that points out to the parents that family problems are affecting their student. Perhaps keeping adult issues private would be helpful to the child.

- The parents may learn from their child or adolescent what is needed from them to keep their child on track at school. Maybe the excessive responsibilities given at home are causing their child to be depressed and anxious.

- The parents may refocus on what their child or adolescent's emotional needs are from them and may learn that those needs are minimal, such as ten minutes of reading or time on Saturday to take a walk and just talk about a variety of things. They may also learn that yelling and name-calling hurt their children, causing them emotional pain that keeps them from focusing at school.

The bonus to this sort of intervention is that once families are involved, student success can skyrocket, which leaves the school counselor to attend to other issues. The family learns how each member can assist the student, systemically changing the interactions around school work. When I was working as a school counselor, I routinely invited families to campus to meet with me and their student. I rarely had to meet with them more than twice. This is because when the school counselor involves the family system, perceptions change, particularly using the solution-focused approach. A student who had formerly been perceived by his parents as a poor student might learn that he merely needed assistance at home with homework. His teacher says that when he is assisted slightly in class, he turns in his work correctly. These insightful sessions serve everyone well and allow the school counselor to be an important instrument of systemic change.

How Helping Families Helps Students

Working with a family in the school setting brings many rewards to solution-focused school counselors:

- Family sessions will help the school counselor understand what it is like to live with the family and determine how the child or adolescent is supported, or not supported, at home. The setting also provides safe opportunities for the child or adolescent to talk about his concerns and needs. If, after interviewing the family, the school counselor learns that the family is not capable or responsive to what the child or adolescent needs, he or she will brainstorm with school staff who can begin meeting some of the needs.

- By observing family discussions, the school counselor has the opportunity to ask everyone involved if the strategies being used to address the issues are working to achieve the desired goal. If they reply no, the counselor then has a chance to gain their attention by suggesting that everyone talk about doing something in a different way.

- It is the systemic change that occurs when people in a family system change their behaviors that has the best chance of helping an adolescent change his or her behavior permanently.

- Family involvement will give the school counselor a chance to plant new, encouraging ideas about the adolescent within the family and give them a new way to perceive and then interact with the adolescent at home. When new perceptions are provided, new reactions are inevitable. New reactions have a domino effect on others, which continues the process of change.

- The school counselor will become an instrument of change, entering the system and providing a new structure, influence, and direction for the family to address their concerns, one where they see themselves and the adolescent as more competent than they previously did.

- The school counselor will help the family see that they are not helpless because the conversation will enable them to identify exceptions to times when the problem occurs.

- The school counselor will assist the family in seeking to help their adolescent rebuild a reputation that begins at home and follows her to school, where she has support. When both school and home work together, things get better.

Just Fix Her While I Go to the Mall

Many times in private practice, I would go into the reception area where an adolescent and parent were waiting. After greeting them, the parent would often tell me that she or he had errands to run and would be back to pick up the adolescent in an hour. Ethically, I couldn't see the adolescent under age eighteen without the parent. As a family therapist, theoretically, I needed to visit with both parent and child. That often led me to inform parents that while I understood they had errands to run, I needed to speak with them. Thankfully, after one session, the parent saw the helpfulness of meeting with the adolescent and me and often returned to therapy with the adolescent for the duration of our sessions.

Although it would be any school counselor's dream for every parent to willingly come to family counseling and do whatever it took to help the child, the reality is that such dreams don't always come true. Many times, when parents contact school counselors to get their children or adolescents fixed, they don't know to look at their own actions that bear on the child's or adolescent's behavior. The example of a family therapy session in the next section, written by Elliott Connie, a family therapy graduate student at Texas Woman's University, shows how change can occur throughout a family when parents change their approach to each other, even if unwillingly at first.

A Case Study: How Change Can Occur Throughout a Family, by Elliott Connie

Douglas was thirteen years old and attending the eighth grade at the time I was working with him and his family. He had been dealing with attention deficit hyperactivity disorder and conduct disorders for most of his life and as a result had been placed in several out-of-home placements during the past few years. In fact, Douglas's behaviors had become so severe that he was sent to live with his grandmother so he would not do physical harm to his siblings, mother, and stepfather.

While he was in therapy, incidents of aggressive behavior were drastically reduced so the family decided to bring him home. Throughout therapy the mother and stepfather had been attending sessions that were held at the grandmother's home, and Douglas had not been to their home in several years. The mother and stepfather decided to allow Douglas to stay at their home for one night during the upcoming weekend. A therapy session was scheduled the next day.

Before the home session, the therapist received a phone call from Douglas's mother who informed the therapist that there were severe problems on the previous night involving Douglas, herself, and the stepfather. The mother was very emotional as she explained that Douglas had become upset and aggressive after she had a verbal altercation with the stepfather. The mother explained she was afraid because she did not know if her marriage could survive the fight. The therapist met with the family, and knowing that Douglas and his two younger siblings were home, the therapist brought pizza to keep the children busy while the parents and therapist met. As the therapist approached the front door, the yelling could be heard. The following excerpt is from the session.

THERAPIST: What would be helpful to talk about today?

MOTHER: I would like to talk about our marriage. If Douglas is going to come stay here, we have be sure we are not fighting in front him.

STEPFATHER: I agree; I just don't know how I can get that into her head.

THERAPIST: Get what into her head?

STEPFATHER: The fact that I love her and would never leave her and my family for anyone or any reason. All of the arguments we have are because she is accusing me of wanting to leave.

MOTHER: That is because you ignore me. I don't feel like you even want to be here. You don't make me feel special anymore, and I am scared that you want to leave.

STEPFATHER: I am not going anywhere, I LOVE YOU and I would never leave you. (This statement was made while the stepfather was yelling, crying, and punching a wall. The stepfather then stood up from the couch where he was previously sitting.)

THERAPIST: Do you feel ignored right now?

MOTHER: Yes.

THERAPIST: Tell me about times when you do not feel as ignored by [your husband].

MOTHER: That is easy: when he is touching me. I feel like the only person in the world when he is touching me.

The stepfather then sat back down on the couch next to the mother and placed his hands on her cheeks and began crying.

STEPFATHER: I love you; you are everything to me.

MOTHER: (crying) I love you too and I never want to lose you. I just want you to be happy.

THERAPIST: I am curious. Are you feeling ignored by [your husband] right now?

MOTHER: No, I love this.

STEPFATHER: I do not feel nagged either.

MOTHER: This is so cheesy, but it worked. I feel completely different than I did at the beginning of this session.

THERAPIST: How can we use this to help you guys each feel not ignored and not nagged by the other in the future? It appears to be very effective from what I have just seen.

MOTHER: Since this is so cheesy I will ask him for "cheese" when I am upset and feeling ignored.

STEPFATHER: I will sure give it to her because I don't want to be nagged. (laughter)

I saw the family once a week for another month, helping them to adjust to Douglas having longer, more frequent visits in their home. The couple reported that they continued to use the "cheese" intervention they developed and have noticed a drastic reduction in arguments. As a result Douglas began to show the same improvement while in their care that he was showing at his grandmother's home. During the last session, the couple informed the therapist they are making plans to buy a home large enough to house Douglas and the grandmother, something they believe would have been impossible months before due to the high levels of family conflict. Douglas also showed dramatic improvements in school as well.

Circles, Triangles, and Squares

Systems theory teaches that the many circular, interlocking, and sometimes time-delayed relationships among its components are often just as important to understand as are the individual components. As Elliot Connie found in the previous case, by helping the parents to reconcile their differences and find another method of expressing their needs, Douglas began to act more appropriately. In most families, when the parental system is in sync and operating well, children and adolescents feel safe and rarely act out. However, when the parental dyad is out of sync, an unrest permeates the system. In order to call attention to that unrest, adoelscents act out and children have tantrums or do poorly in school.

At a seminar once, a school counselor asked me what she should do with a sixteen-year-old girl who was extremely disrespectful to her mother. The girl said that all she wanted to do was run away from home so that she could do drugs. The school counselor had tried suggesting ideas to the girl about finishing high school and looking toward college, but the girl refused to listen. As I talked more with the school counselor, she eventually mentioned that she had recently met the girl's mother, whom she described as tyrannical, rude, and critical of her office staff. It began to make sense as to why the girl was unreasonable and disrespectful to everyone else. The school counselor told me after the seminar that she now planned to visit with both mother and daughter the next week, with the intention of talking about respect between them both.

Change the Familial View, and You Change the Student

In the movie *Dangerous Minds* (1995), teacher and ex-marine Louanne Johnson accepts a full-time job at East Palo Alto High School, realizing that the students in her class are intelligent but their social problems keep their reputation from being respected. She soon learns that she either must give up on them due to their violent and disrespectful tendencies toward her or learn how to cooperate to get the students' attention and help them learn. One such student was Raoul, a street-smart Hispanic young man. One day he got into a fight with another boy and was expelled for three days. Ms. Johnson had tried talking to Raoul about his strengths and abilities, even stroking him for the good work that he handed in occasionally. But nothing worked.

One day Ms. Johnson drove to his home in a ghetto neighborhood and spoke to his parents, who were surprised to see her. Raoul was present. At first, the father took charge of the situation and assured Ms. Johnson that Raoul would be punished severely for the trouble that he caused at school. Interrupting him, Ms. Johnson told the parents that she was not there to make sure he was punished. Instead, she was there to tell them "what a pleasure it is to have Raoul in my classroom. He is very bright, funny and articulate . . . in fact, he's my favorite."

Stunned, the father glanced at his son and said, "It's a miracle!" Ms. Johnson smiled at Raoul, who then smiled back.

What happened when Ms. Johnson entered the system of her student? Prior to the visit, chances are that the parents saw their son as a future dropout. When he came home from school, they probably never asked about homework. Instead, he waltzed back out the door to keep company with his street friends until dawn. Now, however, the story changes along with Raoul's new-found reputation. My hunch is that when Ms. Johnson left, the parents' hope in their son returned. In the future, they might ask him when he comes home from school, "Do you have homework? Your teacher said you are smart. Go study."

This movie is based on a true story. Raoul graduated from high school.

What! Me Do Family Counseling? All I Do Is Schedule!

Yes. There is time. I know the demands on your schedule. As an elementary school counselor, I found that good times to see families were when they dropped off their child at school. Then the parents went to work. As a high school counselor, I had slightly more flexibility in that parents could come during the day or after school occasionally. My job was then to give teachers warning that the student would be absent from class occasionally. I found that by seeing families, I could do more proactive activities. By visiting with families and focusing on how the family can assist their child or adolescent at school, I was able to help the family to change their interactions enough so that the student could literally return to class.

Just Go Once Around the Block with a Family

Meeting with families at school is different from private practice, where families are seen up to six times by a solution-focused therapist. As a school employee, you will likely be seen as a professional ready to deal with school issues only, and that will keep your sessions brief. In fact, meetings may be brief (approximately thirty to forty-five minutes), and most do not have to continue past two or three sessions.

Since you will not charge a fee or request paperwork to be filled out except for a consent form, such as the one provided here, the chances that a family will come to see you will increase.

When it comes to scheduling a family session, consider a variety of times that can work for families, making their acceptance of your invitation more appealing. I rarely had a parent turn me down for an early morning session before work or on their day off. They appreciated the school's taking such a strong stance to help their adolescent. The consent form is useful, particularly when a student's parents are divorced and have joint custody. If this is the case, both parents may need to sign a consent form in most states, because both parents have discretion on the kind of medical or mental health services their child receives. A fax will work from the noncustodial parent in most cases. It also provides a legal document that protects the privacy of the student and family. If you do not have a state license in counseling, your counseling records are open for examination by school staff unless your district has a specific policy that states otherwise. The form protects you professionally. Keep it in a safe, secure place, away from academic records. It should never accompany cumulative folders to other schools.

Consent Form for Family Counseling

Date: _____

School: _____

Student: _____

Grade: _____

I give _____,

School Counselor at _____
School, my permission to provide counseling for my child and family. I understand that the discussion is confidential and will not be shared with anyone, unless court ordered and I approve.

Please check one:

_____ I have sole custody of my child.

_____ I share joint custody of my child.

_____
Parent

_____
Parent

Getting Teacher Cooperation

When I worked with families as a school counselor, I found that most teachers or administrators welcomed such involvement, granting a pass from class for a student to attend the session. The teachers who are involved simply need to know that you need time with the student, who will make up any missed work. Be sure that both parents and student understand what information they need to convey to the teachers. Give this information with plenty of notice so that it does not take the teacher by surprise. Students are sometimes reluctant to bring in their parents, but often they report later that the joint session was worth their time. Again, it is the systemic change that occurs when meeting with the family and offering new ways of thinking that leads to longer-lasting change.

Solution-Focused Script for Working with Families

The following steps may help as you meet with families about a variety of issues, including poor school work, anger, frustration, disrespect to teachers, and depression. You will notice that the steps follow the same protocol for working with individual students and teachers. The difference is that you have many more voices to hear from and talk about exceptions.

1. **Join.** Introduce yourself and learn everyone's name. Ask about where the parents work, and ask them to tell you a little about themselves. Also ask the parents to tell you some strengths of their child or adolescent before getting started.

2. **Hear the concern.** Ask everyone, especially the student, what they want to talk about that would be helpful to them.

3. **Set goals.** After you hear the concerns, help the family focus on what they want instead of what they don't want. Ask them to tell you how they will know when things are better. Help them to get specific:

- What will be happening (instead of what will not be happening) that will tell you that things are better?
- Who will be doing something differently? Who else? Who else? Ask everyone this question.
- How will these changes be helpful?
- How will they affect your family life?

If some of the goals seem unreasonable, such as asking parents to get back together instead of divorcing or asking the adolescent to bring up grades too quickly, ask:

- What will that do for you?
- What would a small portion of that look like?
- What would be a way to begin achieving that on a small scale?

4. **Identify exceptions.** After the family defines the goals from the questions in step 3, say to everyone: "I'd like each of you to think back to a time when a little of this was happening." After they have replied, continue: "Where else has this happened? In what kind of situation, even outside the home, does the goal happen even slightly?" Listen and ask for everyone's responses, and write them down.

5. **Set tasks together.** Each task should be based on an exception that was discussed by a family member. You do not need to suggest them. Instead say, "You have each described some times when the problem was not as much of a problem. Let me read them to you." Then read each exception and continue: "On a scale of 1 to 10, with a 10 meaning that you have achieved exactly what you wanted in your family and a 1 meaning that you were nowhere near achieving it, where would you each put yourself?" Again listen to the replies and continue: "If you were to move up just one place until I see you again, what would you say you could each do to accomplish that, based on what I just read to you?" End the session, and ask for feedback. As you end the session, ask the family, "What did we do in here today, if anything, that you found helpful?" This is valuable information for you and the family to verbalize. It will help you feel motivated to continue working with them and it will send the family a message that you are sincere in working for them. From that information, you will learn what to continue doing.

Use the blank Solution-Focused Script worksheet to assist you. Copy the page when your session is over and hand it to the parents. That support will increase the chances that they will follow through since it is written.

Solution-Focused Script:
A Worksheet for Helping Families

Join. Introduce yourself and learn everyone's name. Ask about where the parents work, and ask them to tell you a little about themselves. Also ask the parents to tell you some strengths of their child or adolescent before getting started.

_____

_____

_____

_____

_____

Hear the concern. Ask everyone, especially the student, what they want to talk about that would be helpful to them. Fill in their answers.

_____

_____

_____

_____

_____

Set goals. After you hear the concerns, help the family to focus on what they want instead of what they don't want. Ask the family members to tell you how they will know when things are better. Help them to get specific. Fill in their answers.

_____

_____

_____

_____

_____

Solution-Focused Script (cont.)

Identify exceptions according to all present. Fill in their answers.

_____

_____

_____

_____

_____

Set tasks together. Each task should be based on an exception that was discussed by a family member. Fill in their answers.

_____

_____

_____

_____

End the session and ask for feedback about what was helpful from the conversation. Fill in their answers.

_____

_____

_____

_____

Make a copy of this sheet for the family.

Next meeting: _____

Before the family leaves, set another appointment one to two weeks away. Make sure to call and confirm the appointment a day in advance since families are busy, and once things improve, they may decide that they don't need to come back. If when you call they report that things are much better and don't see a need to continue, let them know that you are pleased and available should they need to see you in the future. The following case shows how the steps presented helped a middle school student teach her parents what she needed.

I Need Parenting . . . Now!

Sophia, age twelve, was a soccer star extraordinaire. Adopted as an infant, she was the younger of two children, her older brother being her parents' biological child. Sophia had a rebellious tendency that sometimes kept her from seeming respectful—except on the soccer field. Her coach, she reported, would never put up with any rebellion or disrespect; he would make her run five miles if she did that.

When Sophia was arrested at her school for spray-painting graffiti on the walls at school, she was placed in an alternative school with strict rules and consistent consequences. She did well. In fact, for the first time that semester, Sophia did well academically as well as behaviorally.

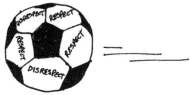

When Sophia's parents brought her to family counseling, they were still at a loss. It seemed that although Sophia had done much better at the alternative school, she remained disrespectful and belligerent at home. Our conversation went as follows:

LM: So what can we talk about here today that would make our time together productive?

MOM: We need to know how to settle her down at home, like she is at school. We don't want any more situations where she gets arrested either.

LM: So you want her behavior to improve. What would that look like?

MOM: She would be more respectful to myself and her dad.

SOPHIA: (cursing) Why would I do that? You don't do anything for me . . . ever. I ask you to take me places and help me with things, and you never have time. You always say, "When I get around to it."

LM: Sophia, I am curious about something. Your parents say that you are doing quite well in the alternative school. Tell me what helps you do so well.

SOPHIA: I don't know. I guess it's because I earn points each day, and when I do, I get privileges right then. I know that they will happen too.

LM: What does it do for you to know you can depend on those rewards?

SOPHIA: I guess it makes me pay attention to what I do.

DAD: Now, Sophia, we have done the charts at home for you before. We set up an allowance, and you still didn't cooperate.

SOPHIA: Yeah, because you would forget to give it to me. You would say, "We don't have the money today. Wait until next week."

DAD: We can't help that I lost my job.

SOPHIA: No, but you just never follow through with anything.

LM: What would be better instead, Sophia, so that you could begin to show your parents a side of you that they don't see as often—the one you have at school?

SOPHIA: I'll tell you what I need. First, a chart with dates on it so that I can do my chores, and they can be written on the chart so I don't forget. Second, an allowance that my parents could afford that I would get each week, based on what I did right. If I messed up one day, they could subtract that day and give me the allowance based on what I did do right at the end of the week. Friday is good. Third, privileges that they would follow through with and I could depend on.

Honestly, at one point, I was unsure who the adults were in the office as Sophia presented a mature side of her that seemed genuine. Sophia basically described what worked for her at the alternative school and tailored it to her home life. Her parents listened to her three ideas and then described that it was true that they often did not follow through. However, by talking to her parents about how determined they were to keep their daughter on track, we were able to contract that they would sit with Sophia, work out the chart with her assistance, and try the technique for one week.

After one week, Sophia's parents described their daughter as doing more around the house without being told and being more respectful of her parents. When I asked Sophia what her parents had done differently, a technique that I have found helpful to parents because it comes directly from their child or adolescent, Sophia answered, "They are following through with what they told me they would do, finally."

Case Study: Helping Families to Recognize the Student Differently

Once families see their influence in solving issues of their children, they become quite helpful. However, some parents still have difficulty in seeing their part. When this happens, school counselors can use externalizing problems as a strategy, since it minimizes blame and increases family cooperation. This case describes how sixteen-year-old Joey was able to improve his own behavior when the issue was not him but tension.

Joey, a sophomore in high school, had been a star athlete for most of his school years. He had played baseball since preschool and had excelled at the sport until this year, when he was dropped from the team for failing three classes. Depressed and rebellious at home, he came to counseling with his mother, stepdad, and brother. The school was concerned about Joey's failing grades and his tendency to engage in fights.

In my first meeting with Joey and his family, his mother expressed her concerns about his father's murder when Joey was two, Joey's violent outbursts toward her and school, and her fear that he would fail his sophomore year. Joey's stepdad described his relationship with Joey as stable but was concerned that Joey had recently stopped talking to him and was choosing to stay out late with his friends instead of studying or being at home with the family.

As I listened to the family's description of the problem that they felt was bothering Joey, I watched him stare at the floor and sink deeper and deeper into the couch, as if succumbing to the problem and its claim on his life. The family was desperately concerned, and their concern was burying Joey and creating a sense of hopelessness. They had confronted him enough to drive him away from any responsibility for his own actions. Instead their confrontation had perpetuated his rebellion. The last thing I needed to do as a counselor was to help them create more of the same hopelessness by trying to probe or understand what was troubling Joey, thereby giving credence to the fact that there was indeed a terrible problem.

Look Beyond the Problems to the Person

If I had been trying to help Joey and his family a few years ago, I might have examined educational assessment forms, cumulative folders, and test scores. I might have asked the parents about the consequences they were currently presenting to Joey in that he was failing three classes. I might have asked personal questions of the parents regarding their family life, searching for reasons that this problem was occurring yet keeping my boundaries as an educator. In an attempt to get to the root of the problem, I might have looked for sequences in behaviors, interactional patterns that did not work, or sibling rivalry between the younger brother and Joey. I might have questioned the stepfather-stepson relationship and asked more questions about Joey's biological, deceased father. Instead, as I met with Joey, I refocused and tried to think differently about the situation. I was more interested in searching for Joey's competencies rather than perpetuating the problem through probing for more understanding of what Joey was doing wrong. Joey's sad appearance reflected that he obviously knew enough about the problem that had brought him to counseling. In fact, by this point, he seemed to be feeling that *he* was the problem.

It has been my experience as a teacher, school counselor, and therapist that adolescents respond with rebellion, resistance, and sadness when they are blamed or criticized. I was interested in Joey's opinion and solutions to his school problems, and I knew that to gain his cooperation in counseling, I needed to align heavily with him against the problem. I knew he was competent in at least part of his educational history, because he had in fact succeeded in school up to this point. He had also succeeded in doing well at a sport. Most important, he had come to counseling willingly with his family. With these exceptions in mind and an assumption that Joey wanted things to be different, I began the session by expressing my concern for the family's worries and then asked:

LM: How will you know when things are getting better for all of you?

After a few minutes of silence, the family replied:

MOM: Things will be better when I don't worry as much about Joey's grades or his outbursts at school. I will receive fewer phone calls about Joey's behavior and will feel confident to go to work without worrying.

STEPDAD: The tension that seems to perpetuate the family life will be less prevalent, and I'll be able to stay off Joey's back and do more things with Tommy [Joey's younger brother].

TOMMY: I'll be able to play with Joey without being afraid that he will beat me up, and I'll have friends over more often because there will be less yelling.

JOEY: I don't know, I guess school will be better and everybody—family and school—will be off my back.

Listening to the family's description of the problem, I asked about the tension his stepfather had described and how each of them kept this tension around. I explained to the family that problems are often maintained through interactions and that persons influence the life of the problem. With this in mind, I addressed each of the family members:

LM: I've often learned that problems are what I refer to as maintained—you know, that possibly people keep problems around by their behaviors with each other. Can you each tell me how you might possibly keep this tension in your family?

MOM: I badger Joey, I worry too much, I yell at Brian [stepdad] when I worry about Joey. I complain too much about his low grades. I get so frustrated that I keep nagging him to study, and of course, the more I nag, the more he refuses to study.

STEPDAD: I pick on Joey. My dad and I used to punch each other, and I used to think that playing around with Joey would lighten him up. Wrong! I do let things get to me and then jump down Joey's throat.

TOMMY: I yell back at Joey when he bugs me. I tell on Joey to Dad and Mom, he gets in trouble, and then everybody yells. Then I guess I aggravate him when his friends are over. It's fun.

JOEY: I don't do my school work, don't come home on time, and yell back when they yell at me. I get mad pretty easy.

As each of the family members described how they contributed to the tension, Joey began to look up at his family and me instead of at the floor. He seemed to feel less blamed, and the family backed off from blaming him as well. We continued to talk more about times when the tension was not as prevalent.

LM: Joey, take me back to a time when school was better and the tension your dad talked about wasn't in control of your life.

JOEY: Last year. I passed all my classes last year.

LM: How did you do that?

JOEY: They have this class at school called Academic Opportunity, where you go for help when you need it. I went when I needed to, and I passed.

LM: Really! By the way, aren't you passing four classes now?

JOEY: Yes.

LM: Tell me which ones.

JOEY: Math, English, home economics, and art.

LM: That's great! What's your secret to doing that?

JOEY: I don't know. I do my work in class and just hand it in.

When Things Were Better at Home, They Were Better at School

Joey brightened considerably and became more forthcoming instantly. He began to describe additional ways he had passed classes in the past and strategies he was using now to pass classes. He recalled that a few years ago, his mom had praised him and rewarded him with time they spent together. He also mentioned that she had been reacting differently lately, not noticing his passing grades and barely giving him a pat on the back. According to Joey, she was correct to be concerned about her badgering: her efforts to encourage him had backfired.

Joey then turned his attention to his stepdad and reminisced how at one time they had gone over his homework together before he turned it in. His stepdad admitted that he had become negligent in checking Joey's work recently and recalled that he did enjoy checking Joey's work in the past. As Joey described his past successes, his mother mentioned her concern about the violent outbursts at school. Joey admitted that he had a temper, but by this time in the session, he too was changing his thinking as he mentioned that on more than one occasion since eighth grade, he had learned to curb his temper. I was curious about his ability to curb his temper, especially since that was an issue brought to my attention by the family and school. I asked him to describe how he did this:

> JOEY: One day at school, I was sitting with six of my friends at lunch. We got up to get some food, and when we came back, a bunch of guys had thrown our books on the floor and were sitting in our seats. It took about fifteen seconds for me to clench my fists and get ready to fight.
>
> LM: Did you fight?
>
> JOEY: No.
>
> LM: How did you stop?
>
> JOEY: We asked them would you please move, and then I noticed the coach watching us. I slowed myself down.
>
> LM: Wow, you asked them to move first?
>
> JOEY: Yeah.
>
> LM: Has that helped in other situations?
>
> JOEY: Yeah, it has.
>
> LM: That's incredible. Tell me.
>
> JOEY: With my mom once, she was yelling at me and grabbed me. I was mad but I kept my cool and didn't hit her.
>
> LM: Amazing.
>
> JOEY: I would never hit my mom. I love her.

Just Avoid the Tension

The initial session ended with a simple task: the family was asked to focus on easing the tension. By easing the tension, the tension remained externalized (Epston & White, 1990). As the family discussed how they maintained the problem, they discovered what they might do to make it less dominant in their relationships. Joey had stated his specific strategies to control anger and pass some classes at school, and he had expressed how important his mom was to him. He indeed had the resources he needed to escape from the tension. I noted to him and his family that there were simply too many occasions when he did not allow the problem to influence his behavior for this not to be the case. The other family members, hearing the exceptions I solicited from Joey, agreed that the tension was the problem at hand. In an effort to assist the family in noticing more times when the tension was not interfering with their family life, I asked Joey and his family to do the following: "During the next week, I'd like you all to notice times when, purposefully, you do not allow the tension to interfere with your family life. Joey, I'd like you to notice when school works, especially in the four classes you are passing, and notice specifically how you are doing that."

By offering a task to notice when the problem was less bothersome, Joey and his family were more likely to see relief and experience themselves as more competent. It was important that Joey experience himself as competent so as to lessen any dependency on his family and teachers to succeed in school behaviorally and academically. The ability to gain independence from the problem is clearly a self-esteem builder and motivating agent for change in adolescents.

Within a week, his stepdad again began checking his stepson's work, and his mom stopped badgering her son. After three weeks, Joey had raised his grades to passing. Tommy, following his parents' lead, bugged his brother less, resulting in more pleasant times together with Joey. Interestingly enough, in a future session, his mom said to me, "I started noticing what he passed instead of what he was not passing, and the times we got along instead of what went wrong that day." This was a nice outcome of the first session task, and since I had only suggested that the family look for exceptions, her behavior change was her own decision. I made sure I gave her credit for such a nice way of relating differently to her son.

I have provided the Case Notes worksheet that I used with Joey's family and a blank form to use in your own counseling. Give a copy of the case notes to the family to review and use if the problem attempts to take over again. Whenever I have given my notes to families, they appreciate being a bigger part of the solution, and it keeps them on track as the case note sheet makes it to the refrigerator, the hall of fame for important documents.

Case Notes for Joey's Family

Name: _Joey Smith and Family_ **Date:** _____

Presenting problem according to family members:

Joey's angry outbursts, failing grades, isolation from family, and reluctance to follow curfew.

Externalized problem (if applicable):

Tension

Goal (State in behavioral terms about what will be happening):

Joey will have fewer angry outbursts, and he will make passing grades in school. Mom will notice when Joey improves and will not hear from the school as often with complaints about Joey. Stepdad and Joey will get along once again and do homework together. Tommy will play more with friends his age and bother his big brother less. The tension will be replaced with better interactions among the family members.

Problem maintenance:

Mom badgers Joey.

Stepdad yells at Joey.

Tommy tells on Joey and complains about him.

Joey gets angry, doesn't come home or do schoolwork on time.

Exceptions:

Joey is age appropriate for his grade in school.

Joey is passing four of six subjects and does so by Academic Opportunity course training and by turning in all work.

Joey has been in difficult situations and has not had an angry outburst by responding politely before losing his temper.

When Mom was supportive and complimentary of Joey in the past, he did better in school.

Case Notes for Joey's Family (cont.)

When Stepdad checked Joey's schoolwork, he was more patient with him, and Joey did well.

When Tommy did not tattle on Joey to his parents, there was less conflict between the brothers.

Joey loves his mother very much and does not want to hurt her.

Joey came willingly to counseling and seems to want his life to change.

Task (developed from exceptions only):

Ask the family to fight off tension as they have at times, based on exceptions, and notice how they do so for a week. Ask Joey to pay more attention in school regarding how he passes other classes.

Case Notes: Externalizing Problems with Families

Name: _____   **Date:** _____

Presenting problem according to family members:

_____

_____

Externalized problem (if applicable):

_____

Goal (State in behavioral terms about what will be happening):

_____

_____

_____

Problem maintenance:

_____

_____

_____

_____

Exceptions:

_____

_____

_____

_____

Task (developed from exceptions only):

_____

_____

_____

Bargaining Power: Just Meet Me in the Middle

Previously in this book, I used an alteration of the scaling question between two elementary students who were fighting. Using the scaling question differently, placing a 5 in the middle and a child at opposing ends of the scale, the students focused on moving toward a mutual goal. The same idea for using the scaling question can be helpful to families, particularly when one member of the family does not feel as if the other family members are working as hard as he or she is. The following case illustrates this dilemma.

Sam, fifteen years old, was referred to counseling after he was arrested by police for carrying a knife and possessing a small amount of marijuana. After attending day treatment in a nearby psychiatric facility for ten days, he and his family began family therapy. As Sam began to lobby his family for recovery of his car (he had a hardship license) and other privileges, he became quite frustrated when his parents refused to comply with his wishes. Instead, they told Sam what it would take for him to recover his car and other privileges. Sam looked at me and said, "See, they never compromise." I was concerned that Sam truly believed his family did not want to work things out and saw him determined to try to get his way. I proposed the following scale to Sam:

1	2	3	4	5	4	3	2	1
				goals here				

LM: I'm going to draw a scale with both of your goals in the middle. I'm then going to put you and your family on a scale, with you at one end of the scale and your parents at the other end, since you are disagreeing at this moment. Sam, when you look at the scale, where do you see yourself in regard to meeting the goals that you both talked about? Where do you see your mom and dad? And Mom and Dad, where do you see yourselves on this scale? Where do you see your son?

1	2	3	4	5	4	3	2	1
Sam				Drug free				Parents
				Respect				
				Trust				
Plan:								Plan:
No Plan								Return his car after 3 weeks
								Allow him to see friends who don't use drugs
								Earn privileges from meeting curfew

The parents continued to list what they were willing to do to move forward on the scale and what Sam needed to do to move forward as well. Together, they negotiated that Sam could eventually reclaim his car when he got to a 4 on the scale by getting clean drug screens for three months, associating with nondrug friends, and his parents' receiving no calls from the school regarding discipline problems and skipping class.

As the scale shows, Sam had not defined what he was willing to do to reach the goal; he was more concerned with what his parents would do. The scale assisted him in seeing how his parents were willing to compromise yet he was not. He became very quiet and then began to collaborate with everyone

When Parents Don't Know the Answer, Ask About Work

As a marriage and family therapist in addition to being a school counselor, I know that not all sessions go just as I plan. Sometimes parents are at a loss with their child and can't imagine things getting better. They have difficulties identifying times when their offspring did better and see only problems now. When this happens, consider talking to the parents about their profession, for within their professional and even personal lives, most parents use strategies that work for them. Help them to see how these strategies that they use outside their family can be used at home too. Consider, for example, the following traits:

Secretary: Patient and understanding, problem solver

Physician: Thorough, bedside manner, seeks answers and offers ideas

Attorney: Objective, factual, listens, is supportive

Teacher: Structured, methodical, tries to be helpful

Construction worker: Creative, listens to directions from others and complies

When working with parents, I ask the following questions about their professional and personal relationships, particularly when I am searching for exceptions:

"What would your boss say your best asset is in working with others?"

"What would your partner or friends say you do that makes relationships work?"

"Would the way you respond at work be different from how you do things at home?"

"If you pretended that your son/daughter was your client or colleague at work with the same type of behavior, what would you do differently?"

These questions help parents examine their competencies elsewhere. When typical parenting strategies do not work, many parents sense that perhaps the situation is beyond their control. By helping them to identify exceptions outside the family, they begin to realize that there may be solutions that they use in other places that could work at home too.

Summary

According to Brian Gerrard (1997) at the Center for Child Development at the University of San Francisco, 85 percent of the students referred by teachers, parents, and other staff members have problems that are related to problems at home. Although the school counselor may be helpful in speaking to the referred students about the symptom of the home problem that occurs at school, unless the home problems are addressed, the chances of change for the student are minimal.

Seeing families in a school setting recreates the sense of communities that schools are the pillar of society. Today's families experience stressors related to finances, legal issues, divorce, substance abuse, custody issues, marital discord, parental neglect, and even siblings in gangs. Where do they turn? If the school has some basic services such as individual, family, and group counseling available to its students and parents, many issues can be addressed. By using a solution-focused approach, the school counselor can be an integral part of getting help for families in regard to helping their children be more successful.

The school counselor should not be a marital counselor and should not see families to help them deal with financial or legal issues. However, the school counselor can help families process their part in the solution for the student. By working with families to help them develop strategies to assist their children, the school counselor can also help families see the power of family counseling. Then referral sources can be provided that are available in the community.

Schools get stuck when they focus on linear issues. By expanding to a circular way of thinking and considering the interlocking pieces that create problems for students, there is a better chance that students can get the help they need to at least cope with issues at home.

The school has always been a pillar. Help resurrect yours again.

Solution-Focused Training Exercise: Chapter Eight

Look through the list of students with whom you are working now, and identify one whom you feel stuck with. Call the student's parents and schedule a family counseling session, mentioning that the session intends to help their child or adolescent do better in school.

Prior to the meeting, gather your thoughts about what might be troubling your student, and jot them down:

_____

_____

_____

_____

_____

_____

After you meet with the family, write down your new thoughts. Were your assumptions about the family correct? Incorrect?

_____

_____

_____

_____

_____

_____

_____

Write a note to the family, thanking them for their time.

Chapter Nine

Disciplining Differently

Behavior Transformations

Discipline is remembering what you want.

—David Campbell

Effective discipline has been a concern of educators for decades. Behavior modification approaches, corporal punishment, in-school suspension, and expulsion have been a few of the "solutions" educators have tried to gain the attention of students so they might change their behaviors. Looking at today's schools full of violence, rebellion, and disruptions, these approaches have turned into boxing matches with students, parents, and special interest groups. They may work for 70 percent of the students in school, but what about the other 30 percent? They need another approach to help them deal with their personal and home issues and begin seeing themselves differently. They need to know they matter to their school. It's the only way to help them change. They have to know they are valuable.

It's Time for a New Approach to Discipline

The ideas in this book are not designed to address any specific behavior problem. Rather, they address them in a general manner. The solution-focused approach encourages school staff to develop and implement a new atmosphere for students that discourages problem behavior and encourages competencies. This chapter suggests new ways of dealing with behavior problems and with students who have not responded to typical school interventions. The ideas presented are suggestions for helping students who are *bothered* by disturbances to begin seeing themselves differently. By seeing themselves differently, as this book has reinforced, they begin to act differently.

To begin, we start with a case about a very different approach to a familiar problem.

The Challenge: Creating Opportunities for Change, by Brian Cade

The dialogue in this case, written and contributed by Brian Cade, a colleague from Sydney, Australia, shows how thinking differently about a problem and redescribing behaviors to a young man threatened by expulsion challenges him to change. I am grateful to Brian Cade for writing this selection.

The Target

Jack, age thirteen, was brought to see me by his parents because he was constantly in trouble at school. He was endlessly battling with his teachers and was also regularly fighting with his peers and with boys. He had been suspended from school several times and recently had been threatened with expulsion. This would then be the third school from which he had been expelled in just over two years. He was running out of options.

As his parents outlined the problem, he sat looking disinterested and bored. After a short time, I asked the parents to wait outside and saw Jack on his own. He seemed quite happy to tell me about what was happening at school. He agreed that he was in trouble constantly but expressed no concern about it.

Aligning with the Student Against the Situation

COUNSELOR: What made you decide to be so helpful to everybody?

JACK: What do you mean?

COUNSELOR: Well, I am sure that there are other kids in your class that play up. Isn't that right?

JACK: Yes.

COUNSELOR: Do they get into trouble as much as you do?

JACK: Not usually.

COUNSELOR: That's what surprises me about you. You seem to have become so helpful to them. Whatever they might do, you seem to be the one that the teacher picks on. It's as though you have become such a big target that the other kids can hide behind you and get away with things. How did you decide to be so helpful?

JACK: I don't know what you mean.

COUNSELOR: It sounds as though your classmates can get away with all sorts of things because you have such a reputation as a troublemaker that when the teacher turns around, you are the first person he or she looks toward. You then get busted, and the others seem to get away with it. Isn't that what happens? In fact, I bet there are lots of times that you get busted for what the others have done even though you have done nothing wrong.

JACK: Yes. So?

COUNSELOR: So, nothing. I am just impressed with how helpful you are to your classmates. Have they ever thanked you for it?

JACK: No. (He looks puzzled.)

COUNSELOR: What? Do you mean to tell me that you often take the rap for all these other kids, and they don't even thank you for it?

JACK: Of course, they don't.

COUNSELOR: Good grief! (Then, after a thoughtful pause) Have the teachers thanked you?

JACK: What are you talking about?

COUNSELOR: Well, you make it so much easier for them. Surely they have expressed their appreciation.

JACK: What do you mean?

COUNSELOR: You save them the trouble of trying to work out who it was that was mucking up. The teachers can just turn around and bust you and thus save themselves all the bother of trying to work out who the hell it was that really made the noise, or whatever it was that attracted their attention.

JACK: You're crazy!

COUNSELOR: Are you sure that the teachers have not thanked you for your help?

JACK: I'm not helping them.

COUNSELOR: You're not? But haven't you found that the other kids in your class are often mucking up but the teacher always looks at you first, even though you might not have been doing anything wrong? And haven't you often been busted for things that the others have done? The real culprit then just keeps quiet and gets away with it?

JACK: Sometimes.

Redescribing the Problem

COUNSELOR: So how come you keep acting like such a big target so that whoever mucks up or whoever starts the fights, you are the one who is the center of attention and gets busted?

JACK: It just happens.

COUNSELOR: Do you mean you don't do it deliberately?

JACK: Of course, I don't.

COUNSELOR: Would you prefer it to be different?

JACK: I don't care. (Profanity)

COUNSELOR: So you are happy to get busted for what the others do? I'm impressed. How come you're so generous? Why do you put yourself so much on the line to be so helpful? I bet none of them would do the same to help you. (Silence)

COUNSELOR: Are there other ways that you help them by being such a big target?

JACK: I'm not helping them. You're nuts.

COUNSELOR: I don't understand. By being such a big target whenever there is trouble, you draw to yourself the attention of all the teachers. They expect you to be the troublemaker, and so they automatically look toward you. Isn't that right?

JACK: I guess so.

Opening Up Possibilities for Goal Setting

COUNSELOR: But what would happen if you stopped?

JACK: What do you mean?

COUNSELOR: Wouldn't you feel responsible that by keeping out of trouble, you were the cause of their getting into trouble?

JACK: No.

COUNSELOR: Are you sure you'd want to be responsible for the other kids getting into trouble?

JACK: I don't care. (Profanity)

COUNSELOR: You'd be happy to try to stop being such a marked man, a big target, even though it meant that the other kids would have to take the rap for what they do?

JACK: Yes.

COUNSELOR: Are you sure you want to take that degree of responsibility?

JACK: (Holding his head between his hands) This is crazy!

COUNSELOR: Sure, but what about the teachers?

JACK: What about them?

COUNSELOR: Their job will be much harder if they have to work out for themselves who it actually is who is mucking up.

JACK: So?

COUNSELOR: Are you sure you want to be responsible for making your teacher's job harder?

JACK: Of course I am. Why would I want to get myself busted all the time to help them?

COUNSELOR: That's what I was thinking. Why would you?

Task Development

COUNSELOR: I don't know, but I guess you'd need to find ways of being a smaller target, of keeping a lower profile, of keeping your nose clean. Do you know what I mean?

JACK: I guess so.

COUNSELOR: It won't be easy. Everyone expects you to be a troublemaker, kids and teachers.

JACK: So?

Encouraging Student Competency to Solve the Problem: Making It His Agenda

COUNSELOR: It could take a while to turn it around. How will you handle it, for example, if you manage to become a smaller target, if you manage to keep your nose clean, and yet you still get into trouble either because some of the kids set you up or because the teacher assumes it must have been you? Will you be able to take your medicine, however unfair it might be, without fighting back so that you avoid being pushed into becoming a big target again?

JACK: If I wanted to, I guess I could do it.

COUNSELOR: Look, I don't want to kid you. If you decide to do this, it could be really tough. I would advise you not to try it unless you are really sure that you want to do it and that you can carry it through. Do you know what I mean?

JACK: Yes.

COUNSELOR: Would you prefer to think about it for a week or so?

JACK: No. I guess I can give it a go.

COUNSELOR: Are you sure?

JACK: What do you want from me, for me to sign it in blood?

COUNSELOR: No, it's not that. I just want you to be sure what it is you'll be taking on. After all, the teachers and the other kids won't know what your new plan is, and they'll be treating you as though you are the same as you were the last time they saw you. They'll be seeing you as a troublemaker, as someone who is easy to wind up and get into trouble. In a sense, you'll be on your own with no one to help.

JACK: I don't need any help.

COUNSELOR: Well, if you're sure, I wish you the best of luck. Don't be too disheartened if it doesn't work out straightaway. You might find that there are going to be lots of times when you'll be struggling against the urge to fight back. What I'd like you to do, if you don't mind, is to take particular note of all the different ways that you can find of resisting the urge to do the sorts of things that both your teachers and the other kids will be expecting you to do based on the past. Will that be okay?

JACK: I guess.

COUNSELOR: Also, if it is not too much to ask, would you be prepared each day to draw a picture of a target that represents what size of target you think that you were that day? If you were as big a target as you have ever been, draw it about this size [I demonstrate by drawing a large target on a piece of paper]. If you manage to avoid being a target at all, just put a dot. If, on any day, you are somewhere in between, draw it to whichever size, somewhere in between this one and the dot, that represents how well you think you have done. I think it might be best to take a big sheet of paper and, with a ruler, divide it up into squares so that one square represents one day. Can you do that?

JACK: Okay.

MONDAY	TUESDAY	WEDNESDAY	THURSDAY	FRIDAY

Brian Cade mentions that during the conversation, it was important that there was no hint of challenge in his voice or his demeanor. All of his responses reflected curiosity tinged with puzzled incomprehension. A challenge would doubtless have represented just a more-of-the-same kind of approach that had clearly not worked in the past. It would have reflected a change in behavior as being the counselor's agenda, not Jack's, in the same way that up until then, it had been his teachers' and his parents' agendas, not his. In Cade's experience, people change only in ways that reflect their own agendas.

Enlisting Help from Parents and Teachers: Noticing What's Better

Cade continued to see the parents in therapy for a short while yet saw Jack separately. He took the parents' concerns seriously but also asked them if "they would be prepared to back off and, for a while, leave things to Jack to try to sort out." Cade felt it important that they did not ask him at all how things were going to avoid having it again become their agenda, not Jack's. They agreed. In the event of their getting further complaints from the school, he asked that they be prepared to take the position with Jack that they were sorry that he still seemed to be having troubles and that they hoped he would finally be able to sort things out. End of response. They were prepared to do this.

Cade suggested that the parents contact the school and let them know that they had sought professional help and to ask the staff if they would be prepared to look for any signs, however small, that Jack was making efforts to improve his behavior. Cade also suggested that they let the school know that it was the counselor's opinion that whatever his intentions, it might not be easy for Jack to change such an entrenched pattern of problem behavior in just a few days or even a few weeks.

Would they be prepared to give him the benefit of the doubt for a while in order that he not be too quickly discouraged? Cade often calls schools personally, but in this situation, he felt the parents, who were highly motivated, would do well being more involved in resolving the problem. "It is easier to back off if you have an alternative thing to do."

Target No More

At the next session, Jack did not find it easy to stay cool or conceal a degree of pleasure when he showed Cade the diminishing size of the targets he had drawn on his chart. The parents received feedback from the school that his behavior had clearly improved. With delight, Jack told Cade several stories of how some of his classmates had been in more trouble over the past couple of weeks than was usually the case.

Over the next few months, the ongoing therapy concentrated not on times when Jack "relapsed" but on the different ways he found, day by day, to avoid the urge to rise to the bait and the ways he got back on track after the lapses. It was important that changing the pattern at school remained solely Jack's goal. When Cade encouraged Jack, he did so following Jack's lead. "It is rarely helpful for a therapist to appear more enthusiastic for any change than the client. The slightest hint of that would have undoubtedly led to resistance on Jack's part."

At a six-month telephone follow-up, Jack's parents confirmed that although Jack was certainly still no angel, he had settled down considerably; his grades were improving, he was no longer constantly receiving detentions, and his possible expulsion from school was no longer an issue. During the call, Cade spoke to Jack briefly, and Jack gave the following explanation: "It's easy, I just keep my head down behind the couple of big targets that are sitting near to me. They're too stupid to see what's happening."

Creating Relationships with Students to Gain Respect and Compliance

Nan Lovelace, a vice principal in Arlington, Texas, has been so successful in her work with students facing expulsion or in-school suspension that she's commonly referred to as "Mom" by her students, who visit her long after they finish junior high. What's her secret to "enlisting" the troubled adolescents who show up at her door? "I ask them, 'What do you want in your life?'" She remarks that many students are quite often put out by being expelled or in suspension and at first resist her assistance. She doesn't give up, however, when she meets such resistance: "I ask them if they know where they want to go in life. Typically they don't know. I then explain to them that if we went on a trip to Florida and didn't have a map, how would we [she and the student] get there?" The students often become quiet and reserved at that point. Lovelace then tells them that she's there, and if they are interested, to come back and talk. "I'm not going to call you from class; you can come see me. I'd love to get to know you."

This approach, as Lovelace describes, beckons many similarities to the solution-focused approaches presented in this manual. Her conversations often go as follows:

Goal: "How do you want things to be in your life?"

Exceptions: "What are your abilities and strengths that will get you there?"

Problem influence: "What might keep you from getting there?"

Task development: "How will you watch out for future problems and solve them with your abilities?"

As a vice principal, Lovelace said she has many opportunities to "open the door frequently, but never go in until they invite me." Her observation that the students need to be ready to work before she begins her mentorship has proven correct time and time again, as she encounters less resistance and more success with her approach. The following dialogue is an example of how Lovelace might approach a student facing suspension:

VICE PRINCIPAL: Do you have a plan for your life?

STUDENT: No.

VICE PRINCIPAL: Would you like to have one?

STUDENT: No.

VICE PRINCIPAL: So you like being expelled in trouble like this? Looks like a crummy way to live. Man, I'd much rather see you in different circumstances. We could probably have a pretty good time.

STUDENT: (Silence)

VICE PRINCIPAL: Tell you what, I'm here for you. You seem like a neat kid. I'd love to get to know you and together work on a plan. Let me know.

Lovelace says her invitations are rarely turned down. Her students obviously sense her hope for their lives, her interest, and her curiosity in their abilities and strengths. She does not send for the students to come to her office, even if she has an inkling that they are interested. She waits, often until the second time they come back, making sure they are invested in their own change process. Later, when a student decides that he or she is ready, Lovelace begins with a new dialogue that is goal oriented and focused on competencies:

VICE PRINCIPAL: Let's pretend you just won the lottery. How much did you win?

STUDENT: Fifty million dollars!

VICE PRINCIPAL: Great! Let's go on a trip, okay? You and me. Where would you like to go?

STUDENT: California.

VICE PRINCIPAL: Why California?

STUDENT: I've never been there.

VICE PRINCIPAL: Great. Good reason for going there. You have good ideas. I love California, but you know, my car is really crummy. It has real problems. Let's buy a new one with some of the lottery money.

STUDENT: Okay. A Ferrari.

VICE PRINCIPAL: My kind of companion. I need cool clothes for a car like that. Let's go to the mall on the way to the car dealer.

STUDENT: Okay.

VICE PRINCIPAL: Now, we've got our car and clothes and we're off. Where's the map?

STUDENT: I don't know.

VICE PRINCIPAL: It's kind of hard to get there if we don't know where we're going. Let's see, where could we find one?

STUDENT: The library.

VICE PRINCIPAL: Now that we have a map and we're on our way, everything has been great until we get to the desert and we have three flat tires. Three! I'm hot, thirsty, hungry, and the vultures are flying. Help!

STUDENT: What?

VICE PRINCIPAL: Help me, I don't like it here. What will you do for me? I'm old, I'm hot, and I don't like it here.

STUDENT: I guess I can go for help, and come back to get you.

VICE PRINCIPAL: Great idea. Get going.

Lovelace then talks to the student about how this metaphorical account of a trip is similar to goal setting and that life is full of "flat tires." Lovelace then compliments the student on his or her problem solving (flat-tire pumping) in the trip description. With this renewed hope, the student and Lovelace create a goal sheet similar to the My Goals worksheet shown here. The student then concentrates on learning how to "fix the flat tires" in other areas of his or her life, using his or her abilities. The metaphorical description of problems as flat tires connects the student with reality and lessens resistance through belief in his or her ability.

The Student Success Diary, also shown here, has been added to Lovelace's goal identification to collect and compile the successes of students for later visits. The diary sheets can be photocopied and given to the student. Lovelace inspired my development of this diary when she described routinely writing notes to her students and recapping the student's successes, adding her compliments. The notes often end up pasted on mirrors, refrigerators, and other visible spots. Her colleagues, who remark on her effective, brief approach, have tried her ideas even more "briefly" to discover that words of kindness and hope by an administrator make tremendous differences in the lives of their students as well as their own. Less stressed, Lovelace has time to walk down the hall and greet the kids and say: "Wow, nice to see you out here and not in my office!" Lucky kids.

My Goals

Name: _____ Date: _____

My goal (Stated in the positive, for example, "I want to graduate from college"; I want to become an electrician"):

What I've done before that might keep me from getting there:

_____

_____

_____

_____

My abilities that will get me there:

_____

_____

_____

_____

How I'll "pump up the flat tires" (use ideas from your ability list):

_____

_____

_____

_____

How will that change my life when I begin to do this, on a small scale?

_____

_____

_____

_____

Student Success Diary

Name: _____ Date: _____

What's been going well for me lately?

_____

_____

_____

_____

_____

How have I done this? Who has helped, if anyone?

_____

_____

_____

_____

_____

What can I continue to do on a small scale to reach my goal?

_____

_____

_____

_____

_____

Helping Students Choose an Alternative Plan to Discipline

School counselors often have an opportunity to help students bypass punishment by simply processing with them alternative ways of relating to school staff. When this opportunity knocks, it can intrinsically change a student, which then has an impact on her teachers and school staff. How one approaches such an unhappy, disgruntled student is "all in the conversation," as the following case study by Nicole Shannon illustrates.

Rena, age thirteen, was referred to interventionist Nicole Shannon at Monnig Middle School/ Applied Learning Academy in Fort Worth, Texas, because of her disrespectful attitude toward her English teacher. When she arrived at the interventionist's office, Shannon asked Rena why she had been referred. She said she was referred because her teacher hated her and wanted to send her away to alternative school. She told Shannon that she was close to being placed in the alternative school if she was referred one more time. Shannon wrote this description as she spent time working with Rena:

I began by asking her if she had ever been sent to alternative school before and she said "yes," she was sent last year. I said: "Wow, how have you made it through twenty-four weeks of the school year without being sent to the alternative school?" She replied, surprised, that she was just lucky. I then asked her what she had been doing that had helped her to remain at school so far. She said that she had been trying to do better but now she did not care because she really believed that her English teacher hated her. I asked her if there was another teacher at school that she felt did not hate her. She said "yes." I asked her what she did that helped the teacher to not hate her. She said that it might be because she does not talk in that class and that she is on time to that class.

I told Rena that I was very proud of her for not talking in that class and commended her on getting to that class on time. I asked her when she did those same things when she was in her English class, and she said "never." She told me that her friends were in the English class and she likes to talk to them. I told her that it sounds like she must be well liked by her peers and that I suspect that she has a lot of friends. I then asked her if she would like to get her English teacher off her back. She said she did not care. I asked what she did care about, and she said she did not want to get placed in alternative school again because she would then have to go live with her grandmother.

Rena and I began talking about what it would take for her to stay in school. I asked her how was it that she was able to remain in class during the rest of her school days and not be referred. She said that her friends were not in those classes so she did not talk as much. I then asked what she thought she could do to not talk as much in her English class. She said she could try to not sit by her friends. I told her that I thought she had a great idea and that she must be rather mature to come up with an idea like that. Then I asked her how she could do that. She suggested that she could ask her teacher to move her away from her friends. I said that sounded like a great idea and asked if she would like to try that. She said "yes." Together, we composed a letter to her teacher asking her to move her away from her friends and then sent a copy of the letter to her vice principal, letting him know what she was trying to do.

The next week when I checked in with Rena, she had only been referred out twice since we had talked, which was a dramatic improvement. My plan is to continue to seek her expertise in lowering those referrals.

What did Shannon do that made a difference in Rena's actions? She stepped into the worldview of Rena and became an ally against the situation. By doing so, she was able to sympathize with the situation and then make Rena responsible for changing her actions to achieve a better outcome. If Shannon had begun the session discussing what Rena had done wrong, chances are that like many other adolescents, Rena would have felt accused by yet another adult and then rebelled. Another important aspect of Shannon's intervention was her ignoring the fact that Rena said that "she did not care." Most preadolescents and adolescents *do* care, but their integrity often gets in the way of admitting so. The solution-focused approach helps the school counselor see past this pathology and keep moving forward to solutions.

Mentorships: Courses in Responsibility

Teachers have always perplexed students, who wonder, Are they human? Many teachers report the surprised looks on students' faces when their students see them in the grocery store, at the mall, or at the park. Do teachers really exist in other places besides behind their desks? The "teacher mystery" can be used perhaps in a mentorship role with students in trouble by inviting them into the teacher's world. By creating such a mentorship, a student's eyes might see the teacher as someone who works hard to provide an interesting class session, see the teacher as someone who is not an enemy but an ally, or provide the one-on-one nurturing a student may be craving from the very population he or she may not be noticing.

The process might begin with the disciplinary process already in effect. However, instead of sending a child to an in-school classroom where he or she is isolated and labeled as bad, he or she is placed in a position similar to an office aide, with responsibilities that grow as competencies do. Teachers are chosen on personality similarities. The teacher with whom the student was disruptive or disrespectful is not initially chosen as the mentor. This relationship may take time. Instead, at the initial faculty meeting, the principal might support the school counselor to announce:

This year, we are providing a mentorship program for our at-risk kids. This program means that you will be asked to be a mentor for three students, unless you desire more! When a student is placed in your care, you will meet with the student and the counselor or administrator initially to learn how your personality and his or hers are matched for mentorship. Thereafter, the student will become your personal aide and will do whatever you need him or her to do. The student will not be identified as carrying out a "sentence," but instead will, I hope, blend in with other office workers. This process will take place no longer than two weeks, based on the in-school suspension time he or she would put in otherwise. The student will be told initially that he or she has a choice to participate or be placed in a cubicle for the duration of the suspension.

Each week the mentor teacher uses the scaling question and, with the student, looks at the progress to set a goal for the next week. Once the student meets the goal, he or she student returns to class. Thereafter the teacher asks the student to stop by and check in weekly, so that separation does not occur, but instead, a friendship develops. The importance of this exercise is in developing rapport with an educator, the population the at-risk student tries to resist. By lessening resistance and showing care, validation, and attention, the teacher has the opportunity to be perceived differently. Again, when perceptions differ, so do behaviors.

Surrounding and Defeating the Problem in Teams

The comradeship often experienced in the team approach has opened up opportunities for creative teaching. In addition, the teachers who work together in planning their lessons know the students they encounter every day. This common knowledge about students offers some marvelous opportunities for teams to go one step further in their planning and discussion of handling student behavior problems. For example, a school counselor can help a team of teachers address concerns about a particular student. The

referring teacher could ask what others have found that worked with a particular student—call him Stephen. Each teacher could then discuss what they have observed about Stephen when he was behaving better in class. The questioning teacher can write down the suggestions, and the team leader might

request that all the teachers be on alert for Stephen this week, noticing and complimenting him when he behaves better. The teachers can, for example, note their strategies on a guide sheet using the Team Strategies for Students worksheet shown here. This approach might also include teachers sending Stephen a note during the next week or two, describing to him what they have noticed him succeeding at behaviorally.

In addition, any other exceptions that describe places where Stephen is in control of his own behavior can be identified and implemented. In one elementary school, a frustrated school counselor noticed that one of her students who was constantly referred for discipline never acted up when he was helping an adult or when he waited for his bus. She decided to offer that privilege as a reward: he could assist the crossing guard in front of his school several times each week, based on good behavior in the classroom. His behavior dramatically improved.

An additional way of assisting students with the team approach is to have the student attend the team meeting. This is especially valuable if a student does not understand what the teachers are concerned about.

Team Strategies for Students

Name: _____   Date: _____

Team Member: Strategies for Behavior:

_____   _____

_____   _____

_____   _____

_____   _____

_____   _____

_____   _____

_____   _____

_____   _____

_____   _____

_____   _____

_____   _____

_____   _____

_____   _____

_____   _____

_____   _____

_____   _____

Putting On the Pressure

A fourteen-year-old female student relayed to me this wonderful intervention that occurred for her one day at her middle school, and it points to the power of teams:

STUDENT: I guess I had not been doing as well as I was before these last six weeks. I'd kind of gotten lazy. One day last week, all my teachers called me into the conference room. I knew I was in deep trouble. Instead, do you know what they said? They said they were concerned about me. They said I was a good kid and that other students really looked up to me and that I could really help them out. I was shocked. Then they went around the room, and each of them told me something good about myself. I've never had anything like that happen to me at school.

LM: Wow, what else happened then?

STUDENT: They told me my grades had dropped, but they had my folder there and showed me how I had done so well early in the year. They asked me if I needed anything from them so I could improve. I couldn't believe it. It was real cool. I told them I didn't know right away, but I would think about it. They told me they were going to watch me very closely and ask me if I needed them again.

LM: They must really believe in you.

STUDENT: I guess so. It was awesome.

The student went from grades in the 70s to 80s and 90s in six weeks, and her behavior improved dramatically. She had previously dropped out of several activities, but after the conference, she began to get tutoring and join new activities. Her mom was impressed with the initiative of the school to call this conference with her daughter. The daughter felt a positive pressure to improve and a sense of support that she had not recognized before. The teachers who were clever enough to devise such a conference gave this student a belief in herself that she needed during the troubled time she was going through. The teachers also changed their image in the student's mind and the student "paid them back" by being more supportive of the teachers during class time.

How wise of the teachers to approach the student in this way. The conference was a respectful, compassionate, and empowering experience for the student. The student felt supported and saw herself as important to the teachers. The conference took ten minutes from class preparation before school one day, and the results lasted the rest of the term. Focusing on when the student did well, mixed with concern, empathy, and compliments for a plan of action, equaled student success and impressed the parent as well. A guide for conducting such a conference is included here. The We Believe in You worksheet can be filled in by teachers who cannot make the conference, but there is power in numbers. If the student has been working with an administrator, ask for his or her comments as well, and give a copy to the student.

We Believe in You!

Name: _____   Date: _____

1. Our concerns:

_____

_____

_____

_____

_____

2. What we've noticed about you and your successful times at school:

Teacher: _____

_____

Teacher: _____

_____

Teacher: _____

_____

Teacher: _____

_____

Teacher: _____

_____

Teacher: _____

_____

Teacher: _____

_____

Summary

According to thefreedictionary.com, discipline is "training expected to produce a specific character or pattern of behavior, especially training that produces moral or mental improvement." Are the disciplinary strategies at your school affecting your students in a manner designed to produce moral or mental improvement? Or do those strategies convey punishment? Do the strategies come across as a collaborative means to help students improve their academic performance, or merely teach them consequences?

These are tough questions, and a school counselor and school staff are wise to consider their answers. In addition, if the current strategies are not working, the school staff is even wiser to revise them. An integral part of the solution-focused approach is to stop doing what is not working. Many schools then say, "What else can we do?" The solution-focused ideas in this chapter will serve such a school well.

Solution-Focused Training Exercise: Chapter Nine

This week, as you teach, counsel, or work with students who struggle with behavioral problems, transform your thinking by redescribing the behavior differently to yourself and the student. Remember that definitions or descriptions of what's wrong with students do not lead to solutions; abilities do. Avoid the "barbed wire fences" that labels can produce. Instead, verbalize a new description of the behavior, and align with the student to fight the behavior so it frees the student to lower his or her defenses and see you as an assistant, not the enemy.

Use the chart below to write down descriptions of student behavior that your school has defined for certain students. Next to the description, write what has been tried. Then change the description to a more possibility-oriented description. See how the intervention changes as well.

Student Behavior   Current Strategy

_____   _____

_____   _____

_____   _____

_____   _____

_____   _____

New Description   New Strategy

_____   _____

_____   _____

_____   _____

_____   _____

_____   _____

Chapter Ten

Helping Students Deal with Dangerous Habits and Difficult Situations

It's all right letting yourself go, as long as you can get yourself back.

—Mick Jagger

Lee, age fifteen, loved marijuana. He began smoking it at age twelve and told me that he used it four days a week after school and on the weekends. His father was unemployed, and his mother took in sewing to support the family, which had moved from Pakistan. When Lee forgot to hide his stash in a friend's car and took it into school one day, he was sent to alternative school. There he listened to drug abuse counselors and watched videos that taught the dangerous side effects of drug use. Lee told me that he laughed through the videos because he knew that he didn't have a problem. He could quit any time; he just didn't want to. His parents came for the first session at the alternative school, something that I often requested with students who were bothered by substance abuse issues.

Lee was candid with his parents and told them that he had no intention of quitting smoking marijuana. Seeing that Lee felt it wasn't a problem for him, a common thought of adolescents, I took a different approach from that of his drug counselor and asked him how smoking marijuana helped him. He told me that it helped him to mellow out and relax. At home, he said, his parents fight all the time because his father lost his job and then his mother yells at him to do his chores. This, he said, had gone on for several years. I told him that I understood but was concerned. He said "Miss, I can't promise you anything like quitting. I've got too much going on." I told him that I didn't want him to promise me anything. Instead, I was interested in what *he* wanted. He quickly sat up and

209

said, "I want a car." His father said that he could not afford a car and that if Lee wanted one, he would have to get a job and start saving. Lee said that he had been filling in applications for some neighborhood grocery stores and was waiting for the managers to call.

Lee's goal gave me an idea. I began talking to him about how unfortunate it would be, someday in the future, when the marijuana habit interfered with his getting a car. He seemed puzzled. I mentioned that sometimes grocery stores do drug screens. How awful, I said, that marijuana could ruin his chance at a car. He was, after all, such a good student. (He made B's.) I then went on to commend him on wanting a car and wanting to be independent. I also commended him on knowing that he needed a job and taking action to get one. He was, I said, being rather responsible for a fifteen-year-old. His parents began looking at him slightly differently, smiling at their son and acknowledging that he was indeed a "good boy."

At the end of the session, I told Lee that all I wanted him to do during the next week was to think about the car and how he could keep the marijuana from interfering with his goal of getting one. He said again, "Miss, I can't promise you anything." I then acknowledged with a smile, "I don't want you to. I just want you to think about what you want."

A week later Lee told me that he had not smoked marijuana since I had talked to him. He began our conversation, "Miss, I can't promise you anything, but, you know, it would not be fair if pot interfered with my getting a car. I don't know if I can stop using it. I think I can, but for now, I need to get a job."

I saw Lee throughout the last two years of high school. Occasionally he would slip and smoke marijuana, but his habit decreased dramatically. When I saw him recently in a computer store working full time, planning to go to a nearby community college, he was bright and articulate as he described how he had graduated from high school, landed his job, bought his car, and had a new girlfriend. He looked different, and I mentioned that to him. He leaned in and quietly said: "Yeah, I stopped doing some things that were interfering with my life." I had the chance to tell him in return, "Sounds like you made a good decision."

Gain Respect by Respecting the Need for the Habit

Not all students bothered by substance abuse issues make good decisions like Lee did, but this approach has provided me with a respectful way to work with adolescents who think drug use is helpful to them in some way. Most people use substances (alcohol or drugs) or engage in cutting, eating disorders, or other dangerous habits to help them deal with life or enjoy life. Those who use healthier coping skills have a hard time understanding such unhealthy behaviors and often scold those unhealthy persons, alienating them and making them rebel even more. It seems more helpful to try to understand how the behavior is helpful, not why students use substances or engage in these behaviors. This change will earn the students' trust, and once they begin to trust the school counselor, they may be open to considering healthier alternatives.

The following question is one that I often use with adolescents engaging in harmful behaviors: "I am trying to understand how this activity helps you, but I have a question for you to think about: How will you know, someday soon, when this problem gets bigger than you?"

Students are caught off guard by this question. What makes this question work? Adolescents are, by nature, egocentric. When they begin to think that anything—their parents, school, the police, and even their problem with cutting—could possibly get bigger than they, they stop and think. Many students I have asked this question have given me answers such as the following:

- I will drink all of the time.
- I will not have any money because I will spend all of it on drugs.
- I may cut deeper and bleed more.
- I would stop going to school.
- I would give drugs to my sister.
- I would fail all of my classes.
- I might lose my job.
- I wouldn't care about anything else.

I write down their answers as they tell me and continue to ask, "What else?" until I have at least seven or eight answers. I then make a copy of the list, keeping one for my file and giving the adolescent the original. I tell them as they leave: "I realize that you aren't ready to make a big change right now and don't want to talk about it. But I am concerned that someday this may get bigger. This week, watch for signs that it is in control."

Whether it is my phrasing or my sincerity, most of the students I have worked with and continue to work with come back and tell me that they often continue to think about whether they should cut back on their habit. I again acknowledge to them that I am quite impressed that they were thinking of changing. I then ask how much the problem was interfering that week. When I learn that it interfered slightly with school performance or their home life, I mention that it is unfortunate that it is taking over their life. Then we begin talking about how the student can begin to regain control of the habit so that it doesn't control him. This conversation continues in our sessions, and each week we discuss times when the student did not use, and I inquire, "How were you able to do that?"

Educate Yourself First

There are many ways of working with students on the issue of substance abuse and harmful habits, and I suggest that the solution-focused school counselor learn as much as possible about the substances and habits that students are engaging in. Have pamphlets available for students to read on all types of subjects, and place them in your school where students can get them discreetly, such as a wall-mounted shelf near your office or in a quiet hallway. Keep it stocked. Many students have misinformation and make their decisions accordingly. Help them make better decisions with better information.

Scare Tactics: Do They Really Work?

Schools have made many attempts to stop students from using drugs and engaging in self-harming behaviors. Each spring there are staged alcohol-related accidents that take place in front of high schools to demonstrate the lethality of drinking and driving. These programs mean well, but they primarily get the attention of the students who participate in the staged accident, while the rest of the student body gazes at the project casually.

When I was a high school counselor, our school staged the Shattered Dreams program, which involved many devoted community members. That program, created by the Texas Alcoholic Beverage Commission in 2001, is a fine educational program that combines the dangers of drinking and driving and educates students about the consequences. It has definitely contributed to the knowledge base of students, particularly juniors and seniors in high school, about alcohol abuse and use.

The students who were allowed to participate in the program were those who received parental permission. The other students who perhaps needed to be involved in such a program were not allowed to because their parents did not want to participate with the student. After watching the process, I found that the speakers who talked with the students in the assembly that followed the staged accident had the most impact. Students were quiet and stunned as people who had lost their child to an accident spoke of the sadness that had enveloped their lives forever. Students cried, and many left the gym somber. To follow up, I spoke with students in several classes later that day and asked them: "Raise your hand if you have known someone who has been injured or killed by a drunk driver."

To my amazement, in each classroom that I visited, at least three students out of twenty-five raised their hands. I then talked with the class for a while on what it was like for them to recall their friends being involved in such an accident. I asked them what impact it had on them. I asked them what those friends might advise them to do on prom night, which was approaching. The responses I received seemed genuine and thoughtful, and the message that circulated throughout the classroom was theirs, not mine. I thanked them for their time and left.

The solution-focused approach helps to cultivate such conversations in an effort to:

- Understand what the adolescent's viewpoint is on a timely subject
- Help the adolescent develop alternative strategies for dealing with pressures
- Respect the adolescent's feelings and need to comply with peers' expectations
- Create an opportunity to think differently about a sensitive subject
- Construct a new strategy that fits the adolescent's viewpoint and goal

This experience taught me that whenever school counselors, teachers, or other school staff members design and implement a prevention or proactive program, it is important to involve students in the design, intervention, and discussion. There is ownership when the questions used are personal ones. Opportunities for such questions and discussion are unfortunately frequent, with the current state of affairs. When a world event occurs, ask students "What do you think about this situation?" and "If you were president, what would you be thinking of doing?" These questions hone in on the adolescent's competency and send a message of respect for their opinion. Nothing improves a classroom atmosphere more than one where respect is mutual. Seize the teachable moment!

Relate It to Them First

Consult with your principal, associate principals, student council sponsor, and counseling colleagues about the next community project designed to help your students make good choices. Check out how the program is to be planned and executed and see how the students will be involved. Push for programming that involves student input, consulting with student council members as well as students who rarely get involved. When at-risk students become involved in healthy programs, a ripple effect occurs that is unstoppable. Their peers begin to take notice as the at-risk student supports the program. This creates an influence on a population that needs attention and gives these students opportunities to mingle with healthier students.

Make sure that the programming teaches as well as reaches students. And get the faculty involved, asking them to integrate ideas into their classroom. For example, I was involved in an HIV-AIDS prevention program that was written for the American Red Cross (Metcalf & Chilton, 1994). This project involved each classroom teacher and requested that the teachers integrate the informational subject matter into their lesson plans. All teachers were to use the information in their lesson plans as appropriate. These are some of the activities suggested:

Social studies: Teachers asked: "How have other epidemics affected various societies?"

Art: Students painted or drew the many "faces" of diseases such as HIV.

Language arts: Students read stories of the Holocaust and talked about the devastation of losing human life.

Math: Students examined the statistics of HIV complications and how its numbers could multiply if a cure was not found.

Science: Students discussed how HIV was contracted and how it could be prevented.

Physical education: Students researched athletes who had contracted diseases such as HIV and had their careers destroyed.

Because the material was integrated into the regular classroom, the week that the program was presented, the students were inundated with information that was applicable. And since their teachers promoted the program through their participation, the message was clear: we took the time to share this with you because you matter to us.

It may be helpful to recall the following phrase that Michael Durrant, author of *Creative Strategies for School Problems,* mentioned, when developing and promoting programs: "What is needed is an opportunity to experience competence." Create it, and they will come. And they will listen.

Death and Loss: Ideas that help

Parents often call the school counselor when a death in the family occurs. The way that people deal with death is unique to who they are. However, after a period of time, well-meaning people often encourage those left behind to move forward. But what if the school client is not ready to move forward? Stay where the client is.

The solution-focused approach offers questions to assist school clients with dealing with loss. The following dialogue shows a method of cooperating with a student grieving over the death of her grandmother. The student had struggled with thinking about when times were better for her and had difficulty moving past her grief:

LM: Debbie, you have obviously been through a lot with the death of your grandmother. I know it might be hard to think about this, but when is it that this tragedy bothers you the most?

DEBBIE: At night when my grandfather gets very sad and quiet. He still lives with us.

LM: So does that mean that maybe there are other times, then, when things are slightly better for you?

DEBBIE: When I'm at school and see my friends.

LM: Tell me what you are doing during those times that helps.

DEBBIE: It gets my mind off her, and I think about other things. My friends really do try to help by asking me to sit with them at lunch and do things after school with them.

LM: When else are things slightly better for you?

DEBBIE: My mom will take me out for a walk or to the grocery store when Grandfather gets sad. Also, I'll go to my room and listen to the radio or do homework to get my mind off of it.

LM: It's amazing that you know how to cope so well. I am still impressed that you continue to come to school, pass your classes, and even come talk to me regularly. How have you managed to make such good decisions for yourself?

DEBBIE: I don't know. I guess I know I need to come to school. My mom says it's important and that it will help me get over this.

LM: Debbie, what will be going on for you in the near future that will tell you that you are going on with your life and focusing less on this situation?

DEBBIE: I'll get back into playing soccer again. When my grandmother became ill, my mom didn't always have time to take me to practice. She said we were going to start again when I was ready. I guess she and I will have more time together.

LM: Since you have told me today how you've been coping so far, what would you like to do more of during the next few days that might help?

These competency-based questions helped Debbie see that she had been emerging from the tragedy and had gone on, although sometimes painfully. These questions are useful for students and teachers dealing with illness, a death in the family, sexual abuse, physical abuse, emotional abuse, or other traumatic situations. The premise of the questions is that people survive and are the most productive in the healing process when they discover what works for them individually.

Frustration versus Motivation: Where Do You Score?

Ng-Chia Moi Lee is a school counselor in Singapore whom I met while presenting these ideas there. I was impressed with her diligence and creativity in helping her students to identify what they wanted to work on in counseling. Many students, she said, were frustrated with school situations and home problems and were often so frustrated that they chose to simply sit and not talk. Moi Lee designed a hand ruler (shown here) with the numbers 1 to 10, similar to the scaling question. She uses it to help her secondary students begin to identify where they are on the ruler in regard to feelings such as anger, anxiety, hatred, stress, fear, behavior, and performance. Moi Lee finds that the students who are not verbal are at least able to point to a number. That serves as a starting point. What is unique about Moi Lee's strategy is that in addition to asking students where they are on the ruler, she also asks them to scale *her* part as the school counselor in the counseling session. "When I am scored at a 7, I feel good about my job. If it is lower, I talk with the student about what we need to do to raise the score in our next discussion."

Moi Lee's ruler is a good way of scaling a student's weekly progress. If the student rates herself a 5, the school counselor can compliment her on making it halfway and then talk about what actions the student could take to score a 6 during the next few days. Her teacher can also be scored by the student, and if the score is low, the student can be asked what the teacher might do to raise the score. The mere idea of discussing numbers on a scale is often easier to discuss than real issues.

Scaling Ruler

Anger, Anxiety, Hatred, Stress, Fear, Behavior, Performance

Side 1

Scale of Feeling

a bit _____ very

| 1 | 2 | 3 | 4 | 5 | 6 | 7 | 8 | 9 | 10 |

Side 2

Desperation Meets Imagination

Like some adolescents, many children share frustrations and have even fewer methods of coping with their feelings. Jenny Jacobs, a school counselor in Flower Mound, Texas, worked with a ten-year-old child in her school who became very upset whenever it rained. She learned from the child that her parents had divorced and that she and her mother had moved to Texas, far from her verbally abusive father. The father was apparently so upset that his ex-wife took his daughter away from him that he told them to think about this: "Whenever it rains in Texas, that means I am going to come down and hurt you both." These words were so harmful that Susie burst into tears whenever the first raindrop fell. In spite of his threats, the father still had supervised visitation rights, and Susie was not only having to cope with the springtime rain showers, but had to think about the upcoming spring break when she would have to visit her father.

Working with Susie, Jacobs used the miracle question to help Susie step out of the story that had been written for her by her father and construct a new story regarding the rain using finger puppets. Jacobs began as follows:

JJ: Let's talk about what you will say to your father when you see him next week.

SUSIE: Okay.

JJ: I have some puppets here. Let's pretend that one is you and the other is your father. Here we go. "Hi, Susie, how is school?"

SUSIE: My dad would never ask me about school. I don't think it matters to him that I get good grades.

JJ: Okay. That seems hard for you. Let's do something different then. Would you like to draw while we talk?

SUSIE: Yes.

JJ: Okay, listen to this question. Suppose tonight when you were sleeping, a miracle happened. When you woke up, it would be raining, but you wouldn't be afraid of the rain. What do you think you would be thinking about to make that happen?

SUSIE: I read a book about something like that once. I think it would look like this.

Susie began to draw rain clouds, but instead of drawing raindrops falling from the sky, she drew hamburgers, lemons, and other kinds of food. Jacobs's intervention was helpful to Susie in that it allowed her to reconstruct a story that was less scary than the actual situation. As the session concluded, Jacobs continued to ask about the miracle day when rain looked like hamburgers and lemons. Jacobs and Susie had a good time talking and laughing about the new "rain."

One week after the session, it rained. Instead of crying and feeling anxious, Susie was able to stay calm. When Jacobs visited her on that rainy afternoon, Susie was able to visualize the rain as hamburgers, lemons, and strawberry jelly.

Situations such as the one that Jacobs worked with can be frustrating to school counselors, yet the solution-focused approach offers a way to be helpful. Being able to construct an alternative story for a child or adolescent who feels frustrated and unhappy is rewarding for both.

A Good Time to Lie

Children and adolescents lie for a variety of reasons, and often the adults in their lives spend a lot of time telling them that "telling the truth will get you into less trouble than telling a lie." We have heard this line and perhaps have said it ourselves. It rarely works. One adolescent told me that he lied because his parents were too strict and he was determined to have a few more minutes of television time. Other children tell me that they are afraid of being in trouble, so they tell lies to stay out of trouble. Unfortunately neither strategy works for them either.

One method that I have used with children and adolescents that lends itself to cooperate with the child's or adolescent's belief that lying can be helpful to them is to say: "Tell me a good time to lie." The first response back from both children and adolescents is usually, "But there really isn't a good time." It's almost as if suddenly all of the adult's messages come to the surface and the child acknowledges them. Then I can acknowledge their wisdom that there is never a good time to lie, and together we talk about times that they have lied that did not work for them. The goal of such an odd but alternative conversation is to give the child or adolescent a new perception of lying. Then I ask the student to go through the next day or two and ask himself or herself, when tempted to lie, "Is this a good time to lie?"

If the parents are involved, I ask the student to decide if it is a good time to lie, and if it is not, to go to his or her parent and say, "I have thought about it, and this is not a good time to lie, so I am going to tell you the truth."

I instruct the parents to be delighted when this happens and to hug their child or offer some other positive response. This allows the parents to see a new effort on behalf of their child, and it gives the child a chance to prove that he or she is thinking before lying. The sequence of events changes, the meanings of the lie change, and new behaviors have a chance to emerge.

Trading Coupons for Frustration, by Nishani S. Grigsby

Teachers often ask whether the solution-focused process is applicable to all students. I often reply that as long as a student has an average cognitive ability, the process can be helpful. The following story was written by Nishani S. Grigsby, now a school counselor, who used the solution-focused approach as a special education teacher in Fort Worth, Texas.

Katy is a twenty-one-year-old student with mental retardation and a medically fragile condition due to a rare liver disorder. At age nineteen, her full scale IQ on the WISC [Wechsler Intelligence Scale for Children]–III was 45. Her verbal score was a 52 and her performance was 48. She is still being educated in public school, which will continue until her twenty-second birthday. Her parents frequently seek care from a long-time respite provider named Amy. There was a brief period where the family terminated services with Amy. During that period, Amy had another child. The family recently requested Amy's respite services again.

Katy began acting anxious, and when I inquired of her job coach what had changed, her coach mentioned that she was going to Amy's again. I asked Katy to come and visit with me in my office. . . .

NG: Tell me about what happens at Amy's.

K: The kids yap and Amy spanks them. They cry. They fight. The kids get on Amy's nerves.

NG: What do you do when all of that happens?

K: I go to my room. I clip coupons. I run away.

NG: You run away? How often has that happened?

K: One time.

NG: What happened after you ran away?

K: My dad came and got me, and told me don't run away.

NG: Can you think of a time when the kids are not fighting?

K: Yes.

NG: Tell me what things are like then.

K: She takes me places.

NG: Where do you go?

K: Sometimes Amy takes me to Sonic or Mexican Inn. I help her load the dishwasher, I help empty the trash. I help with the groceries, I get candy or gum. I watch TV alone in Amy's bedroom.

NG: What do you like to watch?

K: Scary movies.

NG: What else is happening when things are better?

K: I notice Christian [Amy's son] is growing big. Coupons. Alexis [Amy's youngest daughter] goes to my house.

NG: So let's talk about what you can do when things are feeling a little uncomfortable.

K: Cut coupons.

NG: That sounds like a great idea. I want you to close your eyes and pretend that you are asleep. When you wake up things are different. What would that be like?

K: There would be a castle, fresh fruit, hash browns, Tater Tots, coconut cream pie, key lime pie, pecan pie, and three kids.

NG: Who are the kids?

K: Britney Spears, Nick Lachey, Jessie McCartney. Music playing at the house. We had punch, Chex Mix, nachos, Fritos. We see movies called *Strangers.*

NG: What else will be in the castle?

K: Bahamas, hunks with big muscles going horseback riding. I have a boyfriend who buys Cherry Cokes. I talk to him on the phone. Hunks go scuba diving in the Bahamas. There are hot girls.

NG: What do you do in the castle?

K: I eat peas, mashed potatoes, onion rings. I want to make another story.

NG: What is the title of this story?

K: "She Has a Garden."

NG: Okay. Tell me about the garden.

K: She grows onions and cucumbers. One day me and Mom went to Wal-Mart and saw Brad Parker with big muscles and a Fossil watch. Saltwater taffy, Cherry Coke, Tater Tots. Amy went to bingo at 6:45. Watched *Saw II.* We bought pickles, Pam Spray. She bought Hungry Jack, gave it to Erin, I got $20.00. I bought DVD *Survivors.* On Monday February 6, I had a birthday. That's it.

NG: Both of your stories sound very interesting. Which one is more like the place you would like to be when the kids are getting on Amy's nerves?

K: The castle.

NG: One of the things you mentioned doing in the castle that you liked was cutting coupons. Is that something that you can do at Amy's?

K: Yes.

NG: When the kids are fighting, do you think you could go to your room and cut coupons?

K: Yes. [Nishani noticed that Katy brightened up substantially after their talk and whenever she had a tough day at Amy's, Nishani would invite Katy to want to talk about the castle. It became her reprieve. It became her solution. Even in a special education classroom, the solutions developed from exceptions that only Katy could dream of.]

Crisis Calls

When a sixteen-year-old girl died at home one morning, the news swept quickly through her local high school, and hysteria broke out in the hallways. Immediately the counselors took the most distraught students to a comfortable classroom, where they began talking with the students. After the students calmed down and were able to begin processing what had happened, the counselors began talking to the students in this manner:

"Tell us about Lauren. What was she like?"

"What do you remember about her that is important to you?"

"How can we begin to honor Lauren?"

"Where shall we begin?"

The questions asked of the students who were mourning the loss of Lauren were influenced by those of Michael White, who composed elegant questions for clients who had suffered personal loss. White (1989) wrote, "I formulated and introduced questions that I hoped would open up the possibility for persons to reclaim their relationship with the lost loved one" (p. 29). Freud's wisdom about the importance of understanding and acceptance is captured in these words: "Freud . . . suggests that the completion of the mourning process requires that those left behind develop a new reality which no longer includes what has been lost. But . . . it must be added that full recovery from mourning may restore what has been lost, maintaining it through incorporation into the present" (Myerhoff, 1982, p. 110).

The process of working with the students led them to design a banner for Lauren on which they wrote notes and affectionate remarks. The banner was laid across the auditorium stage for a week so that any student could add a message. When completed, the banner was given to Lauren's parents.

Helping school clients deal with death often means helping them to identify the influence of their lost loved one. Michael White, in his article "Saying Hullo, Again" (1988), wrote of dialogue that describes how the school clients recall their loved ones and how their loved ones saw the school clients. For example:

"If you looked through your grandma's eyes, what would she say she missed seeing you do each day?"

"When you remember how she enjoyed watching you do that, how does that bring fond memories of her back to you?"

"What do you recognize about yourself when you have those fond memories, that Grandma recognized?"

"What can you do, just for today, to honor your grandma, based on what you have told me?"

These questions allow the school client to go back in time and revisit the loved one, rekindling the warm memories that were once occurring and place them in a new context . . . one where they recreate a new memory, according to what the loved one enjoyed. This revisiting gives the school clients a chance to move at their own pace through the grief process. Amazingly, most school clients move quicker through the process because the questions respectfully do not ask them to move forward until they are ready. Instead, they move forward because they are ready.

Critical Questions That Work to Increase School Client Capacity

How can the solution-focused approach work in a crisis situation? Because of its versatility and ability to cooperate with a student's feelings, the solution-focused process helps to calm students by asking them to think about what they can do at the moment to bring about a small bit of change and relief. The following mini scenarios, written by Trigg Even, an interventionist at Mansfield Independent School District in Texas, show how the model can offer relief and direction to even the most challenging situations:

- *Conflict or harmony?* A student left home and avoided school for several weeks because he could no longer handle the conflict with his mother and his stepdad. When given a chance to process how it was helpful to him to leave home, it became apparent to him that his problem behavior indicated his sincere desire for harmony. He then made a bold decision to return home and begin a process of family counseling.

- *Help my friend . . . I mean, me.* A student presented herself to the school counselor to talk about her friend's self-injury, depression, and suicidal thoughts. By cooperating with her need to "help" and commending her on knowing what healthy behaviors looked like, counseling quickly shifted to helping this young woman with her own feelings of depression and self-injurious behavior.

- *Breaking up.* An opportunity, not an end. A sixteen-year-old refused to accept his girlfriend's attempt to end their relationship. His ensuing behavior, said school staff, was obsessive, stalking, scary, and potentially dangerous. In counseling, he eventually accepted the breakup and learned to cooperate with her refusal to reinstate the relationship, recognizing it as an opportunity to invest in his friendships with male friends.

When adults empathize with students and acknowledge their pain and feelings, most of these young people are able to understand how they are trying to resolve their own issues, albeit unsuccessfully. By listening and then asking questions such as the miracle question, students are able to set their own direction. The following guide for crisis situations offers students the chance to be heard and then to decide what they want different in their lives. The guide can be used for individual situations or a mass disaster. From there, the solution-focused school counselor becomes a coach who helps the students understand how they had solved other critical situations before.

Solution-Focused Crisis Intervention

1. Listen and empathize with the student. Refrain from any advice giving or telling the student that things will be better. Whether this is the case is uncertain, and the student often knows that. Recognize and relate to the student that the "stuckness" that he or she feels is due to an attempt to get resolution. Let the student know that you notice the efforts.

2. Set a goal for the moment. The goal may be impossible, such as to bring back someone who has died. Nevertheless, listen, empathize, and agree that such a goal would make things better. Then ask what the goal would do for the student. Continue with this inquiry until an achievable goal develops. For example, if a student says that her mother would not have died, ask how her mother being alive would help. If the student says, "She would be there for me," acknowledge and help the student explore who else is there, even if only slightly.

3. Talk about the exceptions that enabled the student to make it thus far. This understanding gives students confidence and empowers them to realize that they have made it through other trying times.

4. Set strategies based on past successes and exceptions. Only ideas presented by the student should be discussed as possible solutions or strategies to cope at the moment.

5. Use the scaling question with the student before ending the session to see where he or she would rate the session's productivity. This response will help both you and the student know what was productive.

6. Follow up and ask, "What's better?" when you meet again to keep the student on track and focus on progress.

Summary

This chapter emphasized the need for the solution-focused school counselor to cooperate with the thoughts, beliefs, and needs of students, particularly when a crisis occurs or when a student's method of coping can be destructive. Although it is sometimes obvious to a school counselor that the student needs a new strategy to be successful, suggesting or advising one to a student who is upset can lead to the student's feeling disempowered instead of empowered. Moreover, when ideas are suggested that do not fit with the student's worldview or match the goal of the student, the likelihood of failure increases.

School clients in crisis don't know where to turn, and sometimes the crisis is so intense that even the school counselor can become uncertain about which way to go. Using the solution-focused ideas in this chapter will guide you while working with such students. Remember that students are resilient, able, and strong. Your role in creating a new awareness, a new story, or a momentary solution is to tap into the student's expertise, even though it may seem difficult to identify at the time. Trust the Force.

These questions help students set goals that are meaningful to them. When goals have personal gain, the likelihood of following through is better.

- With all of these issues occurring at once, which one do you think would be best to focus on?
- If your teacher were here, what do you think she would say you could do to make things better for you?
- If your best friend were here, what would he say would make your friendship better?
- I know things are difficult. What would you suggest doing differently, just for a day, to begin moving forward?
- What do you think your teacher would say you could do to get her to back off?

Solution-Focused Training Exercise: Chapter Ten

This week, when a serious concern is brought up by a colleague or student, instead of giving advice or reaching for another resource, ask these questions:

"What will you be doing differently when things are better for you?"

"How have you coped so far?"

"What does that say about the person you are?"

"What can you keep doing until things begin to get a little better?"

"What can we do at school to help?"

Let the school client guide you to where he or she needs to go to feel safer. Then ask yourself what your school can do to avoid another crisis.

Bibliography and References

Berg, I., & Steiner, T. (2003). *Children's solution work.* New York: Norton.

Davis, T., & Osborn, C. (2000). *The solution focused school counselor.* New York: Brunner-Routledge.

de Shazer, S. (1985). *Keys to solutions in brief therapy.* New York: Norton.

de Shazer, S. (1988). *Clues: Investigating solutions in brief therapy.* New York: Norton.

de Shazer, S. (1991). *Putting difference to work.* New York: Norton.

Dolan, Y. (1991). *Resolving sexual abuse.* New York: Norton.

Durrant, M. (1990). *Creative strategies for school problems.* New York: Norton.

Epston, D. (1989). *Collected papers.* Adelaide, South Australia: Dulwich Centre Publications.

Epston, D., Freeman, J., & Lobovits, D. (1997). *Playful approaches to serious problems.* New York: Norton.

Epston, D., & White, M. (1990). *Narrative means to therapeutic ends.* New York: Norton.

Fulghum, R. (1993). *Maybe (maybe not).* New York: Villard Books.

Furman, B. (2004). *Kids' skills.* Australia: St. Luke's Innovative Resources.

Gerrard, B. (1997). *School-based family counseling: A new paradigm.* San Francisco: Center for Child and Family Development. Department of Counseling, University of San Francisco.

Keeney, B. (1983). *Aesthetics of change.* New York: Guilford Press.

Keeney, B. (1994). Conference remarks at the Salesmanship Club Workshop, Fort Worth, TX.

Kuehl, B. (1996). The use of genograms with solution-based and narrative therapies. *Family Journal, 4*(1), 5–11.

Lipchik, E., & de Shazer, S. (1988). Purposeful sequences for beginning the solution-focused interview. In E. Lipchik (Ed.), *Interviewing* (pp. 105–117). Rockville, MD: Aspen.

Metcalf, L. (1991). Therapy with parent-adolescent conflict: Creating a climate in which clients can figure out what to do differently. *Family Therapy Case Studies, 6*(2), 25–34.

Metcalf, L. (1998). *Solution focused group therapy.* New York: Free Press,

Metcalf, L. (2007). *How to say it to get into the college of your choice.* Upper Saddle River, NJ: Prentice Hall.

Metcalf, L., & Chilton, S. (1994). *PALS for life.* Waco, TX: American Red Cross.

Metcalf, L., & Thomas, F. (1994). *Qualitative Studies in Family Psychotherapy,* DOI: 10.1300/j085V05N04–06; pp. 49–66.

Miller, S. (1996). *The miracle method.* New York: Norton.

Miller, S., & Berg, I. (1992). *Working with the problem drinker.* New York: Norton.

Myerhoff, B. (1982). Life history among the elderly: Performance, visibility and remembering. In J. A. Ruby (Ed.), *Crack in the mirror: Reflexive perspectives in anthropology.* Philadelphia: University of Pennsylvania Press.

O'Hanlon, W. H. (1994). Informational sheets. Omaha: Hudson Center for Brief Therapy.

O'Hanlon, W. H., & Weiner-Davis, M. (1989). *In search of solutions.* New York: Norton.

Peller, J., and Walter, J. (1992). *Becoming solution-focused in brief therapy.* New York: Brunner/Mazel.

White, M. (1988). *Saying hello again: The incorporation of the lost relationship of grief: Collected papers.* Adelaide, South Australia: Dulwich Centre Publications.

White, M. (1989). *Selected papers.* Adelaide, South Australia: Dulwich Centre Publications.

Index

F

Failure, 22

Families: challenges of, 8–9; changing dynamics of, 67–68; compromises within, 184–185; conducting therapy for, 168–183; housing move of, 6, 59, 87; importance of helping, 164–165; involvement of teachers in, 168, 171; overview of, 163–164; scaling questions for, 184–185; solution-focused scripts for, 171–175; training exercise for working with, 187. *See also* Parents

Fielding, L., 147–148

Fighting, 21, 59, 130, 190

Freeman, J., 80

Frolov, D., 111

Frustration, 215

Fulghum, R., 95

Furman, B., 132–133

Future, language related to, 36–37

G

Gerrard, B., 186

Gifted students, 97–99

Ginott, H., 87

Goal setting: in competency-based conversations, 65–66, 70–72; in crisis intervention, 221, 222; to discipline students, 192–193, 197, 198; in family therapy, 171; miracle questions in, 113–115; in relationship building, 62; with secondary students, 35, 184–185; with teachers, 105; vagueness versus specificity in, 35, 70; worksheet for, 198

Grigsby, N. S., 217–219

H

Habits, 130–131. *See also* specific habits

High school students. *See* Secondary students

HIV-AIDS prevention programs, 213

Homework, 11–12

Honesty, 217

Hopelessness, 23, 39–40

Household chores, 175–176

Hyperactive students, 1

I

Illnesses, 6, 37–38

In Search of Solutions (O'Hanlon & Weiner-Davis), 16, 43

Independence, 63

Innovative Resources, 48

Intelligent students, 97–99

Internalizing problems, 45–48, 62

J

Jacobs, J., 216

Jagger, M., 209

K

Keeney, B., 36

Kids' Skills (Furman), 132

Kuehl, B., 55

L

Labels: case scenarios related to, 30–33; for elementary school children, 127–129; power of, 30; and problem redescriptions, 34–35, 36; for secondary school students, 146; and solution-focused guidelines, 16, 17–18

Language: of alternative stories, 29–30; and assumptions of educators, 36; consequences of labels in, 30; to convey hope, 39–40; to discover past experiences, 73; of elementary school labels, 129–130; to externalize problems, 45–50, 62; to find past successes, 40–43; of note writing, 38, 39; overview of, 29; of praise versus curiosity, 43–44; in relationship building, 61–63; to scale down problems, 53–55; specificity in, 35; and students' worldview, 34–35; in student-teacher conferences, 91; and teachers' assumptions about change, 36–37; training exercise for, 29–30; for working with complainants, 77

Learning skills, 132

Lee, N.-C.M., 215

Lesson plans, 94, 213

Lipchik, E., 53

Listening: and alternative stories, 34; to build relationships, 61–62; in crisis intervention, 221

Lobovits, D., 80

Long, T., 51

Lovelace, N., 195–196

Lying, 217

13–15; simplicity in, 19; steps in, 104–107; traditional method of, 40

Problems: definition of, 69–70; perceptions of, 61–62. *See also* Redescribing problems

Punishment, 32, 72, 200

Q

Questioning: to address complainants, 77; to assess students' problem solving, 74–75, 103; in college application process, 158; in competency-based conversations, 66–68, 69–75, 79; in crisis intervention, 222; to deal with death, 214, 220; to defeat bad habits, 130, 131; to define problems, 69–70; to evaluate teacher effectiveness, 44–45; to focus on past successes, 41–43; key words and phrases in, 39–40; to scale down problems, 53–55, 134; to schedule classes, 157; for skill development, 133; of working parents, 185–186. *See also* Miracle question

R

Realistic thinking: versus miracle questions, 114; solution-focused guidelines and, 21–22; and specificity of language, 35

Rebelliousness, 177

Redescribing problems: case studies of, 191–192; guidelines for, 36; and labels, 34–35; and negative thinking, 23–24; training exercise for, 207. *See also* Problems

Referrals, 90–91

Relationship building: case scenarios related to, 111–113; for discipline purposes, 195–196; guidelines for, 61–63; in teacher mentorships, 202; between teachers and students, 91, 94

Reminders, 133

Reminiscing, 66–68

Reputation, students', 59–60, 149–155, 161

Resistance, to change. *See* Change, resistance to Respect: for habits, 210–211; of teachers' feelings, 94–95, 96

reteaming.com, 133

Rewards, behavior, 202

Ripple effect, 18–19, 44, 213

Roth, J., 134

S

Satir, V., 18

Scaling questions, 106; to assess frustration and motivation, 215; in crisis intervention, 222; and mentorship for discipline, 202; for nonverbal students, 215, 216; overview of, 53–55; and resistance to change, 103; for secondary students, 184–185, 215–216

Scare tactics, 212–213

Schedules, class, 156–157

Schneider, A., 111

School attendance, 37–38

Secondary students: aligning with worldview of, 19–20; competencies of, 177; competency-based conversation example of, 63–68; goal setting with, 35, 184–185; guidelines for working with, 159–160; labels for, 146; mentorships for, 201–202; and miracle questions, 115–118; normal conflicts between parents and, 63–64; overview of, 145–147; punishment of, 32; reputations of, 149–155; respecting habits of, 210–211; scaling questions with, 53–54, 184–185, 215–216; scare tactics for, 212–213; self-image of, 149; training exercise for working with, 161; and working parents, 185–186

Self-image, 149

Self-perception, 45–46

Senior release time, 156

Sexual abuse: of elementary school children, 133–139; externalization of, 51; solution-focused guidelines for, 16–17

Shannon, N., 200–201

Shattered Dreams program, 212

Shaw, G. B., 163

Skills, students', 132–133

Socializing, with students, 61

Solution-focused approach: guidelines for, 16–24; overview of, 15–16; versus problem-oriented approach, 13–15, 69, 104; school district's introduction to, 9–10; staff members' concerns about, 9

A Solution-Focused Approach to Conversations: Guiding Questions Cheat Sheet, 78–79

Solution-Focused Script worksheet, 172–174

Counseling Towards Solutions Workshops

The ideas in this book are available as workshops and can be presented to school counselors, teachers, staff members, social workers, school psychologists, therapists, and more. All workshops are presented by Linda Metcalf, Ph.D., and can include the following agenda:

1. Introduction to the solution-focused approach and its usefulness in a variety of school settings, processes, and programs.

2. Guiding solution-focused ideas and their direct application to a variety of school issues, explained with the use of many case studies.

3. Application of solution-ocused ideas to school issues such as discipline, classroom management, parent conferences, special education/IEP development, teacher-student relationships, parent-school relationships, and more.

4. Explanation of narrative therapy and its application to school issues: how to externalize problems so that the student becomes empowered and the school staff sees beyond the pathology, toward the strengths of students who are challenging.

5. Specific ways to work with adolescents to rebuild reputations, and how to use the miracle question and story writing to assist elementary school students see themselves differently. Additional ideas for helping students bothered by depression, anger, sexual abuse or trauma are provided.

All workshops are very interactive, utilizing brief lecture, motion-picture excerpts, videos of actual cases, role-play exercises, and planning exercises.

To schedule a solution-focused workshop for your staff, please contact:

Linda Metcalf, Ph.D.
5126 Bridgewater
Arlington, TX 76017
(817) 690-2229
dr_linda@ix.netcom.com